The End of the Street

LINDA MELVERN

The End of the Street

METHUEN · LONDON

First published in Great Britain 1986
by Methuen London Ltd
11 New Fetter Lane, London EC4P 4EE
© 1986 Linda Melvern

Typeset, printed and bound in Great Britain
by Richard Clay Ltd, Bungay, Suffolk

British Library Cataloguing in Publication Data

Melvern, Linda
  The end of the street.
  1. News International Strike, Great
  Britain, 1986
  I. Title
  331.89′28107215   PN5124.S75

  ISBN 0-413-14640-5

Contents

Illustrations

Acknowledgements and thanks for permission to reproduce photographs are due to the Press Association for plates 1a, 4b and 6a; to London Post (Printers) Ltd for plate 2b; to Kent Clark for plates 3a and 3b; to David Modell for plates 2b, 5a and 5b; to Andrew Wiard (Report) for plates 6b and 7b; to Stefano Cagnoni (Report) for plates 7a and 8b; and to Rob Bell for plate 8a.

Acknowledgements

I would like to thank all those in the trade unions who decided to give freely not only of their time but of their files. In some cases the truth obviously damaged their case, but they decided that the story was more important. The book took just seven months and many people were bothered with unreasonable requests at unreasonable hours.

Bruce Matthews, Managing Director of News International, told me towards the end of the project that at that time the company 'felt unable to help'. But there were senior executives and managers from Rupert Murdoch's companies who, having worked in the newspaper industry for many years, and realising the historical implications of what they had undertaken in 1985, decided, in the strictest confidence, to talk with me. Some spent many long hours with me and I owe them an enormous debt. I thank them for their honesty and courage.

I also thank the library staff of the St Bride's Institute for helpfulness and patience.

For friendship and encouragement, I would like to thank Paul Eddy, Isabel Hilton, Hank Klibanoff, Florence Mary, Peter Murtagh, Angela Pitts, Michael Pye and Sara Walden. For invaluable local support: Jay and Tuk Novak, Catherine O'Keeffe, Norman Mkhize and the wise Australian John Wait.

I thank Phil Green, whose support and care amazed me. Journalist Cynthia Jabs was invaluable in the last stages. I was lucky to have been able to have the help of the talented journalist, Isabel O'Keeffe, at vital stages of both research and writing. The one person who made this book possible with her commitment, unstinting enthusiasm and journalistic skills was Jane Rackham.

Words cannot adequately express the debt I owe my parents. To them, I dedicate this book.

'The newspaper is of necessity something of a monopoly, and its first duty is to shun the temptations of a monopoly. Its primary office is the gathering of news. At the peril of its soul it must see that the supply is not tainted. Neither in what it gives, nor in what it does not give, nor in the mode of presentation, must the unclouded face of truth suffer wrong. Comment is free but the facts are sacred.'

C. P. Scott (1846–1932)
Manchester Guardian, 6 May 1926

ONE

'Bloody exciting'

They assembled quietly that morning in a room at the Park Lane Hotel, Piccadilly. Rupert Murdoch shook hands with each of the union officials, followed in turn by his executives. There was none of the usual small-talk, only 'good mornings'.

Opposite Murdoch at the oblong table sat Brenda Dean, who represented 4,500 of his employees. She appeared cool and collected as ever – only later would she recall her unease. Murdoch had a glass of Perrier at one hand, polo mints at the other, and when he spoke, he balanced either a pencil or his glasses in his hands.

Murdoch, known for never using a paragraph when a sentence would do, began by saying that nothing could be gained by going over old ground. They were not there to talk about his new printing plant in Wapping. 'The horse has bolted at Wapping,' he said.[1]

This was how the final meeting between News International and the print unions opened on Thursday, 23 January 1986. After years of bitter negotiations, both sides knew the crunch had finally come. The mood was sombre. There was just one half-hearted attempt, early on, to lighten it for an instant, when news photographers asked to get into the room.

'They've got a job to do,' Murdoch said, nodding to let them in.

'What about the mirrors?' asked Bill Gillespie, Managing Director of Times Newspapers Ltd, worried about the reflection of flash-lights in the ornate room. Gillespie, the Irishman known for his winning charm and quick wit, had won the respect of union negotiators by his ability to iron out difficulties with a quiet chat.

'Come on, Bill,' laughed Dean. 'You can't exclude the *Mirror*.' When she had become General Secretary of the Society of Graphical and Allied Trades (Sogat), it had not taken her long to learn of Murdoch's resentment of the Mirror group in general and its chairman, Robert Maxwell, in particular.

Murdoch looked at her. 'You give him what he wants,' he said, referring to Maxwell, who had just successfully negotiated 2,000 redundancies.

'You can have that deal today,' she told him. Murdoch made no answer. 'He just backed off,' she remembered later.[2]

Fleet Street's problems were no secret. For years, newspaper proprietors had grappled with the industry's labour problems: an over-paid workforce using outmoded equipment, over-manning of strictly closed shops with restrictive practices and frequent wildcat strikes. Since purchasing the *News of the World* in 1969, Murdoch had struggled with the all-powerful bedrock of print trade unions, the individual bargaining units known as 'Chapels', with their shop stewards, the 'Fathers'.

Murdoch said he paid an average weekly salary of £300 to his workers at the *Sun* and *News of the World*. 'I have strained myself emotionally and financially to build this business and we have been met with nothing but cynicism, broken promises and total opposition,' he had told them all recently.[3]

But in Fleet Street in 1985, change was in the air – and not just because new Conservative legislation had altered the rules for trade unions. Eddie Shah had added a note of urgency by launching his national newspaper, *Today*, which he intended to publish without the traditional print unions. Shah, a provincial newspaper owner who specialises in 'freesheets', had raised £25 billion for the venture. He was banking on labour-saving new technology to make it profitable at what was, by Fleet Street standards, impossibly low circulation for a tabloid paper. The balance of power was shifting.

When the photographers left the room, Murdoch turned to the General Secretary of the National Union of Journalists (NUJ), Harry Conroy, and said he was surprised to see him. 'I would not have thought this concerned you,' he said.[4]

Murdoch had exempted the journalists ten days before when he had suddenly given six months' notice to terminate union agreements covering 5,500 production workers at the News Group and Times Newspapers.

Conroy said that although he knew Murdoch had only agreed to talks on the proviso that they would concern only

production union members at *The Times* and *Sunday Times* in
Gray's Inn Road and the *Sun* and *News of the World* in Bouverie
Street, he thought he would attend just in case the discussion
got round to Wapping, Murdoch's new printing plant in the
East End of London. He said he did not think the two areas
could be separated. He was there, he said, as an 'observer'.
Murdoch nodded his consent.

Wapping was all that the union leaders wanted to talk about
that day: Murdoch's new, purpose-built plant in London's
dockland, and the *London Post*, the newspaper he said he
intended printing there. The £100 million newspaper factory
was uppermost in the mind of every person in the room. Its
very appearance was startling. It was a fortress, ringed with
razor wire in huge coils, fenced with steel and constantly
scanned by the shifting eyes of closed-circuit cameras. It was
built to be picket-proof.

History had been made in the new plant five days before.
Murdoch had trampled centuries-old Fleet Street traditions
by printing a section of the *Sunday Times* there without union
agreements. The newspaper industry was dumbfounded.

The General Secretaries of the print unions had to plead
with the Fathers not to react with an immediate walk-out
from all Murdoch's titles. To comply with the 1984 Trade
Union Act, they had to wait for a strike ballot.

Murdoch had thrown down the gauntlet on the plant three
months before: he had given the print unions a three-month
deadline to reach agreement on manning his new paper, the
London Post. Murdoch had said he planned to produce both
the *Sun* and *News of the World* there. But he wanted an
agreement on the *Post* first. Until they had that, he refused to
discuss either paper's move from its cramped and decaying
Bouverie Street location to its new-technology future in the
East End.

Two weeks before this final meeting, News International
had announced that the Wapping plant was ready for the
launch of the *London Post*. A skeleton staff was in place for the
twenty-four-hour newspaper. And the plant was also ready to
meet the 'urgent requirements of the News Group's other
newspapers'.[5]

Print union leaders were armed that Thursday with what

was, traditionally, their most powerful weapon: an overwhelming mandate from their members for industrial action. The issue they had chosen for the strike ballot was a guarantee of jobs for life – no compulsory redundancies if any of the papers moved to Wapping.

Murdoch, that day, was poised on a financial precipice. He had come to the meeting knowing that his ambitions for a news empire were on the line. This was a man who thrived on risk. He had just completed the biggest acquisition of his corporate career. He had borrowed a staggering $2.6 billion to buy a movie studio, a chain of magazines and six television stations which he planned to turn into a fourth American television network. Steady profits from his British newspapers were crucial to finance the deal.

News International had said that if the print unions went on strike, the company would attempt to publish all four papers without them in its new plants at Wapping and Glasgow.

All the negotiators at the table that day knew that the stakes had never been higher. They knew they were on the brink of the endlessly delayed Fleet Street revolution. This meeting was about more than jobs, money, policies or principles. The fight was also for a craft, for tradition and ritual, some of which had been in place for centuries. It was a clash of powerful institutions and personalities.

Brenda Dean entered the room that day believing that she stood more of a chance of bringing them back from the brink than any of the others. One of Murdoch's team had recently told her he respected her. His attitude was described as, 'What's a nice girl like you doing mixed up with this lot?'

Dean's union, originally an amalgamation of seven different unions, was over 200 years old. In 1982, there was a complicated merger with the clerical union, National Society of Operative Printers and Assistants (Natsopa). Before this, Sogat's involvement in the newspaper industry was limited to distribution. But Sogat members in Fleet Street now included workers who packed and loaded vans along with messengers in the editorial departments, copy boys and copy-takers in the clerical area, tea-ladies, cleaners, telephonists and librarians.

Dean led the print unions' team that day, a role conferred on her as head of the TUC's Printing Industries Committee. In her soft voice, she told Murdoch that Wapping could not be separated from talks because of the publication there of the *Sunday Times* section five days earlier.

Tony Dubbins, General Secretary of the National Graphical Association (NGA), spoke next, representing 850 members of the craft union. He did not mince words. Agreements with his Chapels had been broken when the *Sunday Times* section was printed, he claimed.[6]

Fleet Street Chapels were traditionally independent from central union authority. The closed shop compelled the Street's employees to be union members. There was also a tradition of inter-union rivalry. The NGA viewed itself as the elite and Sogat members as nothing more than unskilled workers. In some areas, Sogat members worked alongside the NGA. In the press room Sogat people generally ran the presses under the direction of NGA machine minders. Sogat members held copy as NGA 'readers' checked for errors in the composing area.

The NGA was an old-style union, whose members' work was the production of print. The NGA manned the composing room. Members included linotype operators, who set the metal type, and time hands who set the metal into the page. The union traced its origins to the Manchester Graphical Society formed in 1797. But it was not until 1964, when the Manchester-based Typographical Association merged with the London Typographical Society, that the NGA was formed. Smaller craft unions joined later and, in 1982, the notoriously powerful Society of Lithographic Artists, Designers and Engravers.

New technology was threatening the very existence of the NGA. In the commercial sector thousands of its members had lost their jobs. It had eradicated many old typesetting skills. The threat in Fleet Street was the greatest that members had faced: with new technology, copy could be set directly on computers by journalists and tele-ad girls. The union had clung on for as long as it could to exclusive control of a skill no longer needed. To retain power, the NGA had argued to other unions that as it bore the brunt of the revolution, its members should be allowed to transfer to other departments.

Dubbins pointed out to Murdoch, that Thursday morning, that before either of his titles in Gray's Inn Road, namely, *The Times* and the *Sunday Times,* could be printed elsewhere, there had to be negotiation with the Chapels. Murdoch dismissed Dubbins's remarks. 'It's all too late,' he said. 'It's no good coming to me now. You pledged you would do what you could. Now . . . if you want to talk about Bouverie Street we want some kind of agreement.'

The *Sun* was printed in Bouverie Street, where more newspapers were produced every night than in any other plant in the world. The *Sun* was the jewel in Murdoch's crown: it earned his News Corporation £26 million a year. Without disputes, Murdoch had told his shareholders, profits would grow dramatically.[7]

At the final meeting, the *Sun* was more vital than ever to Murdoch. His recent acquisitions had him walking a tightrope. He was stretched so thin that the New York's Citicorp bank organised a loan of £670 million for his TV buys only on the condition that his total borrowing did not exceed his net worth by more than 10 per cent. Murdoch had the bankers on his side because they recognised him as an aggressive, expansionist magnate.

Murdoch had eliminated many of his outside shareholders so that he never needed to pay high dividends. His empire, and the risk, were personal. But that empire still had to pay interest to the banks, or they would lose their faith in him. All the companies Murdoch controlled put together did not earn enough in 1985 to pay the bill for the interest payments that the banks would soon present.

Murdoch's game was a spectacular gamble which defied conservative ideas about a company's finances: to invest in him, you had to believe in him. The power he was buying around the world was far beyond anything that previous emperors of the press could have imagined. Four months before the final meeting, his company paid out $325 million to buy the second half of the 20th Century Fox Film Corporation. His purchase the month prior to that of Metromedia, America's largest independent television network, was the second largest acquisition in broadcasting history, requiring over $2 billion in financing. William Randolph

Hearst may have financed movies, mistresses and a lavish palace, but he never bought an entire movie studio, much less dreamed of a television network.

No one could have predicted that the son of Sir Keith Murdoch, who was knighted for bringing respectable journalism to the *Melbourne Herald*, would become a media magnate with power even Hearst could not have imagined. Sir Keith, as a war correspondent, had disregarded censorship during the First World War to break the story of the Gallipoli disaster. He sent his son to Geelong Grammar School – the Australian equivalent of Eton. The News Corporation's 1985 annual report described Rupert Murdoch as head of a company that was now in 'almost every corner of the world'. The company was 'a citizen of the global village'. This was not an overstatement. The change in the balance of News Corporation's operations from the old to the new world was swift.

Murdoch's method has been described as 'buy, borrow and buy'. His balance sheet by normal standards was highly stretched: borrowings almost all in the form of bank loans. He defied the ordinary laws of commercial gravity and managed to survive.

His ability as a planner and manager was well known. But there were those in the industry who doubted his ability to recruit the creative talent needed to turn round ailing movie and television companies in the most competitive arena in the world. Murdoch was well aware that his new ventures would demand a level of commitment that would push him to the limit.

Murdoch was on his way to achieving a global communications empire spanning three continents. But to do it, he had to sort out the problems with his British newspapers. He desperately needed his UK profits. The golden goose could not be allowed to stop laying eggs.

He had been in London for nearly two weeks before the 23 January meeting. He had reserved a total of four weeks for the British operation – an unheard-of amount of time for him to spend in one country. Ever since he had outlined the 'Post Project' in February 1985 to a few key executives in New York, he had remained, as usual, determined to succeed.

That morning, when Tony Dubbins insisted that Murdoch could not print *The Times* or *Sunday Times* in his new plant without first talking to the Chapels, Murdoch adopted a belligerent tone. 'We have been through this before. Time doesn't stand still.[8]

The next few minutes were historic. Speaking slowly, Dean surrendered the power of the Fleet Street Chapels. She outlined a plan worked out with the other unions that conceded management's right to manage, agreed to binding arbitration on any dispute, gave flexibility between unions, prohibited wildcat strikes and promised ballots before strikes. None of the General Secretaries there that day was sure they would even be able to sell the deal to their members.

But it was the unions' olive branch. To their utter amazement, Murdoch dismissed it. 'If this had come three months ago, the answer might have been "yes",' he said quietly.

Dean would remember that from the start it was a 'funny kind of meeting'. She had sat directly opposite Murdoch and watched him fidget. He seemed agitated, but he was as articulate as ever, speaking without raising his voice. And, as usual, he twirled his spectacles in his hand. 'I just did not believe he was in the business of changing his mind that day,' she said. But she spent the entire meeting searching for the slightest, faint hope of a compromise.

Not even those working closely with her in Sogat knew Dean. In her first job, in a printing factory, she had complained about not having enough work to do. She was approached by a Father who suggested she work for the union, and she was soon secretary to the powerful Greater Manchester Branch Secretary of Sogat, Joe Sheridan. It was curiosity, she says, which prompted her to get to know every detail of Sheridan's work. He was a willing teacher, an old-fashioned trade unionist known as 'Mr Sogat', who never saw her as a threat. He eventually took her to negotiation meetings with members and managements. Dean's face was therefore familiar to members when she stood for election as Assistant Branch Secretary in 1971. She won by an overwhelming majority, setting the pattern for subsequent victories.

The first woman in history to head a big industrial union,

Dean was the daughter of a railway inspector from Salford in Greater Manchester who had left school at 16 to become a shorthand typist. 'I just have to do my nails and have a bath and wash my hair if I've got a meeting,' she has said, 'otherwise I feel I'm not giving my best. It inhibits my performance.'[9] She gave the appearance of a mature and sensible senior secretary with moderate views which she expressed in a polite and reasonable way. 'Managements,' she had once said, to the surprise of some of her colleagues, 'get the unions they deserve.'

Some seasoned trade unionists thought she treated talks with News International as if she were dealing with boy scouts. They complained that she was an inexperienced negotiator whose tactics were too transparent. Dean had come to Fleet Street as an outsider. She was from the provinces, where she had built a reputation – with both members and managements – as a skilled negotiator. She had been appalled by her first experience of Fleet Street negotiations. She once saw a manager 'get up and start talking to the wall' to show how he felt about talking to his opponent, she said.

Dean brought a new atmosphere to national newspaper negotiations. There was now less table-thumping at meetings with management – less of what was euphemistically described as 'male rhetoric'. In the past nine months, the tone and language had changed.

The 23 January meeting was the result of a final appeal she had made to Murdoch and had arranged at the last minute with Bill O'Neill, Vice President for Personnel and Labor Relations for Murdoch's News America Publishing Inc. He had had trouble finding anywhere to meet at such short notice. Initially, O'Neill had suggested the meeting be held in the Times building. Dean said she wanted more neutral ground, and O'Neill asked her to find a place. She had laughed and told him he had a plusher office with more facilities – he could do it.

Bill O'Neill, sitting as usual next to Murdoch, viewed coming to Britain for another round of talks with the British print unions like being ordered back into the trenches. He was Murdoch's global industrial relations troubleshooter on three continents, living out of a suitcase, never far from Murdoch's

side. O'Neill thought negotiating anywhere was easier than in
Britain – in Chicago they had just had their first strike for
forty-seven years and in Boston there had not been one since
before the war. Fleet Street problems were caused by the
unions' 'inability to negotiate', he had said. He believed that
the only law which applied to Fleet Street was the law of the
jungle. 'I guess some people here follow football, some people
collect stamps and some people become Chapel officials,' he
said.[10] Not generally known was the fact that O'Neill was a
former Chapel official himself: he had been a linotype operator
in Sydney until Murdoch had plucked him from the ranks in
early 1975.

Six foot and quietly spoken, O'Neill, who called Murdoch
'the boss', was not a man who went in for small-talk. Some
Murdoch executives would joke that O'Neill would suit
cowboy boots and a stetson, that he should negotiate sitting
on a rocker with a gun at his hip. As it was, his dress attracted
attention. A fitness freak, he favoured tracksuits and sneakers,
and when in London was often seen jogging round the Gray's
Inn Road building. And he liked casual suede jackets. But
even when wearing a suit, which he did for most meetings, he
never took off his famous rings. One could not avoid noticing
them: two large silver rings with turquoise, the stone of the
North American Navaho tribe, the sort of jewellery one buys
at the side of the road in Arizona. No one ever dared ask
O'Neill why he wore them.

The print union leaders first met him at Murdoch's side in
1981, during the purchase of *The Times*, which had landed
Murdoch with heavy losses of almost £15 million a year at a
time when high interest rates were exposing the risks of his
business philosophy. O'Neill had negotiated the staff-cutting,
and the printers soon realised that in any talks he set the pace.
Sometimes, if his list of demands was not met, he would simply
get up and walk out. But print union officials believed that his
word could be trusted and he had earned their grudging respect. He was a man who meant what he said. 'We don't need
you,' he had said to the proof-readers in Gray's Inn Road in
1982. 'We're going to have direct inputting in this place.'

In those days he had a broad Australian accent. But in the
last three months of talks conducted by O'Neill, the union

negotiators had noticed that he now used American slang and
his accent was more mid-Atlantic.

The terms he had put on the table had dumbfounded them:
the unprecedented deal he was after for the *London Post* was
quickly dubbed 'the serfs' charter' by union leaders. There
were four basic demands which O'Neill had drawn up, he
claimed, on a plane between Chicago and New York in late
summer, and they were designed to smash union power. He
was demanding no closed shops, management's right to
manage, dismissal for striking and legally binding agreements.

O'Neill had also devised the Christmas deadline for the deal.
The unions were told that if the terms for the *Post* were
accepted, the talks would be extended for the move of the *Sun*
and the *News of the World* to docklands.

O'Neill was Murdoch's strategist – his front-line man against
the unions. His take-it-or-leave-it attitude throughout the *London
Post* talks had intimidated the unions. When he had presented
the four clauses to the unions' branches, he had often repeated:
'Believe me because I'm playing for real.' 'Playing for real' was
to become a catchphrase among the print union leaders. And
O'Neill had said: 'I have done it in Australia and I have done it
in the US and I intend doing it here.'

O'Neill had once claimed that he was the 'best around',
that he was Murdoch's greatest asset. Dubbins commented: 'I
don't think that's an understatement.'

At the final meeting, O'Neill was playing it as he usually
did. Almost as though he was trying to draw out the NGA
General Secretary, he said: 'Letters to the NGA weren't even
answered. We have really tried to get agreements.'

Dubbins, known for his temper, kept calm. But he was
furious. His union had already conceded more to Murdoch
than to any other Fleet Street proprietor: the NGA had said it
would accept the principle of direct, computerised typesetting
by journalists on the *London Post*. This point had been conceded
on several provincial newspapers, but never to a national
proprietor. For years, the NGA saw direct entry – journalists
typing stories into computers instead of having them typeset
by the NGA – as a threat to its very existence. Dubbins had
been amazed and baffled when News International had
dismissed the offer – it was the NGA's ultimate sacrifice.

Dubbins was the bright young Turk of the print unions. He and Harry Conroy, a traditional trade unionist and General Secretary of the National Union of Journalists, were firm friends. Conroy was a playful man with a fierce sense of humour, gregarious and expansive. But he was to reach despair in the days to come. A Catholic from Glasgow, he describes himself as a 'Christian Socialist'. As a working-class Glaswegian, he disliked what he described as 'southern middle-class socialists', although the description probably fits a majority of his members in the national press.

Conroy had already taken a battering in his first three months as General Secretary. He had barely moved to London from Glasgow when he was swamped by the crisis. He had been 'shocked', he said, when Norman Willis, General Secretary of the TUC, tried to impose a common approach on all five unions involved with News International – the NGA, Sogat, the AUEW, the EETPU and the NUJ. Willis had written to the General Secretaries on 23 December, advising them that no union should 'enter into an agreement or arrangement with News International covering all or part of the operations or groups . . . except with the agreement of the other unions concerned.' Conroy believed this bound his union to the others so as to leave them no room to manoeuvre. 'We were drawn in totally,' he said.[11]

Conroy had been concerned about the presence in recent talks with News International of lawyer Geoffrey Richards. Union leaders had seen the lawyer's attendance as an unwelcome move towards American-style negotiations, and they had ignored a suggestion that they should have a lawyer present as well. Conroy's response was to ask Richards his name repeatedly. He feigned forgetting it at every meeting. 'And you,' he would say, 'what's your name?'

At the final meeting, Richards, a short wily man in his late thirties, but looking much older, had said nothing. He was a senior partner of Farrer and Co., an old and established law firm, advisers to the Queen since 1965.

Alf Parish, the NGA official responsible for national newspapers, had tried to draw out the lawyer during recent meetings. Richards rarely intervened in negotiations and spoke to his News International clients in whispered asides. But

Parish noted he was quite talkative during the adjournments.

Parish recalled a discussion at one stage about legally binding contracts. 'I asked Richards if he could distinguish between law and justice. He didn't even see what I meant,' said Parish.

When the discussion turned to ending closed shops, Richards, in a rare interjection, had asked: 'What exactly is your objection?'

Parish's curt reply had been instantaneous. 'In your profession?' he asked. 'You dare talk to me about closed shops.'[12]

Parish had a reputation as a skilled and witty negotiator. His sharp repartee was often quoted with hilarity by other union officials. In March 1985 he was negotiating with Murdoch's Bouverie Street management team in the Waldorf Hotel after a sudden stoppage at the *Sun* when the talks were interrupted by the telephone ringing. Parish picked it up and said into the receiver: 'No Rupert, we're far too busy . . . No, look we can't talk to you . . . we're too busy . . . no, I said . . . can't talk . . . sorry.' And he put down the phone. 'Every one of Murdoch's team,' he recounted, 'had got up and rushed to the union side of the table, shouting for me not to hang up. "Get the operator, get the call back." One of them grabbed the phone and was desperately trying to get the hotel switchboard.' Parish was roaring with laughter. The call had been a wrong number.

Parish had been responsible for the NGA members in Fleet Street for only just over a year, but he was an experienced Street negotiator. Now in his mid-50s, he had been Assistant General Secretary of the elitist Society of Lithographic Artists, Designers and Engineers (Slade), and had been responsible for the union's merger with the NGA in 1982. Dubbins had taken a risk with his appointment: the NGA man already in the job was popular, and in spite of the amalgamation there was still a distinction between NGA and Slade members. But in a short time Parish had earned the respect of the Fleet Street Chapel Fathers. He was known as a man with his feet on the ground who understood the industry better than most.

Parish prided himself on gauging atmosphere. Almost as soon as Murdoch had led his team into the room for the final meeting, he knew it would be what he called a 'tramline' meeting – that it would stay on the same track throughout.

*

Murdoch seemed off-hand. He seemed more abrupt than they had ever seen him. Then, suddenly, he delivered a bomb-shell.

'It's too late for Tower Hamlets,' he said. 'Gray's Inn Road and Bouverie Street will have reduced manning. We will employ some hundreds of your members.'

'Christ,' thought Conroy.

'Some hundreds?' Dean asked. 'How many?' She thought he ought to have the decency to specify, but Murdoch refused to be drawn. Dean asked for an adjournment.

Murdoch rose and led his negotiating team out of the room. Everyone on the union side was shocked. Parish thought there was nothing much to discuss after what they had heard – there seemed no point in talking about tactics. At a meeting on 30 September, when the unions had been given a Christmas deadline for the *London Post*, he had come away with a feeling that no matter what had happened in the past, there was now something concrete to talk about. Then, he had seen possibilities for constructive discussion and a way forward. Not any more.

Twenty minutes later, when Murdoch walked back into the room, Dean told him that although they found his proposals totally unacceptable, they still hoped to avoid a dispute. 'We are prepared to sit down and talk with you,' she said.

'I haven't got rich pension funds,' Murdoch said. Parish's immediate thought was that Murdoch was scoring points: he was again referring obliquely to rival publisher Robert Maxwell. 'Maxwell hasn't got a new plant to go to,' he thought.

Murdoch went on: 'There will only be state compensation.' Dean asked him again what he meant by 'some hundreds'. Murdoch refused to say. She pressed him and he still refused. She said she then looked straight at him.

'Is it negotiable?'

There was a pause. She thought, all he needs to say is 'yes' and she was ready to tell him there would be no strike. This was the chink she had been waiting for.

Murdoch said nothing. Dean could not believe it. She said later that this was the moment she realised they had failed. She turned to the man sitting beside her, the man who knew her as a shrewd, intelligent woman, but who still called her 'the girl'.

There was a sense of expectation. Bill Miles, Sogat General Officer, leant forward. Nearing retirement, Miles, with his snow-white hair, was the most seasoned Fleet Street union negotiator in the room. His oral attacks on management were well-known to them all, but when Miles spoke it was always with an air of righteous indignation, as though he was the most reasonable man ever to have walked down a Fleet Street pavement.

He was a charming man who counted many newspaper proprietors among his friends. There was not one proprietor in Fleet Street who did not have time for him, including Rupert Murdoch. In 1969 he had supported Murdoch's take-over of the *Sun* and, with others, had opposed an attempt to turn it into an independent, non-profit-making, pro-Labour daily. He believed the ownership would lead to more jobs and pay for his members.

Miles described himself as an industrial salesman – selling deals. He had worked very hard building up a relationship with all Murdoch's management team in Fleet Street, particularly in Bouverie Street with Bruce Matthews, the Managing Director of News Group Newspapers Ltd.

'He'd always thanked me for the help I had given but he used to say he did not believe I was speaking for all my members,' Miles had said with a laugh. 'There's an element of truth in that,' he had told Matthews.[13]

At the September meeting, Miles and Murdoch had collided by chance during one adjournment in the gents at the Inn on the Park hotel.

'This is a bit grim,' Miles had said to him.

Murdoch, said Miles, had replied that the last thing he wanted to do was 'screw you lot into the ground', but he was having problems with the 'bloody NGA'.

Miles had replied: 'I can't do anything about them.' He would remember that conversation.

Fleet Street was his life. Miles had come from poverty in West Ham; he had spent some time in an orphanage and gone into print quite by chance when he left school at 14. He had been elected from the shop floor and became a Father on the *Daily Express* during its zenith. For nearly twenty years he had been a full-time official, and for the past thirteen had direct responsibility for national newspapers. He understood proprietors and he knew his members. In the last few months, Brenda Dean had depended on him more than ever.

Miles had been taking notes throughout the meeting on the back of the letter Murdoch had issued to his employees the day before. It read: 'I am writing this final appeal to all of you on Times and News Group Newspapers to continue to do your jobs.' What infuriated Miles was a particular paragraph about lost copies: 'Can I tell you that between October, when our talks began, and Christmas, Fleet Street newspapers, governed by 'trust and honour', lost 2,750,000.'

The tirade he levelled at Murdoch this time was typical Miles. He spoke at a rate of knots. How could Murdoch talk about millions of papers lost? He had distorted statistics. 'You're counting the strike at the *Guardian* when our members were locked out,' he said. In the last year the losses on the *Sun* and the *News of the World* had been less than 1 per cent. Miles was getting more angry. He told Murdoch that the industrial relations team on his papers behaved like gun fighters.

In his usual quiet tone, Murdoch replied: 'We came to this meeting at Sogat's request. There is no point in going over old ground.' Then he looked straight at Miles and said of Sogat's future in the new plant: 'Bill, the horse has bolted at Tower Hamlets,' using the name for the new docklands plant he insisted all his executives use.

Dean decided it was time to change tack. 'The AUEW is included in these talks,' she said, turning to Les Elliott, London Divisional Organiser of the AUEW, who was representing his 192 members working for News International. He told Murdoch the strike ballot for his union was in progress.

'So you are saying the AUEW is at me as well,' replied Murdoch. Dean told him the AUEW was part of a joint approach, as they shared common concerns for their futures.

'Do you intend printing all the titles in Wapping?' asked Dean. Murdoch had bought thirteen acres in Wapping back in 1978. He needed a new production site, he had said, for his most successful paper, the *Sun*, as well as for the *News of the World*, because there was no room for increased print runs in

Bouverie Street. Building work in Wapping began in 1980 and negotiations for manning the plant started between O'Neill and the unions in May 1983. At the beginning of 1984, News International proudly showed a video to Bouverie Street Fathers of what they called 'our super new printing plant'. But in March, O'Neill returned to the States: the talks were breaking down. They re-opened in September and continued until just after the announcement of the *London Post* in March 1985. Dean pointed out that her members had all believed that Wapping was built to produce the *Sun* and the *News of the World*. 'The result of the strike ballot would have been greater,' she said, 'if it had been taken after you had printed the section of the *Sunday Times* last weekend.'

Tony Dubbins interrupted. He was known for getting himself wound up at meetings, although he claimed his temper was always under control. Years back, as an NGA official in the provinces, he had said he wanted nothing to do with Fleet Street. But once he became General Secretary, he was fascinated with its problems. Negotiating, as far as he was concerned, was a game of skill, and it was one which he enjoyed.

He told Murdoch that the company had led them to believe that the plant was to print the *Sun* and the *News of the World*, not sections of the *Sunday Times*. The decision to print the section had breached agreements and, he claimed, had broken guarantees which the Chapels had been given. So the assurances they sought from Murdoch now were quite reasonable.

Murdoch looked at him squarely and said he was five years too late for Wapping. If the unions had come to him with their offer two years ago, there would have been a deal. 'I told you in September,' he repeated laconically. 'I am not prepared to let time stand still.' He said their members had not woken up to the problems early enough. The Chapels, with their demands for more money, had vetoed any possibilities. 'Your only reaction has been to put a gun to our heads,' he said. He provided three times the number of jobs necessary at five times the level of wages. And his was a company which had expanded and had taken over 'sick and ailing newspapers'.

He was now offering five-year legally binding contracts, and wanted total flexibility of staff – who would be chosen by the company – and he also wanted mobility between his plants. 'I want to keep all the plants open and I want to print newspapers,' he said. There would be 'some hundreds of jobs' but they would all be secure and well paid.

Miles could not believe that Murdoch understood what he was asking. 'You're a busy man,' he said crossly. 'You have got lots of interests outside the UK and you have been fed a lot of false information from your people here.' He told Murdoch that recent strikes had been due to his members being locked out by the employers. Ninety-nine per cent of them were decent people. 'My members are not bingo numbers,' he said. 'Whatever Maxwell is . . . he has never set out to destroy trade unionism.'

O'Neill interrupted. He said there had been no movement during his twenty hours of negotiation with the unions. 'We can go back and point at the problems of the past years but it won't get us anywhere. We are not all black on our side and you are not whiter than white.'

'There's a change now,' Bruce Matthews added. Matthews, Managing Director of News Group Newspapers, was a man with a deeply lined face that made him look permanently exhausted. He was one of Murdoch's trusted lieutenants. Both O'Neill and Matthews reported directly to Murdoch – union leaders thought this often worried Matthews. They noticed he sometimes looked at O'Neill before he spoke.

Bouverie Street was his home. He thrived on the cut and thrust during the constant warfare with the Chapel Fathers. He had almost lost his Australian accent. Matthews could be easy-going and great fun to be with and had become close to many of the union leaders over the years – Bill Miles was a particular friend. Union negotiators believed that Murdoch made most of the decisions and his executives were nothing but go-betweens. Matthews only negotiated with the amount of rope given him by the proprietor. But there was not one print leader in the room who disliked him.

Matthews's tone that day surprised Miles. He told the unions that the company had given them every opportunity to reach agreement. When the company began talks on Tower Hamlets, the unions had taken the position that no one should lose

their job. 'Other people have got concessions,' he said, referring again to Maxwell's agreement with the unions to
eliminate 2,000 jobs.

Bill Gillespie, Managing Director of Times Newspapers, was
also liked by the print unions. He was approachable and sometimes difficult problems were solved after an unofficial word
with him. He was often used in this way and Miles and Parish
had felt grateful to him. But that day it seemed he wanted to
goad them. In his familiar, soft Irish accent he said: 'The cost
of investment and the cost of the union demands have made it
the economics of a mad house.'

But Dubbins was not to be drawn by rhetoric. There was
no more time for threats. He said he had recognised the ser-
iousness of what faced them. He wanted as much information
from Murdoch as he could get. 'Are you saying that the
proposed agreement for Wapping is the one you are thinking
of for Gray's Inn Road?' He could not believe Murdoch now
wanted the 'serfs' charter' at his existing operation.

'Yes,' said Murdoch. It was then, Dubbins said later, that
he realised Murdoch had already made up his mind about the
dispute.

Murdoch continued speaking. He told them he would
eliminate the composing, stereo and plate-making areas.
'There will be flexibility for the unions to work out the
numbers of jobs between them.' His tone held no hint of
sarcasm. 'There will be statutory redundancy for volunteers
and the numbers will be achieved by compulsory redundancy.'

Dean asked if they could now negotiate with the company
for agreements which would cover all his plants. 'Three years
ago, yes. Now, no,' said Murdoch. She asked for another
adjournment.

Murdoch wandered into the hotel lobby. Reporters
gathered round him.

'How is it going?'

'So far they have been quite lively,' Murdoch replied. 'Both
sides are pretty vigorous.' But he said he did not think the
unions were in a mood to go very far. 'We will see.' He turned
back to the room. 'We are not going to lie down and play
dead,' he said. Parish noticed this. He thought it strange that

in the middle of negotiation anyone should wander out and talk to reporters.

Murdoch came back into the room for the last time. Dean said she had two final offers for him. The unions would go back to where it had all begun: she offered to negotiate a deal for union members in Wapping and she would negotiate the TUC seven-point plan.

'I reject any recognition for your members in Tower Hamlets,' said Murdoch.

The atmosphere was becoming oppressive. The room was silent. Murdoch finally put his hands on the table and pushed his chair back. At that moment the talks broke down.

'It was one of those meetings when you just know it's over,' said Parish, who did not get up from his chair when Murdoch led his team out of the room. He sat there for a few moments. He thought that although the company had been 'playing for real', it had been with a fixed deck. He had a feeling they had spent the last three months negotiating for a paper which had never existed.

It was noon, Murdoch stepped into the lobby and gave a quick press conference. He said the meeting had ended calmly and cordially. 'We have a lot of respect for many of the individuals concerned and I think it is tragic that they have missed these opportunities.' The company had been begging for six years for an agreement for Wapping. 'We would have given them all sorts of things,' he said. Murdoch looked baleful.

Helen Hague, a member of the *Financial Times* Labour staff, thought Murdoch seemed unusually bullish. 'I think they are determined to take me on,' he said of the unions. 'I am amazed . . . they seem to roll over and play dead for Mr Maxwell. And we, on the other hand, have created thousands of jobs in this country. We've picked up ailing, dying newspapers and breathed new life into them.'

Patrick Wintour from the *Guardian*, who had been following the story closely, asked Murdoch about Wapping. Wintour knew that the printing capacity had been tested there over the last three months. 'There has been nothing covert there,' Murdoch told him. 'Everything has to end some time . . .' But

Wintour interrupted. Had not Murdoch done a deal with the electricians, the EETPU, who had been working in the plant? 'We have nothing with the electricians' union at all,' he replied.[14] He said there were 'some hundreds' of employees with individual contracts.

Would he take legal action if the unions did go on strike? 'If they break the law, we will move, of course, at once. But I don't know about things like that. I think they moved their funds out of the country some time ago.'

Wintour wanted to interject but another reporter, sensing deadlines were at hand, asked if Murdoch had a message for his readers. Murdoch smiled. At the September meeting he had endeared himself to the newspaper journalists by beginning the conference without waiting for the television cameras. It was Murdoch the newspaperman, who in his twenties had spent two years as a sub-editor on the *Daily Express*, who replied. 'Hang on in there. We will get to you. If we miss a day or two, we will be back.' And he walked away.

All Dean said publicly after the meeting was that everything put to Murdoch had been rejected. 'I rather got the feeling that the company did not want a settlement.' She was less talkative than usual. Privately, she said later: 'We are going into the likes of which we have never seen before.'

When Miles walked out into the lobby, an industrial reporter he knew was waiting for him. 'It's bloody awful,' was all he said. He thought Murdoch had miscalculated. From the beginning of the meeting he had found Murdoch's manner brash and objectionable. 'Here we all were,' he said later, 'trying to get the whole thing back on course and it was all brushed aside.' He believed that if there was a dispute it would be short-lived. The company would have to be back negotiating and it would be sooner rather than later. 'We'll be back round a table trying to sort out the mess we haven't sorted out today,' he said.

Tony Dubbins and Harry Conroy walked out of the hotel together and went into the nearest pub for a pint. Dubbins was shocked at Murdoch's audacity. 'We had given him an olive branch and he'd broken it in two and beat us round the head with it.' He knew they were on the brink. 'Now, it was if and when and who started it.'

Both men knew that the company could respond to any strike by immediately sacking employees on the grounds of broken contracts. The two of them calculated Murdoch's problems. They knew the *Sun* was crucial to him: he had to keep it on the streets or be forced down in the intensely competitive popular newspaper market. They knew he could produce newspapers in Wapping. Dubbins had evidence in his files that there were members of the EETPU in the plant, but neither of them knew how many. But they thought they could bank on Murdoch being unable to print the massive 4.5 million copies of both the *Sun* and *The Times*. Even if he could print, he would have great difficulty with Sogat's members who helped with the distribution of the papers – this was the key.

Dubbins believed that Murdoch, through his action that day, had made himself the villain. It seemed as though Murdoch just did not 'give a damn' about public relations any more. He would surely lose public support for what he had done – it was that support which both General Secretaries knew had to be maximised.

Conroy wondered how much support to expect from his own members, the journalists. He believed that the *London Post* had been a cover and a sham from the start – he had already told his members as much. He thought Murdoch intended all along to transfer production of all four papers to docklands. He knew Murdoch would not be able to operate in Wapping without journalists. They had been instructed by his union not to cooperate with publication of the titles in the East End. But he could not predict how they would behave. Dubbins thought they would hold fast, particularly at *The Times* and the *Sunday Times*.

Murdoch had left the hotel through the back entrance with two bodyguards. After lunch with his negotiators, he went straight to Wapping, where in the past few weeks the catchphrase – in an imitation of Murdoch's Australian accent – had become: 'Bloody exciting, ain't it? Bloody exciting.'

Gang Warfare

Ray James always went to work in a conservatively tailored navy blue suit with a freshly laundered white or pale blue shirt, carrying a black briefcase. Walking up the front steps of 30 Bouverie Street, under the Victorian Gothic black and gilt clock, he looked as though he had just stepped from one of the shiny executive Mercedes parked sometimes in the narrow street.

A short, chubby man with thick, wavy, grey hair, his was one of the most well-known faces in the building – and in Fleet Street. Ray James was the Street's most powerful 'Father' – head of its largest Chapel. From his office he decided if there was peace and production in the *Sun* machine room. He had 700 printers in his charge and he allocated their jobs, their shifts and their time off. He controlled their holidays, hours, overtime and working practices. And his was a closed shop: James would only employ those men who came from the machine branch of his union, Sogat, which acted as his labour exchange.

The strength of any Chapel depends on the Father, elected by members yearly in a secret ballot. Some candidates had fought like mad for the job, attracted by being out of overalls and into a suit, but had underestimated the position's responsibility and power. Not 'Jamesy'. He was sure of himself. He did as he pleased. He had his own territory and he was proud of its strength.

It is the nature of the job that a Father is also responsible for the welfare of his men – a Father in the true sense. Jamesy's office door was often shut as he sorted out a problem with one of his men, most often about marriage or drink. But although he appeared easy-going, with the air of a holiday-camp comedian, he could sometimes be a hard disciplinarian. A machine man out of favour could find himself in a noisier and dirtier job than the one he already had. And there was always the ever-present threat of a man's union card being taken away, which would make him unemployable.

James had first been elected Father in 1979 with a majority of 300, and only two men had ever dared challenge his leadership. It is said that a Father successful in wage negotiations is bound to be re-elected, and it was James's reputation in the company that he was always after more money. 'They always thought I was carping on about it,' he says. One of his favourite stories was about how he coerced a manager to pay the rental on his home telephone: he simply refused to take late-night emergency calls.

The machine room job is dirty, noisy and can be dangerous. And machine rooms can be vicious places to work: the description used in the printing trade is 'volatile'. There is a lot of drinking, and arguments between the men are sometimes sorted out physically rather than verbally. Chapel power is absolute. Managers are mere bystanders and are never trusted. Only the Father and the union, as far as the men are concerned, are capable of sorting out problems.

An ambitious Father could look to the union for higher office. Fleet Street provides more opportunities for a union career than most industries and one day a senior Sogat official sitting in James's office – no more than a cluttered cubby-hole next to the canteen on the first floor – suggested he run for branch office.

'Why should I?' he had said with his typical chuckle, which even those who knew him well were never sure how to take. 'I'm at the top already.'

Ray James and his machine men prided themselves on being the best print workforce anywhere. They produced more newspapers in Bouverie Street each night than in any single plant in the world. The circulation of the *Sun* – the world's largest English-language daily – was just over 4.1 million and the paper contributed a massive cashflow for Murdoch's News International.[1] It was the company's greatest newspaper asset, and James, in his dealings with the Chapel, the union and the management never forgot it.

If there was one person in the building James could not stand it was Kelvin MacKenzie, the *Sun*'s tough, irreverent Editor, a man not many dared or cared to stand up to. His

shouted orders in the newsroom rarely lacked a profanity.
When James and the Editor 'eyeballed' – a common word
in the trade – those in the vicinity would just stand and
stare.

The sheer size of the print run and the lack of a northern
printing plant meant the presses in the *Sun* machine room had
to start rolling at 8 p.m. – two and a half hours before any
other Fleet Street paper. If a late story broke, when time for
deadlines was dissolving and with the massive presses geared
to go, the *Sun* Editor and James would come into contact.

James was firmly of the view that the success of the *Sun* was
certainly not due to the Editor. It sold for page three, the
sports pages and Hagar the Horrible, the back-page cartoon.
And James was not someone who missed an opportunity to
say what he thought. There was once a furious row between
James and MacKenzie in the small lift which serviced the
back of the building. When James got out, he was shouting:

'It's not your fucking editorials that sell 4 million. This
fucking paper sells 4 million in spite of your editorials . . .
Your editorials couldn't sell four fucking quire.' Both men had
to be held back from each other as the doors to the lift closed.

James would also strike out at those for whom he had a
grudging respect – like the Managing Director, Bruce Matthews. During one dispute, when James's men had stopped
work, the door of his Chapel office had flown open and
Matthews had marched in. Matthews was really mad, but no
one was allowed to walk into James's office like that.

'I said it was his fucking firm but he was in my office,'
recalled James, saying he told him to leave. Sometimes it was
better to do as James said.

James's popularity was due to his sense of humour. When,
in April 1982, the *Sun* had announced a 'Best Worker in Britain' contest offering a prize of £5,000, James had entered. He
wrote:

In 1969 the *Sun* newspaper in its present form was started
and the department which I am recommending, the
Machine or Press Room, came into being. At this time the
department consisted of seven machines being used to
produce three-quarters of a million newspapers per

night. . . . Through management's application in recognising the needs of the public with regard to the style of
a popular newspaper the . . . circulation has increased four-
fold. The number of machines used is 22, at least half of
which must be at least 40 years old.

Each application had to be signed by 'the boss'. 'Un-
fortunately,' James wrote to Matthews, 'in the end I could
not get anyone to countersign the document.' And he added:
'My conclusion is that the good will is not as good as I thought
it was and must be only one-sided – from my Chapel to management.' [2]

There was certainly a need for good will in Bouverie Street.
The machine room was known throughout the Street as the
Black Hole of Calcutta. The conditions were appalling: the
unions had been told by a factory inspector in 1984 that the
building could only last another eighteen months.[3] As the
circulation of the *Sun* had increased, extra machines had been
packed in: the management had been so desperate for space
that it had once considered buying the pub next door,
knocking down the walls and installing presses there.[4] And
there was no space for changing rooms. The several hundred
machine men coming off shift, faces grimed with ink and
grease, had to share eight showers – some of those in a building
across the road.

During summer spells the machine room was boiling hot,
with heat generated from the massive presses and from the
foundry. In one corner of the basement there was a tarpaulin
to keep out the rain. Round the old copper tea urn – tea is the
traditional printers' drink – which had been gurgling in a
corner of the one-acre machine hall since the building was
opened in 1930, there were cockroaches and mice, and one
machine man remembers someone finding a dead rat. Tramps
would wander through the works entrance in Whitefriars
Street and sleep among the reels of newsprint.

The faster the presses ran, the louder the noise, and every
night the massive machines were pushed to their limits. In the
middle of the room, the noise level sometimes exceeded 100
decibels.[5] A code of practice issued by the Department of
Employment in 1972 stated that there should not be continu-

ous exposure to over 90 decibels. When the 1974 Health and Safety Act was passed, ear protectors were provided, but there were always problems: to be really effective, the ear protectors had to fit properly, and there were constant complaints and demands for re-fitting.

Like all Fleet Street machine men, James can remember his initiation to the machine room in the 1960s – working on the dreaded fly. The fly hands sat right up to the machine at the 'folder', where the complete papers left the press. They would take off the bundles in quires and put them on a conveyor belt which would send them to the warehouse for dispatch. James remembers first learning the variety of sign language machine men use – talking was impossible through the noise of the machines and the loud ringing of the bell when the presses start to roll. He remembers not being able to see across the machine room for a thick fog of fine ink spray and tiny particles of paper dust which looked like snow. When men came out of a machine room they got 'the bells' – a ringing in the ears which could sometimes continue until they woke the next day, when their pillows were sometimes black with printer's ink.

Ink spray was a particular problem in Bouverie Street because of the confined space. The faster the machines, the worse the spray became. After the 1974 Health and Safety Act, newspaper managements had investigated the possibility of low-mist inks. But the complaints from the Bouverie Street Chapel continued. Fears expressed by union health and safety representatives seemed justified when in January 1986 the oils used in newspaper ink were defined by the International Agency for Research on Cancer as a Group Two carcinogen.[6]

James and his men believed that whatever slight improvements were made in health and safety were due solely to the Chapel and the union. It was the same with wages and hours worked. At 54, James admitted he had had over twenty years of good living from the trade. It was true that he had two men for every job. The 'blow' system – the break period – meant that some men worked one hour on and one hour off. Some worked four hours on and four off. Keeping the staffing levels high was a policy not just of the Chapel but of the

London Machine Branch of Sogat, one of the most militant in the union.

'If we work 20 hours per week it is still the longest week in the Street – they average about 15 hours,'[7] James had once told the News International negotiator Bill O'Neill during a discussion on manning. 'I should point out to the company that we are not interested in blood money – we will not be selling any men.'[8]

'Looking at our conditions it wasn't unreasonable,' he says. 'No one could have stood that machine room from 7 p.m. until 4.45 in the morning with all those machines running.' Nor did he think ten weeks' holiday or the wages unreasonable. In 1985 he had earned £28,000. When he was elected there were some in the Chapel who said that Ray James had stood because he needed the extra £6 a night which the position paid – at the time he had been buying his council house in Northolt, Middlesex.

On Friday, 15 March 1985, at 3.34 a.m. the noise of an explosion ripped through the *Sun* machine room. A plate had broken on machine ABC 2 in the corner of the room. A sudden break of a plate while a giant printing press is running at speed sounds like a grenade going off. The roaring and the clattering of the machine turns to a screech and metal fragments crash on to the guards surrounding the plate rollers. Fragments of metal can fly through the bottom of the machine to the 'reel' room below, where newsprint is fed into the machine. When machine men hear the noise they instinctively run for cover and duck. There are Fleet Street stories of men with metal fragments in their limbs from breaks and the thought of a plate break terrified them.

In most press rooms a plate break was a rare occurrence. Many printers who had worked for years had never seen one. The mystery in Bouverie Street was that in the last two years there had been a staggering number – over 60[9] – which had caused the loss of hundreds of thousands of copies of the paper. When the plate broke that Friday, Ray James decided he had had enough. Although known by members of other chapels, particularly those of the rival NGA, as a right-winger and a man of peace, this was certainly not his reputation with the *Sun*'s management.

The assistant General Manager was sitting in his office on the Monday following the latest break when his extension, 276, rang. He answered with his usual curt, 'Tony Britton'.

'There's a problem,' an overseer told him. 'The Chapel's double rolling.'

Britton slammed down the phone. Ray James was acting up.

That night James had issued an instruction to his men to apply the safety measure known as 'double-roll locking': the lead plates would be clamped on the machines but instead of immediately starting the machines, the operators would turn the roller one revolution and one extra time to re-check the clamps. Britton knew there would now be overtime claims and, worse, production would certainly be delayed, trains missed, copies unsold, advertising revenue at risk.

Britton and James were old adversaries who pulled no punches when they met. Britton had once been the Father of a Sogat Chapel in Times Newspapers. Out of step with the rest of the Fathers, he had advised negotiating with the management in 1979 – just before Thomsons had closed *The Times* and the *Sunday Times* for a year in a desperate attempt to get new technology agreements. Britton had been lured to the management side, one of several Fleet Street Fathers who 'went over'. Benefits to newspaper proprietors were obvious: they had men on their side who knew not only the politics but the tricks.

James had always considered himself superior to the Assistant General Manager. He was forever pointing out that Britton had been Father of a RIRMA Chapel – Revisers, Ink and Roller Makers and Auxiliaries, the Sogat section for engineers' assistants and cleaners. 'I'm not having a shithouse cleaner tell me what I'm having in the press room,' was one of James's favourite remarks. His nickname for Britton was 'bungalow'. 'Because,' James would chuckle, 'he's got nothing up top.' But James had a certain respect for Britton, who was said to have held his own during two beatings from printers for his stance at *The Times* in Gray's Inn Road. And Britton also claimed to have been in the SAS.

When James finally appeared in his office that Monday night, Britton told him in no uncertain terms to stop double-roll locking.

'Get stuffed,' James admits telling him. 'It's a safety measure. I'm fucking fed up with a company that's not interested in us.' And as he walked out of the door he was goading Britton about 'that brand new building' in Wapping.

This, Britton remembers thinking, was the real reason for the double roll. He believed Ray James was out to prove that the machinery in Bouverie Street was so antiquated that the company had no option but to move his men to the new plant.

'All the unions were pressing for a deal to move to Wapping at the time,' recalls Britton, who had been put in charge of union agreements for the plant, under the direction of Bruce Matthews. At that time, James was eleven men away from a deal with the company for the eventual move, and was furious at what he perceived as deliberate delays by the company in negotiation. He thought the company had been stalling.

What made him even more furious was the company accusation that he had engineered some of the plate breaks. Each time a plate had broken there had been a management enquiry. The company claimed that nearly half had been due to an 'incorrectly bedded plate' – the plate had not been put on the machine properly by an operator – or that there had been a 'foreign body' which had caused the breakage.[10]

'We could make those machines do anything,' James said of the huge presses. 'We could make them talk . . . we bloody had to. When we looked at our production figures and the conditions, we produced a miracle each night.' He swears that no one could make a plate break. 'We couldn't do it and we wouldn't,' he says. 'That stuff can kill you.' James believed that the number of plate breaks was due to the lack of maintenance on antiquated machines. Some of them, like the one the crews called the African Queen and another called the Flying Scotsman, had been in use since 1936. They were, he says, quite simply falling to pieces.

James does not deny that he sometimes pressured the management. He could always apply the sudden imposition of a work to rule. When negotiations with management over staffing had broken down in 1983, he had 'expressed disappointment' and had indicated that 'this could affect the performance in the machine room'.[11]

'You don't rush around so much,' he explained. 'We used to do everything by the book, no short cuts. But really, all those men wanted to do was get the machines ready, press a button and sit and read a book. They didn't want extra work.'

After leaving Britton's office the night of the double roll, James walked down the stairs to the machine room and at about midnight he called a Chapel meeting. In doing so he 'stopped the run', as they say in the Street, and over one million copies of the *Sun* were lost.

At 4.30 the next afternoon James gave the management an assurance that there would be no double-roll locking that night. It was Budget Day – Tuesday, 19 March – one of the most frantic for the newsroom, and the *Sun* was gearing into production. Britton thought it was safe. But at 5.20 p.m. a manager telephoned him and said that the Imperial Father, the head of all the Chapels in the composing area – where metal type is set and fitted into pages – had called a meeting. Britton was curt: 'If they don't get on with it we are not plating up.' This meant the plates would not even be put on the presses. Britton was under instruction from Bruce Matthews that if there was trouble anywhere that night, production of the *Sun*'s Budget issue would be stopped. The next bad news Britton heard was that the linotype operators were refusing to delay their meal breaks, a practice which was agreed between Chapel and management for those times when deadlines were impossibly close at hand and there was a backlog of stories to set into type.

And at 7 p.m. Britton heard that the machine men were double rolling. He decided to stop the run. He immediately rang the electricians and told them to pull the power. He told his managers on all production floors that the Budget paper was dead. And Bruce Matthews went home.

Much to Britton's horror, no one in the production areas would stop work. He found himself in the extraordinary position of trying to stop them. Ray James's men continued to put the plates on the machines; the compositors were carrying on working. No one would leave the building. At almost midnight, two visitors arrived: General Secretary of Sogat, Brenda Dean, with Bill Miles, General Officer, both having hurriedly arrived

from a retirement dinner in the City. The national officers
toured the building and spoke to the Fathers.

The dinner had been the labour movement's farewell to Bill
Keys, who had been General Secretary of Sogat for twelve
years. Dean had spent much of the evening with Neil Kinnock
and Norman Willis, but she had noticed that Bill Miles on the
other side of the room was 'on edge' and continually getting
up to take phone calls. As soon as it was convenient, she had
asked him what was going on. Miles told her that there were
problems at the *Sun*.

Leaving a respectable amount of time for goodbyes, Dean
leapt into a taxi with Miles and headed for Bouverie Street.
Dean went straight to the Machine Chapel office and tried to
get hold of Britton.

'I was told he had gone home, so I got him there,' she said.
'I told him I was prepared to negotiate. I would instruct my
members to run the job. I was then told I would be responsible
for any libel actions and my members would not have insurance cover. I told them that was nonsense.' She determined
to print the paper.

But in spite of her pleas to the electricians, they refused to
turn the power back on, and the plates had been destroyed.

'It was an extraordinary evening,' she recounted. 'I was
wearing a black velvet almost backless dress. I had to keep my
coat on . . . sitting drinking mugs of tea.' It was long after
midnight when the building finally emptied.

The eventual stoppage cost the company not only 23.5
million copies of the *Sun* but 3 million copies of the *News of the
World*. The Sunday paper is printed on the same presses and
there is a union rule that only the Chapel which has put plates
on can remove them – and the presses had remained 'plated'
with *Sun* plates.

For the first time in a Bouverie Street stoppage, the
company took court action against the print unions, under
the 1984 Trade Union Act. On 24 March an injunction was
granted against Chapel and national officials in a ninety-
minute hearing in Mr Justice Leonard's sitting-room in his
house in Purley. The unions' action was outside the law because workers had not been balloted.[12]

Dean was baffled about the eventual settlement. She had

typed the return-to-work formula, agreed after midnight, on a typewriter borrowed from the receptionist at the Howard Hotel. The management had conceded all but that the Machine Chapel would be paid for the eleven-day stoppage.

'They did not want to fight that day,' she said. 'All it did was cost them a load of money.' Looking back, she believes it was 'the start of Wapping'.

The NGA also linked the dispute to Wapping. John Brown, the Imperial Father in the composing room, said he believed the company had deliberately provoked a dispute in order to pressurise the Chapels into reaching a speedy agreement for the move to Wapping. The management strongly denied this. Matthews said he was not 'within 100 miles of getting to a common point'.[13]

As for the plate-break problem, the return-to-work agreement had stipulated that there would be a joint study between management and unions on plate breaks. But meetings were just as acrimonious as they had been. Sogat's Health and Safety Adviser told Brenda Dean: 'This was a very difficult meeting with feeling running high.' Matters were not helped, she reported, by a member of management 'blatantly accusing our machine room Chapel of malpractice'. The meeting had lasted six hours and made very little progress.[14]

A branch official of Sogat wrote to the company: 'I have received reports that during the course of these meetings there have been accusations levelled of deliberate malpractice which could, of course, be said to be tantamount to sabotage.' Plate breaks, he said, were a hazard to the safety of all people at work in the press room. 'It is therefore absolutely inconceivable that the malpractices referred to could have any substance.'[15] In one letter James demanded that the management either 'put up or shut up'.

In May 1985 an Inspector of Factories from the Health and Safety Executive wrote a diplomatic letter to the News Group management. 'The reasons for plate breakages appear to be many and various,' he wrote, suggesting several measures to be followed, including the regular inspection of plate-locking devices. 'Breakages are unlikely to be eliminated entirely. While vigilance is obviously required by those fixing the plates and close visual examination may be required, information from other houses does not suggest that a 'double roll' system of work is absolutely necessary'.[16]

It started as a rumour which went round the Street like wildfire. The linotype operators on the *Daily Express* had hit the magic figure of £1,000 for a sixteen-hour week and even the most militant were beginning to talk about how things had got out of hand. Most NGA compositors can remember when the £200 hurdle seemed impossible, then it was £500, then £800. The rumour was wrong: by the end of 1985, the *Express* men had in fact leapt over the £1,100 hurdle.[17]

The Fleet Street NGA compositors consider themselves an elite – within an elite. Composing-room Chapels kept their wages secret from each other and not even national officers of the union knew how much deals were worth.

The customs and practices which led to the extraordinary composing room salaries were 200 years old. The first ever print union agreement was reached between the principal master printers and a compositors' trade union in 1785. Forty master printers signed a document setting out the scale of piece-work prices which could be charged per line of type. The 1785 Compositors Scale of prices is the first ever trade union agreement, and it was made to keep wages high and jobs secure.[18]

The direct heir of this elaborate 200-year-old system of piece work, the 'London Scale of Prices', was the basis for working out rates per line of type and is still used to work out the piece work in hot metal Fleet Street composing rooms. All linotype operators were piece workers – they operated the clattering, cumbersome and noisy machines smelling of molten lead which look like huge antiquated typewriters. They set the journalists' words into metal type. A proficient linotype operator's hands hardly move. Unlike a typewriter, the keys are stroked not tapped.

The London Scale of Prices, known simply as the 'scale', plagued Fleet Street managements for years. They were powerless faced with a Father who knew how to manipulate the elaborate rules the scale laid down, specifying not only

rates for the lines of type set into type or made up in a page –
and that was complicated enough – but the scale of payment
for an operator walking across a room to pick up the copy,
walking back and marking the paper with chalk. It set the
rate when a man moved a few yards from one machine to
another. Operators were even paid for leaving blank spaces
between the lines of type. Under such a system a man who
had set 50 lines into metal could end up being paid as though
he had typed 250.

The scale had been amended and revised during ceaseless
bargaining over the years. It set the rate for working during breaks – fractions of hours were charged as complete
hours and the scale even specified the rate to be charged if
extra time was needed during the change over to summer
time.[19]

There were different rates for different sizes of type. One-
fourth extra could be charged for lists of names, racing cards
or football results. Badly typed or subbed – corrected – stories
earned one-third extra. Corrections on stories already set were
charged double. And if an urgent news story came in which
had priority the men received an extra payment for setting it.
And there was a payment each time an operator changed the
size of type he was using – the lever used for this was known
in the Street as the 'one-armed bandit'.

Newspaper managements had used the scale as an induce-
ment to get the work done on time: the attitude in the Street
had become 'print at any price', although the scale was a difficult system to monitor and was wide open to abuse. Each
linotype operator would fill in a docket with details of the line
he had set for payment: managers at the *Sun* continually complained they were indecipherable. And with corrections at
double rate there were always complaints about deliberate
errors in typesetting. It would take an operator a few seconds
to change a headline set in the page layout: under the scale,
the same task could take thirty minutes, and quoting the scale
was an ideal way of slowing production.

In 1981 the gap between the salaries of the piece workers
and the staff members working in the *Sun* composing areas
had become so wide that the management decided to tidy up
the scale system. They had tried before. In the mid-1970s a

group of accountants had been called in but had failed to get to grips with the elaborate rules. So the management decided a negotiator who understood the scale was needed. News Group brought in Allan Fisher, an ex-Imperial Father from the *News of the World* who had been a lino man. He knew the grey areas and he knew the fiddles.

It took three years of negotiations at the *Sun* before a ceiling of payment for the linotype operators was agreed – negotiable every year. When details of the agreement leaked out, there were accusations in the street that the *Sun* Chapel had sold out the London Scale. But it guaranteed the *Sun*'s 50 operators £43,000 a year – the highest paid printers in the building.[20] But management was continually reminded that the rate was not high compared with other newspapers.

The elaborate rules and the rituals and traditions of composing rooms have been in operation for centuries – ever since Caxton set up the first printing press at Westminster in 1476. The Chapel was a mutual benefit society, a disciplinary and benevolent institution, almost masonic with its initiation ceremonies and secrets. And there was extraordinary solidarity. The Chapel was known generally as 'the companionship'. There are no apprentices in Fleet Street composing rooms: every man – there are no women – has done a six- to seven-year apprenticeship in the general printing trade and, if lucky, after doing casual shifts during holiday periods, is taken into the Street permanently.

In Fleet Street's hot-metal composing rooms the men only began work when the Father had allocated them a lino machine. No work could start until the Father or one of his committee stood in the middle of the room and shouted, 'Line on, gentlemen.' 'Lines cut' was announced when the edition had gone. 'The line is on' meant the day's work had started. A familiar phrase in the Street's pubs is, 'I'm going to line on.' And there was still the centuries-old 'banging out' ceremony, an emotional moment for any printer when on retirement his colleagues would bang metal to metal as he walked round the room to say goodbye.

Those who worked in composing rooms considered themselves more than factory workers. Setting molten lead type, photo-engraving the etched images of photographs, making up the metal-cased pages which would eventually be taken to the stereotype department where an impression of the page would be made, and reading the proofs, the samples of the pages – this they considered was the work of craftsmen. The speed with which they set the type or the ability to read the reversed words on the metal blocks, was for them an industrial art.

The composing room had a special atmosphere. The compositors wore navy aprons with brass 'charging gauges' to measure the type, a tool of the trade which most had received from retiring printers. The smell of molten lead, the noise and the urgency of the work as deadlines dissolved was a special and precious world for them.

It was in the composing rooms that the fight against new technology had been the fiercest. These craftsmen had fought against the Linotype machine in 1889 when it had arrived from New York. It had been greeted with horror by the members of the old-style craft unions, the Typographical Association and the London Society of Compositors, predecessors of the NGA. Previously the compositor had hand-picked each letter of type, so the machines could mean fewer and unskilled jobs. But through negotiation the unions had managed to keep the machine for the exclusive use of members.[21] Their reaction to photocomposition had been the same: they were craftsmen who would not accept that technology had changed their world.

In the *Sun* composing room there were four NGA Chapels, each for a different process area: the comps, who made up the pages; the linotype operators; piece case workers, who set everything that went into large type, including the headlines; and the proof readers. They were all in the same Imperial Chapel, but fiercely proud of their own craft. They considered themselves to be labour aristocrats of print, and members of the rival Sogat to be mere manual workers who would never aspire to the printing craft.

In the last years in Bouverie Street the NGA men were all too well aware that trade unionism was under threat from a government determined to alter labour relations. The last major battle in the *Sun* composing room was not about rates of pay or hours worked. It centred on the effort by the composing room to support striking miners. Fleet Street trade unionists donated more than £1 million during the 1984-5 miners' strike; Chapel activities became totally associated with the miners' cause. There was a feeling of pessimism, a belief that if the miners lost, the printers would be next.

Throughout the strike the *Sun* stridently supported the government and some editorials and stories enraged NGA union activitists. Their recourse was either to refuse to handle stories they obected to or to have a 'right of reply'. In the past, Fleet Street printers had used these tactics on stories containing references to themselves: in the early 1970s, for example, they had stopped a piece by David Astor, due to be printed in the *Observer*, which detailed their overmanning and restrictive practices. But it was during the 1976/77 Grunwick dispute, when workers in a film processing laboratory walked out for recognition for their union, APEX, that printers extended these tactics to issues outside their own industry. Printers had also tried to interfere with the reporting of the Eddie Shah dispute in Warrington in July 1983. Shah, of the Stockport Messenger Group, had set up non-union subsidiaries with which his NGA members refused to deal. There was a bitter and violent strike. It was a test case not only for the NGA closed shop but for the new Tory labour laws. The NGA lost £1 million in fines.

Demands by compositors at the *Sun* for a right of reply during the miners' strike led to claims that the management was losing control of the editorial content of the paper. This was not something which Editor Kelvin MacKenzie would easily tolerate, but at times during the miners' dispute he found himself with no alternative.

In January 1984, during the mineworkers' overtime ban, MacKenzie hit on the idea of running a *Sun* ballot: 'Miners! Tell us what you really think. This is the ballot that Arthur Scargill won't give you.' The ballot form was set in metal and page two was ready to go to the next process when a young printer arrived on 'the stone', the name for the steel-topped tables where pages are assembled. John Brown was the Imperial Father of the composing room. He instructed the man on page two to do no more work.

Within minutes of this instruction, MacKenzie had stormed

into the composing room. The Imperial Father and the Editor glared at each other across the page. There was a heated discussion. Brown told MacKenzie that the ballot paper interfered with the democratic rights of trade unionism. Page two would not go, he told the Editor, unless there was a disclaimer on the page from the NGA. After two hours of heated negotiation, MacKenzie agreed. Under the ballot appeared the words: 'The members of the National Graphical Association employed on this paper object to the above ballot paper on the grounds that it interferes with the democracy of the National Union of Mineworkers.' And MacKenzie was also forced to agree to allowing 300 words from Arthur Scargill in the next day's paper.

Four months later, in May, a front page was prepared by MacKenzie with a picture of Arthur Scargill at a rally, with his arm in the air, giving what looked like a Nazi salute. The headline, under the banner 'Sun Picture Special' was 'Mine Fuhrer'. When the photograph and the copy arrived in the composing area, all work stopped. Again, tempers were lost. MacKenzie eventually pulled the picture from the page, and in its place, blazoned across the front page, he put: 'Members of all the *Sun* production Chapels refused to handle the Arthur Scargill picture and major headline on our lead story. The *Sun* has decided, reluctantly, to print the paper without either.'

John Brown had an air of timidity, but managers knew that this hid an astute mind and an extraordinary obstinacy. A Father is said to be only as good as his committee, whose members are his lines of communication with his men. Chapel committees throughout Fleet Street varied in the number of members, but always had a Secretary and Treasurer. Brown was the type of Father who used his committee to the full: he cared about his popularity and he would always accept a majority point of view. This gave him extra strength.

During the miners' strike his nickname became 'right of reply Brown'.

'All I tried to do was get some balance,' he says. 'It was the best year we had.'

Brown really did not care about criticism from Tony

Dubbins and other executives from the national union who warned him that if such actions continued his men were heading for trouble. Brown was involved with the Campaign for Press and Broadcasting Freedom and was a member of a secret group of left-wingers within the NGA known as the Shoe Lane Progressives, named after a road just off Fleet Street where the London Region of the NGA once had offices.

On 28 September 1984 'right of reply' caused the stoppage of the newspaper. That evening, John Brown had left Bouverie Street at 6.30 and had just arrived at the junction with Fleet Street when one of his men from the composing room caught up with him. There were problems on the stone. Brown turned round and went back into the building.

A story had been sent down to be set which had outraged some of his more militant members. Brown went straight to the composing room, where work was in progress on all but one of the pages. He was handed a proof of a story and read. 'Miners were rightly once called the salt of the earth. No longer. Too many of them have become the scum of the earth.' Brown could hardly believe it. He had just finished reading when MacKenzie approached him.

'You can't keep on with this, John,' he was told.

Brown told him there would be no more movement on the page unless the word 'scum' was removed. MacKenzie refused.

'Then we'll have a statement saying we are producing under duress,' Brown replied.

MacKenzie laughed. Brown then asked if the NGA could have an advertisement in the paper stating their case.

'No,' MacKenzie told him. Brown next requested that a letter from the NGA be printed. This was also refused and MacKenzie left the composing room.

Minutes later Brown was called to the office of a manager in the composing room. He was ordered to push the trolley containing the page to the next process. 'Push the forme,' he was told. Brown, always one to keep to the rule book, told the executive he had no alternative but to call a meeting of the Imperial Chapel and talk to the men.

'Do that and you're fired,' he was told.

Brown calmly walked out of the room. Minutes later the line was cut – the meeting was in progress.

Copies of the proof were being run off and given to the Chapel Fathers elsewhere in the building. The machine-room men stopped work and were in the reel room having an emergency meeting. Members in the publishing room, where the papers are bundled, had also stopped. MacKenzie telephoned Murdoch. When he put the phone down he ordered the cashiers to close so that the night's wages could not be paid. The paper was lost and what became known as the 'scum of the earth' dispute began.

Ray James was not in the building that night, but when his deputy, Ernie – known as the Weazle – Hardcastle, heard that his men would be losing a night's money he toured the building with one of his committee men to find Bruce Matthews. They found him talking to Murdoch on the telephone.

There are two totally different versions of what happened next, but by all accounts it was a furious scene. Matthews describes Hardcastle and the committee man 'rampaging around the second floor after the newspaper had been stopped'. Hardcastle, he said, 'proceeded to break into a private telephone conversation I was making in Mr Murdoch's office.' When he had finished the call, he said, he had gone into the passage to see what Hardcastle wanted. 'At that moment the Editor, who was obviously concerned at having lost his paper by the action of the various Chapels, came through the swing doors and maybe slightly brushed past Mr Hardcastle as he was standing right at the door.'[22]

Hardcastle's version is that when he realised Matthews was on the phone to Murdoch he left to wait in the small outer office. Seconds later, he says, 'MacKenzie barged through. I said: "Haven't you got any manners?".' Hardcastle says he was then treated to a torrent of abuse.

'I'm fed up with you fucking people interfering in my editorials. Piss off.' Hardcastle also claims that MacKenzie called him a 'little wanker'.

Matthews described this incident in a letter he wrote later to Ray James. He says that Hardcastle had very loudly insulted the Editor.... The Editor was so incensed at this that he became highly critical of Mr Hardcastle.'

Matthews was also angry. Hardcastle described him as 'raging'.

'He said he was sick of the Chapels and we could all go and work for fucking Maxwell.'

Matthews says: 'I realised the situation was getting out of hand and I ordered Mr Hardcastle and his colleague to leave the floor. I did this in the strongest terms, as I believed at that moment the matter would get more serious.'

It was not the insults from Matthews that upset Hardcastle. 'I can take it from him because I know him,' he said. Hardcastle was incensed by the insult from the Editor. Like most production workers, he hated MacKenzie. 'He would charge the working class for breathing. I told him to come outside the building and we'd sort it out on the pavement.'

The machine room called a Chapel meeting two days later and decided to stop work. Ray James wrote to Matthews: 'We will obviously be seeking an unreserved apology from Mr MacKenzie.'

A meeting was eventually held in MacKenzie's office with Ray James, Ernie Hardcastle and Bruce Matthews.

'I had never been in the Editor's office before,' said Hardcastle. 'When I got there there weren't enough chairs and MacKenzie went outside to get me one.' Hardcastle said he jokingly put his fists up and they had both laughed. 'MacKenzie said he had spoken in the heat of the moment,' Hardcastle recalls. The meeting ended in talk about Wapping. MacKenzie told them he wanted to produce six million copies a night in the new building. 'We want to be in a position to print them,' Hardcastle said.

The 'scum of the earth' dispute cost four days papers. The stumbling block for the return was a dispute about which Chapels should be paid for the Friday stoppage: management said no Chapels which had supported the composing room action should be paid. The exception was the machine room.

In the last months in Bouverie Street it began to seem to the Fathers that the ground was shifting under their feet. Three Chapel officials were fired and the Fathers on the *Sun* and the

News of the World believed that these unprecedented moves were designed not only to demoralise their members but to try to shake the balance of power. Kelvin MacKenzie had taken to walking through their composing room and shouting: 'You haven't got much longer, you lot.' And he would laugh.

John Breen, the deputy Imperial Father of the *News of the World* composing room, had received more written warnings and had been suspended more times during his fifteen years on the paper than any other official. A short, wily, self-opinionated man with a lined, bearded face which made him look more than his 48 years, Breen, with his cashmere coat with velvet collar and pointed, stack-heeled boots, was more unpopular with management than any Chapel official. He was known for his quick and vicious temper and for being one of the most politically motivated officials in the Street. He was. Breen had done more than most to support the miners and was said to be able to press-gang anyone into giving money during the strike. He had only attended one meeting of the Shoe Lane Progressives – he had his own political ideas and did not easily fit into a group.

Other Fathers in Bouverie Street hated his arrogance and the way he spoke of the composing room's 'monopoly power'. Breen had wanted Chapel office because he said he was better at it than anyone else. 'If anyone is going to represent me, it's me.' The composing room and the union were his life. 'I love the hot metal skills,' he says. 'I knew no one, no one else could do my job. We weren't producing ball bearings . . . there is an urgency about it and we did a good, clean, professional job.' And it was his skills in hot metal which earned him some respect.

At 11.23 p.m. on Saturday, 6 April 1985, Breen stood in the middle of the composing room floor. 'Line off,' he shouted. The men stopped work. He had called a Chapel meeting, claiming that his men should be paid £2.50 each because of late copy from the journalists. His men were 'sweating to make up time and were overworked'. The copy was arriving in a flood. 'We claimed extra money because we wanted to screw down editorial,' he says, blaming the journalists for late arrival of stories. 'The off-stone times had drifted.' At 11.40 he took a telephone call from a national official of the NGA, who ordered him to instruct his men to resume work. The compositors 'lined on' and continued working.

At half past midnight the men were working on the last edition, which by then was half an hour late, when Matthews walked into the composing room. The Managing Director was in a furious temper. He found Breen on the stone and the two glared at each other.

'I was harangued,' said Breen.

Matthews told Breen he had disrupted the paper for years – that he had stunted its growth. Breen admits losing his 'rag'. He yelled at Matthews. He said that he himself was a 'progressive Father' and said the company was incapable of managing the editorial department.

On Sunday morning Breen was telephoned at home and told he was sacked. In the next few days there was a flurry of activity between Alf Parish for the NGA and the company. There were meetings and lengthy telephone calls. Four days later the sacking decision was reversed and Breen was suspended on full pay pending an investigation. A week later he was reinstated on the understanding that he would not hold Chapel office. That too was eventually withdrawn, but the Chapel was told that any future negotiations with management would have to be conducted by the Imperial Father himself and not by Breen, his deputy.

At the end of September, a reader whose job it is to check the page proofs spotted the words 'no, he is a hero' in a story in the *Sun* about Enoch Powell. The words clearly made the story racist. There was uproar. MacKenzie was furious. He said the words had been inserted in handwriting on a proof by someone in the composing room. Matthews insisted that samples of handwriting be taken from every member of the composing room. John Brown, the Imperial Father, gave instruction that no one comply with the investigation. He was fired. Another compromise was reached, again involving negotiation through national officials. Brown would be taken back and a joint union-management inquiry would be set up to find the culprit. The inquiry never took place.

In October, the Deputy Father of the process department was accused of having disobeyed an order. He was accused of having broken a plate, told the action amounted to industrial sabotage and was fired on the spot. What shocked the other Fathers in the building was that his men did not react by striking, although they continued to pay his wages between them. Again there was negotiation leading to a compromise. The official was eventually given his job back but told he could not start until 1 January 1986.

Ray James had sensed that times were changing. He remembered distinctly the first time he heard the phrase 'management's right to manage'. He had shut down a machine one night in 1980 and the production manager had told him to put it back into operation. 'God, he was a boring bloke,' James remembers. 'We hated each other.' He was told twice to start up the machine. Management, he was told, had a right to manage. 'I said, "Start your fucking machine . . . but you see those blokes, they are not working it."' And James had ordered the crew out of the room.

In the days leading up to the Wapping dispute, it was not plate breaks which caused delayed copies, missed trains and the continuing claims for overtime in the machine room. There was a surprising number of paper breaks. The Production Manager told James that there was nothing wrong with the newsprint and accused his pressmen of negligence and sabotage. When at 4 a.m. on 17 January 1986 the company refused overtime, the crews broke the paper on the machines and lifted the plates before the print run was finished. The last letter to James from the management threatened his members with disciplinary action, including dismissal, if the paper breaks continued.[23]

Whatever the problems, James never blamed Murdoch. He thought him a reasonable 'governor' – he had sent him a telegram of congratulations when he bought *The Times*, and Murdoch had replied that it was 'particularly pleasing' to have heard from him.[24] But James had worked for over twenty years in press rooms where Fathers were used to looking the proprietor directly in the eye. The management set up in Bouverie Street continually confused him: he just could not get used to the idea of an absentee landlord. He felt that management was uncertain and contradictory, and saw his men being used as scapegoats. He truly believed that many of the troubles would be over if only Murdoch was personally involved. How could a successful newspaper proprietor, he wondered, hide behind such incompetent managers? In an unprecedented step, he took to writing to Murdoch.

'... You have members of your staff who find themselves incapable of resolving comparatively small problems ... I hope you do not think my remarks are presumptuous but at the moment I represent 700 of your employees ... who are being manipulated and used in a power struggle,' he wrote in April 1985.[25] He did not receive a reply.

In 1981 he had fired off a letter about what he considered to be Matthews's off-hand manner during wage negotiations: the Managing Director, he said, had not even got up when James had walked into the room and had kept his feet on the desk while he was talking to him. He told Murdoch that further discussion with the Managing Director would be 'damaging', and he asked that they sort out the problem themselves. A curt reply came back: Murdoch was unable to take part in industrial negotiations as this would make 'everything unworkable', and he warned James that because of the fall in the price of sterling the company would be losing £6 million in the next twelve months. To survive, everyone would have to 'do more'.[26]

Such a response never deterred James from his belief that all Murdoch's problems were caused by his managers. Shortly before the 1986 crisis, he wrote Murdoch a detailed three-page letter urging him not to suspend the negotiations for Wapping. 'We have always believed you were extremely pleased with the fact you took the *Sun* over ... I am well aware of the frustration and disappointment you must feel over the whole question of the investment you have made and the new building which is standing idle at Tower Hamlets.' He told Murdoch that the *Sun* would get to the new plant 'in a reasonably short time once we get together'.[27] He did not receive a reply.

On Friday, 24 January it was already dark when Ray James walked back to Bouverie Street from Sogat's London Central Branch headquarters near King's Cross, where, at a packed meeting of Sogat officials, Brenda Dean had announced that the strike was on that night. With the others he had applauded and cheered.

James went directly to his Chapel office and telephoned the Production Director. 'My Chapel's out,' he told him, and put down the phone. Then he went down into the machine room. There he found management taking 'diabolical liberties'. He noticed a group of his men gathered round an overseer, who was handing each of them a letter of dismissal. James grabbed one and read: 'Dear Sir/Madam'. He angrily pushed through the group and picked up a pile of the letters, throwing them violently into a rubbish bin. It was not the letter which had infuriated him. Management had no right to hand anything out to his men; all management contact had to come through him or the Chapel committee. And he ordered the overseer out of the room.

His Deputy Father, Ernie Hardcastle, took another pile of letters to the first floor where, in keeping with the rules, he started giving them to the men gathered in the canteen. But an overseer came up eventually and snatched them back. Hardcastle went back to the machine room to find James.

'A lot of us had been sacked before, but we had always got our holiday money,' he said. 'A lot of blokes wanted to know where their holiday money was.'

About a hundred men in overalls in the machine room had already started work: the machines had been 'webbed up' – the sheets of paper already guided through the rollers. James stood in the middle of the room.

'Clear the room,' he yelled.

The paper was taken out again and for the next hour the room was cleaned. As was customary before any dispute, the large rollers were lifted to prevent damage when the presses were idle for any length of time. Discarded copies of the *Sun* were thrown away, the floor swept and the trolleys which transport the heavy plates were lined in the corner. Only after Ray James was satisfied did he tell his men to leave.

There is an old tradition which has fallen into disuse that the Father is the first in and the last out. It was perhaps this tradition which prompted James to make a final tour in the Bouverie Street basement that night. It took him an hour, walking the three floors, climbing on every deck. He inspected all twenty-five machines – including the African Queen and the Flying Scotsman, which in 1936 had been Fleet Street's print run record holder. He walked past the small locked wooden door behind which was the crypt of the Whitefriars monastery. The cavernous room was empty and his footsteps echoed on the metal floors. The only sound came from the old tea urn, which continued to gurgle.

When James finally left through the swing doors, he saw a security guard in the corridor waiting to lock the room. He walked up the stairs to the works entrance in Whitefriars Street, where years ago printers desperate for work had 'signed on' at the wooden door, hoping to be picked by the Father for a night's shift. James thought he would be gone a long time. But he believed he would be back. It seemed inconceivable to him that his men could go out on strike and not stop production of the *Sun*.

By chance, that Friday night, on a narrow back staircase in Bouverie Street, Bruce Matthews bumped into Tony Isaacs, Imperial Father of the *News of the World* machine room, the only official who had negotiated an agreement to go to Wapping. The two of them were alone. The Managing Director put out his hand. 'I'm sorry, Tony,' he said.

Tony Isaacs has the sort of grin which leads one to believe that everything has come easy. A bullish East-Ender from Bow, Isaacs left school at 15. In his first job in print he had organised a 'rat' shop – non-unionised – and had been sacked after six months. But he did not want to stay in commercial printing companies. He had family in the Street, and he says that the only ambition he ever had was to become a Father in the *News of the World* machine room.

Isaacs was an efficient Father: his letters to management were neatly typed and his files always in order. Isaacs regarded stoppages as a failure in negotiation and they were rare in his machine room. He was a well-prepared and skilled, if ferocious, negotiator who used London slang to the full with his deep gravelly voice. He stuck rigidly to tradition: the Father, not his deputy or one of his committee men, always opened negotiations with management. And when Isaacs started talking, he could go on for forty minutes. Isaacs had a large ego and would be the first to admit his arrogance. But he always tried to negotiate his way out of trouble, and despite his temper the executives in Bouverie Street warmed to his sometimes totally disarming honesty.

There are said to be two types of Chapel Fathers who are poached by management: those who are so obstructive to the company that it is preferable they are out of the way and those who are moderate, effective and efficient. Isaacs was one of the latter. There had been talk in the last months among his Chapel members about him 'going over'. He had been noticed lunching with Industrial Relations Executives. Not that there was anything unusual in that, as Fleet Street Fathers sometimes negotiated with management over lunch – generally in expensive restaurants. 'Knife and forking', it was called. But it was a practice always regarded with suspicion, and since Isaacs had concluded his agreement for Wapping, he had been called 'right-wing' by the union hardliners, who also accused him of selling out. Isaacs never replied directly to the accusation of 'going over'. He would roar with laughter no matter who was asking.

'No one will ever get anything by buying me a meal,' was one of his replies. Another was – 'No one ever offered me enough money.' Isaacs, who earned £22,000, says no one got anywhere by offering him money to get them into a highly paid job in the Street. He said he had been asked once by someone on the golf course.

'I told him to have sex and travel,' he said.

The negotiations for the *News of the World* machine men to go to Wapping started in the Imperial Hotel, Russell Square, on Friday, 13 April 1983, and Isaacs had started proceedings by saying that he hoped the date was not an omen. He told O'Neill that he wanted to improve conditions for his men – he wanted them to get out of the Bouverie Street basement and be the first Chapel in Wapping.

The negotiations were not smooth. The first letter Isaacs sent to O'Neill stated: '. . . your initial overtures are to be likened to the back street abortionist, who not very skilfully performs his operation, removes what he thinks he should and is not particularly worried about the survival of the patient.'[28]

Isaacs complained that the company's proposals cut his staff in half. O'Neill told him that the 100 per cent relief system – the one hour on and one off agreement – would not be operating in the new plant. It had only been agreed, O'Neill said, because of the Bouverie Street machine room working conditions.

'You want two men doing one man's job,' O'Neill said, and went on to ask: 'Could we produce this newspaper with half of your current staff?'

'Yes,' replied Isaacs. 'It would be possible, but no one could work a full night of twelve and a half hours.' [29]

During one meeting, O'Neill angrily told him: 'You have quoted the long nights of ten hours but you only work five hours. We are proposing you work seven and a half hours.'

Isaacs replied. 'We are not going to sell jobs.' At first he had been adamant. 'Currently we have 475 jobs in the Chapel. These will have to be maintained – for all time.' O'Neill's proposals took no account of equipment failure. [30]

But Isaacs sincerely wanted to get his men to better conditions. He used all his negotiating skills with management and he begged, pleaded and cajoled the Chapel. After Tony Britton had taken over the talks, he agreed to lose 90 men. In January 1985 he wrote to the Labour Relations Manager: 'It is with pleasure that I can advise you that my Chapel . . . accepted in principle management's proposals that embrace the Tower Hamlets plant.' [31]

Three months later he was told that negotiations for Wapping had been suspended. He was informed that the meetings with other Chapels had been 'catastrophic'. [32] But Isaacs continued to push the management. He told them that the presses in the machine room were falling to pieces. 'Tower Hamlets is the way out . . . we don't accept talks are suspended,' he wrote to them. And he suggested that the *News of the World* Machine Chapel should go to Tower Hamlets alone. [33]

The last letter Isaacs wrote, in early December, asked for a meeting with Bruce Matthews. Rumour and speculation about Wapping were rife and he wanted to establish their substance. He wanted to know if 'the workforce at Bouverie Street has a future, and if so, what does that future hold for us?' [34]

Just before Christmas he had a reply: 'These are uncertain times in the newspaper industry and as we have consistently stated, the way for your members to safeguard their employment is to ensure the continued and uninterrupted production of our newspapers.'[35]

When he met Matthews late on Friday, 24 January on the back stairs, he told him it was a 'sorry state of affairs'. Matthews, according to Isaacs, said he had not wanted what had happened. 'He seemed physically shaken by it,' said Isaacs. 'He was close to tears in my view.' Matthews shook Isaacs by the hand and walked away.

THREE

The Sun King

Fleet Street has produced some strange, outrageous characters, but no one quite like Kelvin MacKenzie. Descriptions of the *Sun*'s Editor range from 'an ogre' to a 'manic genius'. There are some journalists on his own staff who think he is both.

MacKenzie is an example of Murdoch's ability to pick the right person from the ranks at the right time for the right job. The *Sun* is described by journalists as a 'sub's paper' – the reporters' raw material is always re-written by sub-editors, moulded to a formula and its emphasis sometimes changed. MacKenzie joined the *Sun* subs desk in 1973 and his talent on a popular tabloid was evident then. He could pick a one-paragraph story off the spike and turn it into front-page news. He could spot sensational angles that everyone else had missed and if others thought the truth had been slightly distorted, it did not matter that much. By all accounts he was continually battling with other members of staff.

No one in the Street is hated quite as much as MacKenzie for the way he treats his staff. For example, a feature writer once tried to persuade him to use her article, without success.

She said: 'Well, at least give me E for effort.'

He reportedly replied: 'How about F for fuck off.'

But even his arch enemies will grudgingly concede that there has never been anyone better at the particular brand of journalism which makes the 'Soaraway *Sun*' the paper it is. However soft-porn or trite the journalism, MacKenzie is still Editor of the largest selling English-language daily in the world.

His father was a successful local newspaper journalist. Although he has working-class pretensions, MacKenzie came from a comfortable background and went to a private school in Dulwich. One of his school contemporaries remembers: 'He shouted and swore the loudest. He was a bully.'[1] His reporters would say he had not changed a bit. MacKenzie was Jekyll and Hyde. One minute he could have the back bench laughing – the next minute he would be in a terrifying rage.

He was soon working as an editorial executive. In 1978, he was sent by Murdoch to New York to become Managing Editor of the *New York Post*, bought in December 1976 and turned it from a middle-class liberal newspaper into a sizzling tabloid with junk journalism – famous for one headline quoted constantly in journalistic circles: 'Headless Body in Topless Bar'.

A year later, MacKenzie returned to London as Deputy Night Editor. But he was frustrated because he thought his path to promotion was blocked. He was soon poached by Lord Matthews for the *Daily Express* but within weeks was lured back to the *Sun* by Murdoch, who made him Editor. The first edition of the *Sun* soon became a paper other editors waited for nervously. Sir David English of the *Daily Mail* said once: 'They're shameless. They can't lose.' [2]

MacKenzie had the ability to turn out instantaneous front-page headlines. When he was told that Moors murderer Myra Hindley's lawyer had successfully taken out an injunction against a story, the telephone receiver was barely out of his hands when he shouted: 'Evil Myra Gags *Sun*'. It was the next morning's screaming headline. MacKenzie conceded that some of his own headlines were too much – even for the *Sun*. One which never appeared was: 'Will Andropov pop-off?'

The speed of his particular form of wit, of turning the sordid into the sensational, amazed his journalists and endeared him to many of his staff. MacKenzie always tried to be one of the lads. No matter how offensive, he could always make them laugh, wandering around the newsroom, cracking jokes. He was a great story-teller.

In September 1985 there was a feature series in the paper on Priscilla Presley's life with Elvis. The last day of the series carried a story headlined: 'How could Priscilla do this to our daughter Lisa?' It was Elvis's message to the *Sun* from the beyond through the medium Doris Stokes. One joker picked up a phone and said to MacKenzie: 'Elvis for you.'

Quick as a flash MacKenzie replied: 'Tell him his cheque's in the post.'

'He was born to be Editor of the *Sun*,' said Miles Hedley, a bearded, six-foot sub-editor. 'He could not have been Editor of any other paper.' Hedley is from a Fleet Street family. Murdoch had worked under his father, Peter, who was the 'splash' sub on the *Daily Express* – handling only the front page – and his brother Clive is a *Times* journalist.

Hedley had the sort of talent which made him an excellent tabloid newspaper sub. He loved his work and he admired MacKenzie for his instantaneous decisions about stories. 'It was *Sun* genius,' he said.

Hedley said the *Sun* subs were 'a talented bunch of lads'. They certainly worked hard and they bore the brunt of MacKenzie's tongue: he was not an Editor like some, who lock themselves away. The editorial powerhouse of popular newspapers is the back bench, where decisions are taken about each story's importance and prominence, where the paper is shaped into its exaggerated layout. The back bench and the subs desk were MacKenzie's favourite places on the editorial floor.

He was grudgingly respected for the fact that unlike some Editors he never, as one journalist described it, 'fawned all over politicians'. He gained popularity early on in his editorship when in 1981 he turned down an invitation from the Queen to go to the Palace. Fleet Street Editors had been asked to stop the harassment of the Princess of Wales. MacKenzie refused to attend on the grounds that he was too busy. He considered a meeting with his proprietor more important.[3]

Murdoch and MacKenzie, it was said by the subs, admired each other. The proprietor loved the Editor's tabloid talents and wit and MacKenzie the proprietor's business ability. But there was no doubt who dictated the paper's policy – Murdoch. The Editor would sometimes describe 'the boss' having 'kicked him up the backside'. MacKenzie, known for his fairly liberal views, changed in 1981 to become a strident Thatcher supporter.

Ironically, the *Sun* newspaper was founded in 1911 by printing workers and for years was the official paper of the unions and the Labour Party.[4] Called the *Daily Herald*, it later became the property of the Trades Union Congress. In the 1930s the paper had won the most costly circulation battle the Street had ever known, when proprietors almost broke them-

selves on promotion gimmicks. The *Daily Herald* was the first
paper ever to reach the two million mark.

The paper of working-class politics was renamed and
revamped in 1964 by Hugh Cudlipp, Chairman of IPC, when
its sales were rapidly declining. He renamed it the *Sun*. But
five years later, when the *Sun* had cost IPC over £2 million,
the company decided to sell. The paper's circulation was
dropping fast: it was well below a million and looked ridiculous
against the *Daily Mirror*'s five million.

Robert Maxwell was the first bidder, not aiming for mass
circulation but intending to keep the paper's commitment to
Labour. His plans also included cutting the staff by half. Less
than twenty-four hours after Maxwell pulled out of the deal,
Murdoch was on television announcing that he would publish
a 'straightforward, honest newspaper'.[5] He could print it on
the presses of his other paper, the *News of the World*, in Bouverie
Street, idle for six days a week. And he managed to get 25 per
cent cuts – the best manning agreement in the Street: he had
told the staff he would not start to print unless they agreed.

Two days before the launch of the new paper, an appeal to
readers, written by Murdoch, stated: 'The most important
thing to remember is that the new *Sun* will be a paper that
CARES. The paper that cares – passionately – about truth,
beauty and justice.' And he promised that the paper would
never, ever be boring.[6]

The first issue, on Monday 17 November, carried a picture
of Murdoch's wife Anna, a former journalist, pressing the
button to start the presses, with an accompanying story: 'It's
thank you to the trade unions who bent over backwards . . .
to the journalists . . . the machine men, the wholesalers.'[7]

The speed of the paper's conversion into a racy tabloid
amazed other Fleet Street proprietors. The second issue
carried a picture of 'rich girl Uschi', topless, who had gone to
live with her hippy lover for a life of free sex and marijuana.
Page three showed a girl in a bikini.

At the end of the week, in answer to criticisms that the
paper had no principles, an editorial told readers that the *Sun*
opposed capital punishment, colour discrimination, the
common market and the Vietnam War. 'We are not going to
bow to the Establishment in any of its privileged enclaves.'[8]

Within a year, the *Sun* began to burn its rivals: the circulation shot to and then exceeded two million, mostly at the expense of the *Mirror*. And Murdoch spent money on the paper. In 1972 there was a £1.16 million television campaign and a promotional leaflet was pushed through over thirteen million letter boxes.[9]

By 1976 the *Sun* had caught up with the *Mirror*, and became the largest selling paper in the country. The circulation war had been won with banner headlines, sex, crime and trivia – entertainment, hardly news.

Murdoch's intervention at the *Sun* was then, and continued to be, constant. In his Editor, Sir Larry Lamb, Murdoch found a journalist who reflected his direction: the two had worked together during Murdoch's brief spell as a sub on the *Daily Express*. It was Lamb who had recruited the *Sun*'s journalistic team, known throughout the Street as a bunch of talented odd-balls.

Under the proprietor's direction, the *Sun* newspaper was to poison the world of Fleet Street journalism. To compete in the circulation war, other popular papers changed their image. The trouble was that the imitations were not as good.

But in 1981 sales of the *Sun* were flagging. By the spring, the *Mirror* had caught up and the rival *Daily Star*, launched in November 1978, which had introduced Bingo to the Street, was also taking circulation. Murdoch started his own Bingo game, offering massive prizes, launched a television campaign and cut the price of the paper. Up went circulation, and Murdoch appointed Kelvin MacKenzie, an Editor who, like Lamb, knew what his proprietor wanted.

A year after his appointment, the coverage of the Falklands War indicated to the Street that although the *Sun* had become an 'in-joke', its standards of journalism were no laughing matter. The paper published a scorecard, 'Britain 6 (South Georgia, two airstrips, three warplanes), Argentina o.' In April 'The *Sun* says Knickers to Argentina' became the talk of the Street. There was a series of jokes in the paper under the heading 'Argi-Bargie', and readers were offered £5 and a can of non-Argentinian corned beef per printed joke. But when the paper tried to report the actual news of the war it was often terribly wrong: 'In We Go' screamed a headline – three weeks before any invasion of the islands. And the invention of an interview with a Falklands VC's widow, headlined 'World Exclusive', won the paper condemnation from the Press Council. It was denounced as a 'deplorable, insensitive deception on the public'.

The *Sun*'s coverage of the war led to one of the most vicious mud-slinging matches the Street had ever seen. When HMS *Sheffield* was sunk on 4 May, the *Daily Mirror* printed a leader: 'Calculating and miscalculating politicians started this conflict . . . it is time to prove that peace through diplomacy is the only policy that pays. . . .' The *Sun*, three days later, wrote of its rival: 'What is it but treason for this timorous, whining publication to plead day after day for appeasing the Argentinian dictators . . . we are truly sorry for *Daily Mirror* readers . . . they are buying a newspaper which again and again demonstrates it has no faith in its country and no respect for her people.'

The *Mirror* replied with a leader of its own, headlined 'The Harlot of Fleet Street': 'The *Sun* today is to journalism what Dr Josef Goebbels was to truth. . . . A Labour M.P. yesterday called for the *Sun* to be prosecuted for criminal libel. There is no point in that. It has the perfect defence: Guilty but insane.' A few days later, the *Sun* journalists held a Chapel meeting and a motion was put to condemn MacKenzie for the editorial. It failed.[10]

MacKenzie is credited with writing the most famous headline in the Street in recent years. On 3 May 1982, when all but thirteen of his editorial staff were on strike, 'Gotcha' described the sinking of the *General Belgrano*. It was even too low for the *Sun*, and it was changed later that night to 'Did 1200 Argies Drown?' 'We felt excited and euphoric. Only when we began to hear reports of how many men had died, we began to have second thoughts,' said an editorial director the next day.

'We hardly got any sleep,' said Peter Stephens, Editorial Director of News Group Newspapers, one of the editorial team who worked with MacKenzie during the 1982 journalists' strike. 'We all became totally exhausted. Everyone ate at the office – it was a bit like being in a bunker. Looking back on it, it's amazing that we kept the paper going.'[11]

During the strike the paper carried a picture of a missile with the words, 'Here it comes, Senors'. On 1 May the paper reported: 'The first missile to hit Galtieri's gauchos will come with love from the *Sun*. And just in case he doesn't get the message, the weapon will have painted on the side, "Up yours, Galtieri". . . .' Three days later, the *Sun* reporter on the *Invincible* reported that the '*Sun* sidewinder' had hit an Argentinian bomber. Other journalists covering the war felt so strongly that they sent a joint message to Bouverie Street. Said Stephens in justification: 'Look, we were tired.'[12]

The journalists were amazed at MacKenzie's behaviour during this strike: 'We knew he could do the work of twenty-seven of us,' said Hedley. 'He works six days a week from 11 in the morning until 11 at night as it is.'

A strike by *Sun* journalists was nothing new. Journalists on the *Sun* had a history of militancy. Just like the production unions, the NUJ was aware of the paper's vast profits. In 1978, journalists were becoming increasingly resentful of the wages being paid in production areas. They wanted equal power – they wanted as much trade union muscle and the ability to stop production.[13] They put in a large wage claim and struck for ten days. The dispute cost the company £1.9 million.[14]

It was the *Sun*'s financial success which prompted a strike in 1984. And once again, behind the £3,000 a year across-the-board wage claim was an attempt to reach parity with the print unions.

The strike was a failure. Only two editions of the paper were lost when MacKenzie, who had been working with a few executives, went home because he said he was 'knackered'. The greatest damage for the NUJ was to morale and to relations between the journalists and the printers. Long-standing resentment turned to anger.

The NGA had crossed their picket lines. Senior NUJ officials blame Ken Ashton, then General Secretary of the NUJ, for this.[15] To the striking journalists, not in the confidence of the union hierarchy, the strike was lost because of the printers. It was something they would not forget eighteen months later.

*

John Hill, a *Sun* stalwart, was one of the longest-serving sub-editors on the paper. He had worked with MacKenzie on the subs table for years, and they would often play squash together. When Murdoch was in Bouverie Street, Hill was one of the subs he would stop and chat to.

When Hill arrived in the newsroom on Thursday afternoon, 23 January, MacKenzie was sitting on the back bench. 'On your bike today, John?' Kelvin asked. Hill told him he had left it at home with a flat tyre.

'You won't need a bike where you're going tomorrow,' said MacKenzie. 'You'll need a fucking armoured car.'[16]

It was yet another Wapping joke. For months there had been rumours and speculation. Two senior, bright and experienced journalists, David Banks, the talented and ambitious assistant night editor, and Graham Courtenay, had disappeared. In the summer, Banks said he was going to America to look at technology; Courtenay, who had written the 'Mine Fuhrer' headline, claimed he was leaving to become a press officer for the Middlesex County Cricket Club. No one quite believed any of it.

Rumours about Wapping were growing. In September some staff heard that the plant was being protected with high metal fencing. A dummy issue of a newspaper printed in the plant had been smuggled out. When the talks over manning the *London Post* broke down just before Christmas, there were more and more conversations in the newsroom about Wapping.

In December, Eric Butler, a 62–year-old sub-editor for the sports pages, who had been on the Murdoch *Sun* since it started, remembers some friends from the sports desk going to have a look at the place. They were standing outside the plant when out came the Sports Editor, Terry Clark. 'He didn't know where to put his face,' one sub said.

By January 1986 rumours about Wapping were round the building like wildfire. When the print union announced their strike ballot, some people in the newsroom speculated that the journalists would be provoked into a strike, would be sacked and only a select few, chosen by MacKenzie, would be allowed to go to Wapping.

In the last six weeks some heads of department were away sick. There was a joke that they had the 'Wapping cough'. A select few were secretly, and discreetly, told that they would be going, but they did not actually go. MacKenzie started taking certain people into his confidence. 'It was like waiting for an invitation to a party. You began to worry you were not going to be invited,' said one sub.

MacKenzie later told Hill: 'Tell your mates a new life starts tomorrow.'

Hill said he was quite pleased to hear that. 'I thought Christ . . . something's got to be better than this . . . we'd had nothing but rumours for six months, all the scaremongering.' Hill said he thought he would give the firm one more chance. 'They've been screwed mercilessly by the print unions.'

The NUJ seemed in disarray but the instruction was clear. *Sun* journalists could not think about going to Wapping until there was a deal with the print unions. At a meeting of the *Sun* and *News of the World* Chapels in St Bride's Institute in early January, Harry Conroy, the National Union of Journalists' General Secretary, had said it again. He was given a rough ride. Journalists wanted to know why they should now support the print unions. Conroy kept reminding them of the TUC's collective policy. Some thought he had been evasive. One journalist described Conroy as giving them the 'ABC of Trade Unionism'. On Wednesday, 22 January, at another meeting with Conroy, the Chapel had voted to recognise the instruction not to go.

On Friday, 24 January it became quite clear by midmorning that there would not be a paper that night. Talks between the company and the print unions had broken down the day before, and although no one knew when a strike would be called, everyone knew it would not be long. 'We all knew Bouverie Street was finished somehow,' said one sub. 'We didn't know whether we had jobs or not.'

Some reporters were already packing up their belongings. It was an emotional and apprehensive time. Groups gathered to try to work out what the future was. Some were convinced that Bouverie Street was finished, that the *Sun* would never be printed there again. Others thought such talk was ridiculous.

Most newsrooms in Fleet Street are messy, untidy places. It is the nature of the product, the speed needed for hitting deadlines, that make newsrooms unlike any other office. The newsroom in the *Sun*, like all other areas in the building, had somehow survived with minimum maintenance for a long time. 'It was a filthy hole,' one journalist said. 'But it was home and it was Fleet Street.'

By 6 p.m. on Friday, 24 January, when MacKenzie finally burst into the features room on the fourth floor in Bouverie Street, a short step down the corridor from his office, to address the staff about Wapping, he was facing a bunch of worried, frightened people.

He stood in the middle of the room, surrounded by journalists, some standing next to him. Over a hundred members of the *Sun* staff were crowding into the room when he started speaking. He was cocky and he was self-assured. 'Now,' he started. 'This is a momentous day for the newspaper.'[17] There was talking and shuffling. MacKenzie raised his voice above the chattering. Unknown to him, he was being taped for posterity.

> Seven years ago, Rupert Murdoch decided to build a plant at Wapping, mainly because if the papers were going to be successful he felt the *Sun* and the *News of the World* wanted extra capacity.

The room was becoming quieter, people were settling down.

> For six years he tried to persuade Sogat and the NGA to join with him down at that plant.

MacKenzie raised his voice:

> For six years . . . they said no. Finally, one of the branch secretaries at London Central, seeing the new plant, turned round and said, 'The best thing you can do is blow this place up.' At that point there seemed no further point in continuing to try to get the traditional unions to take part in what was obviously going to be the future.

MacKenzie paused. The room was now completely quiet.

> So off we went from there. And Mr Murdoch went on . . . and we completed it, and as you will see if you read the *Sunday Times* or watch 'Panorama', various things had to be done in secret to get that plant into shape.

He raised his voice again:

Because where we had been on the end of blackmailing, bullying, every single pay round, every single piece of technology that was introduced into the world we tried to introduce into this building – every single time there was a threat that if we didn't turn it away they would shut us down.

By now MacKenzie was shouting.

In a minute-to-minute industry, when they've got you by the balls, you've got to listen. Well, they haven't got us by the balls any more.

He paused. No one spoke.

The situation is simply this . . . the only people that matter any more are the journalists . . . there can't be papers without journalists and it is with this in mind that we are now going to make this momentous step from Bouverie Street down to Wapping . . . tell you a number of things about that . . . first of all . . . we need you. [He paused.] It is you that makes the paper . . . I personally want every single one of you, including those who are ideologically at the opposite end of the pole from me.

Then, emphasising his words by banging his fist on to the palm of his hand, he said very slowly and firmly:

I want every single one of you in Wapping.

Again no one spoke, but there was a sense of relief in the room.

I understand that if for political, industrial . . . even if you can't find it . . . [there was subdued laughter] if you don't want to go then that is a decision for you . . . not a union decision, not a management decision, it is a decision based on what you think your best future is.

He banged his fist against his palm again: 'Enlightened self interest,' he almost shouted. And went on:

In self interest say to yourself, is this my future? Is this the paper's future? If they coincide, for Christ's sake grab it with both hands.

He said they had an assurance their union house agreement would remain unaltered. They had an assurance there would be no redundancies.

'Despite my protestations, Mr Murdoch . . . is going to make an extraordinarily generous pay offer to actually be part of the transfer down to Wapping,' he paused. 'I counselled against it . . . I . . .' his words were lost as the room erupted into laughter.

'How much is it?' MacKenzie ignored the question and just carried on.

'But he insisted that he was not going to play the nasty guy any more . . . he's giving it away.'

'What pay offer?' Again MacKenzie ignored the question.

You all have something to offer . . . when it all comes together it's the paper . . . each one of you contributes something different and something bloody worthwhile. I want it . . . so we continue to produce without a shadow of a doubt the best paper in Fleet Street . . . right, that's it . . . thank you very much.

Then, just as it seemed as though he was about to leave, he said: 'If any of you have any questions, I am quite happy to answer them in the face of fear . . . or worry about the future, security and those sorts of things.'

Bruce Kemble, a feature writer who had been on the *Sun* for only a few years, spoke first: 'How much, Kelvin?' Once more, everyone in the room laughed.

'I don't know,' replied the Editor. 'I have a vague idea . . . it will be resolved on the 28th . . . right.'

Someone asked when they were going. 'The timetable will be that if you gentlemen want to go, a few of you can go tonight.' Then MacKenzie started struggling for words, unsure of what to say. 'Er . . . tomorrow morning, at a hotel . . . er the Tower Hotel . . . take half of you at ten o'clock and half of you at two o'clock.' Others rostered to appear for work, he said, would just appear in Wapping, 'as per normal'.

'Where is Wapping?' someone shouted.

MacKenzie just carried on. 'You can look at the set-up, get to know it, have a go on the machines. We have people on hand to train you . . . and so you can get your security passes because obviously security is an aspect to this which is unfortunate, but must be in the very nature of the dispute; it would be unwise to take less than adequate precautions . . . er . . . and basically . . . bring your own wine, OK?'

He was asked about redundancies. 'Nobody,' he said, 'but nobody is being made redundant. People must stop worrying. The truth is we will be employing thousands more in the years to come . . . not thousands less.'

There was so much general chatter that the next question, asked by Eric Butler, an elderly journalist, was lost to most of the room. But MacKenzie's answer was not.

'If they don't want to go down there. I . . .' he was hesitating. 'I . . . er . . . think the answer to that is er . . . that those who did not go to Wapping . . . would be considered to be dismissing themselves.'

But others were still concerned about where they should be the next morning. 'Ten o'clock tomorrow morning in the Tower Hotel,' he said impatiently.

'What's the new technology?'

'Er . . .' MacKenzie hesitated.

'Atex,' someone prompted him.

'Are we all meeting at the Tower Hotel?' he was asked again.

'What we are going to do, is to split in half . . . er Ken will probably . . .' and MacKenzie was prompted again by Ken Donlan, one of his executives.

'Secondary picketing, Kelvin?' a journalist asked.

'I don't know . . . er . . .' He was unsure, then he found his stride: 'Brenda Dean has given an assurance today . . . I think that most people have been rather impressed by the way that Miss Dean has handled herself. She has given an assurance that picketing will be peaceful. I am sure there will be very odd exceptions. I very much doubt if there will be any violent scenes. I do not expect to see that.'

A question about the technology was lost in chattering. MacKenzie said: 'It is in your own interests to get to grips with it as soon as possible.' It would take a couple of days to get used to the computers, he told them.

'Kelvin, do you expect to get a *Sun* out on Monday?'

'Yes, I do.'

Jean Ritchie, a feature writer, popular with everyone, asked about clearing out their belongings in Bouverie Street. Would they be able to return next week to collect things? 'If it's work things I would take them home,' MacKenzie said.

'That's all been sorted out,' Ritchie said in her clipped voice. 'But we have a few personal things.'

'Really?' said MacKenzie. 'Oh?' There was laughter. 'Look, take everything, O.K.?'

'Yes,' replied Ritchie.

'Is there a newsroom in Wapping?' someone asked.

'This building was never actually designed for doing what it will actually do, it was never intended to have these newspapers there and therefore there are aspects to it that aren't tremendous, but it's a thousand times better than here. It's beautiful inside, smashing canteen, that sort of stuff.'

There was then a rush of questions about the NUJ's directive that they were not to go to Wapping. What would happen if they were expelled by their union for going?

They got a really firm answer from MacKenzie. 'Let me say to you this – I would be astonished by the NUJ chucking out paid-up members. If at any stage it does, perhaps, get a bit nasty, and the NUJ may at some stage threaten, you are journalists you know, you are creative people, you have a lot to offer, you have a value in your own right as distinct from just being members of a trade union. It's no problem . . . honestly, I promise you, there will not be a problem. We will always, always, always defend anyone who has been persecuted by . . . er . . .'

'You?' someone shouted.

The meeting disintegrated into general chat and jokes. None, apart from those closest to him, heard MacKenzie say that the computers in Wapping would be used for direct input. 'It will make your job a lot easier.'

'On the health side?' someone asked about the new technology.

MacKenzie made sure everyone heard what he had to say next. He wanted to draw the meeting to a close: 'I'll tell you what he has got,' he said in a loud voice. 'Rupert has bought some of the world's most expensive chairs, $300 each, they go up and down and round about at the touch of a button. So every effort has been made.'

As he left, he said: 'O.K. Bye, bye, see you in a couple of minutes.' He went straight into his office and telephoned Murdoch, waiting for news of the meeting.

Malcolm Withers, the paper's financial correspondent, who had been Father of the *Sun* journalists' Chapel for seventeen years, ever since the Murdoch purchase, spoke to his members. He told them it was a tremendous decision to make. He had been in touch with the union and the directive was clear: they should not even negotiate the move.

'I will not be going,' he said. 'You will lose your cards. From the time you go, you will be on your own.'

MacKenzie was called back. His mood had changed. He had just received very clear instructions from Murdoch. 'You'll get £2,000 each for retraining. We'll produce this paper with or without you. If you don't come, I'll find another two hundred people.' He was by then so furious that he stormed out of the meeting before fully losing his temper.

Withers then told the journalists that he had received no assurances from management that the union's agreement with the company would remain intact after the move. He had been told that the management would only give their answer on the 'house agreement' the following week.

They decided to call MacKenzie back. He had, once again, spoken to Murdoch. It was MacKenzie the comedian who came back. 'All right, all right, I think on one of the main assurances you seek – since you seem such an untrustworthy lot – anyone would think you were journalists – is that you are worried that at the end of eight weeks, right, the company house agreement is up, introduce the old banging drums, slavemasters and away we go, seven days a week, eighteen-hour day . . . now I put this forward to Rupert and Rupert is dead against it.' The chapel was laughing again.

'And in his place, I am quite happy to assure you that agreement will be standing for another year, right? So you now have basically a fourteen-month house agreement on the same basis you have now, right? So there we are, game set and fucking match. I'll drop my trousers . . . OK?' There were sniggers, but he continued: 'Anybody got any questions, you know, things you really deeply fear this beastly management, paying you on average twenty-five grand a year for a four-day-week ... is going to do to you? Can anyone tell me how much tougher we can be?'

Someone asked again about the health hazards with new technology. 'Yeah, yeah,' said MacKenzie. 'And we are also giving you golden wheelbarrows ... you want zimmer frames or any other health aid ... please, you know, I realise how tough it is to be a journalist in Fleet Street today, or in Wapping.'

He was asked for news of the print unions' dispute. And how would it end?

'If you can tell me how it's washing up ... right, I'd be obliged because we've got no one on strike but we've got no damn paper tomorrow, right? So we lose another three hundred grand, so if you can tell me which way this dispute is going, I'd like to know because I don't know. There is nothing official. There is no set date, no official time, it might be a clever ploy. I'm sure if you asked Rupert Murdoch right now he does not know when it is going to start, and certainly has no idea how it's going to end.'

'Do you accept we have no dispute with the company and we have no agreement to go to Wapping?' asked Ian Blunt, a sub from the features department who had just become the Chapel clerk.

'I don't know whether you have an agreement to go to Wapping. We are going to Wapping. You are journalists who work for us, therefore we say that is where our head office is and therefore it is up to you to decide. There's nothing I can do – I can't force you to do it, as much as I might like to but, er ... so in the event it is up to every single one of you to make the decision. It's not really an answer to your question because I don't know what you are getting at.'

'At the NUJ we have no dispute?' asked Blunt, who was angry. For weeks the Chapel had been asking the management for information on Wapping.

'As far as I know we haven't,' replied MacKenzie. 'I am sure you can find one if you work hard enough. If I bend over any further I'll be in *Gay News* ... sorry about that every-body.'

'Kelvin,' shouted a sub. 'In the event of our being thrown out of the union, would you and the management recognise . . . if we reorganise ourselves into another organisation, would you recognise it?'

'Absolutely. What the NUJ has done for you could safely fit up a gnat's arse. What you have done for yourselves has been incredible . . . you think about it. It's astonishing. I must think of becoming a member. Any other questions. Right, keep on talking.' And he left the room once more.

After the Editor had left the room for the last time, Harry Conroy, the NUJ General Secretary, who had been waiting in the back of the room, stepped forward. With him was Mike Smith, the union's organiser for national newspapers.

In his familiar Glaswegian dialect, Conroy told them he had just come from the TUC. Under no circumstances could they go to Wapping. They were bound by the TUC decision on collective action with the print unions. They were also bound by a decision taken that week by the union's executive instructing all members to work normally at their normal place of work. This decision had been endorsed by all the Fathers on Murdoch's four newspapers.

Conroy was treated with anger. 'We pay your wages,' David Pryke, a reporter in his late fifties told Conroy. 'I want to know what you're going to do to get us into Wapping. Because that's where we're going.' Conroy was accused of not keeping them informed. He was told his executive should have put in more ground work.

Conroy was shaken. 'It was rough,' he said later. 'Very rough.' He had been repeatedly asked by journalists why he thought they should support the NGA and Sogat. 'They were a cynical Chapel,' he said. 'And highly paid. Most believed they had been treated badly by the NGA over the years. Eighteen months before, the NGA had walked through their picket lines.'

Conroy, the traditionalist Glaswegian trade unionist, had kept referring the journalists back to collective TUC action. He told them they had to try to save over 5,000 jobs. He reminded them that at a Chapel meeting the previous Tuesday they had supported a motion that they would not go to

Wapping without an agreement.

One voice of support for Conroy was from Olly Duke, a
layout artist who for months had tried to get the Chapel to
discuss the issue, warning any member who would listen that
Murdoch intended to break the power of the print unions so
that he could print the titles at Wapping with non-union
labour. Since April he had been pressing Malcolm Withers
to hold meetings on new technology and the Chapel's relations with the NGA. He had even organised a petition calling
for a meeting. He felt that Withers was being obstructive
and he wrote to Conroy accusing him of breaking Chapel
rules.[18]

The son of a U.N. diplomat, Duke had joined the paper in
1981. He had been a member of the Socialist Workers' Party for
ten years, his interest in politics starting when he was studying
political science at university in Johannesburg. He used to sell
the Socialist Worker in Bouverie Street. 'About fifteen or twenty
people would buy it from time to time,' he said.

Duke had been critical of Conroy's previous performances
in front of the Chapel. 'He was better,' Duke said of Conroy
that day, 'but it was too little, too late.' Along with many
others, he believed that people had made up their minds before
Conroy even started speaking. Conroy was no match for
MacKenzie.

It was Jean Ritchie who finally proposed the motion. It
read: 'Bearing in mind the verbal assurances from the Editor,
this Chapel goes to Wapping.' Conroy again tried to explain
to his members that they were under instruction. Malcolm
Withers also argued against the move. 'If you go down, you'll
turn into a company union,' he said.

The vote was taken. It was a show of hands. One hundred
members voted to go to Wapping and eight voted against. It
proved to Murdoch the effectiveness of the strategy of taking
the Sun vote first, devised by one of his other British editors
some time before. MacKenzie immediately telephoned Wapping. 'We're on our way,' he said to Murdoch, who replied,
'Fucking great.' He was beaming, executives remember. He
had told MacKenzie that if the debate had carried on, his
final offer to the journalists would have been increased to
£6,000.

When Conroy walked out of the *Sun* and down the steps of Bouverie Street, he stopped for the television crews. He looked, and sounded, shattered that night. 'It was the worst mistake I made,' he said later. 'I had gone through personal abuse and faced a total lack of understanding. I was really depressed – and it showed. I came over on television as a guy who was despondent and tired. You should never allow that to be seen.'

In the newsroom most reporters and subs had started clearing their desks. There were plenty of black plastic sacks available. Some of the copy-takers were in tears. There seemed to be more than the usual number of commissionaires wandering around. One experienced sub who had voted to go, said that he was relieved his future was secure. 'We realised we all had a part to play and there was a great pioneering spirit.'

Eric Butler, who had asked MacKenzie the question about what would happen to those who did not go, said he was in a state of shock. 'MacKenzie told me if I didn't go I would dismiss myself. I'm the longest-serving journalist on the *Sun* and have had one day's sickness, and that's what I was told.' Anger turned to depression when he saw his colleagues forming queues just outside the Editor's office to put their names down for the buses to Wapping.

Olly Duke was also fuming. He said he had stormed downstairs to the composing room where he found John Brown, Imperial NGA Father, standing on a chair addressing over two hundred people.

'John, John,' he yelled. 'My chapel's voted.'

Brown had called the Imperial Chapel together only minutes before by banging a metal block on a completed page. The meeting had been brief and subdued. 'We're all out indefinitely,' he told them. The response was muted. There was almost no discussion. Just as the meeting was ending, Duke had burst into the room.

He was one of the few journalists Brown had time for, and he allowed him to speak to the Imperial Chapel. 'The bastards have decided to go,' he remembers saying. 'I'm disgusted.' When he had finished speaking, he was applauded and cheered.[19] Brown said later that Duke had seemed near to tears.

Brown had returned from the NGA branch headquarters in Doughty Street, just off Gray's Inn Road, where he had been told at a meeting of Chapel Fathers, addressed by Alf Parish, that there was to be a simultaneous stoppage with Sogat that night. But Parish had instructed the Fathers to keep their men in both the Gray's Inn Road and Bouverie Street plants for as long as possible.

Parish's main concern in Bouverie Street that day had been a piece of equipment which the management had installed in the composing room three weeks earlier. The Dia-Press was a machine capable of reproducing the newspaper pages prepared by the hot-metal process for transmission anywhere.

The management had negotiated the use of the Dia-Press with the unions in late April 1985. They said it was to be used to reproduce pages of the *Sun* for eventual printing in Kinning Park, if the new plant in Glasgow ever opened. At another meeting with the unions on 28 May 1985, the management said the Dia-Press could be used to 'fax' pages of the *News of the World* to Manchester, where the Sunday paper's northern editions were printed. The unions heard nothing further about the Dia-Press until Saturday, 4 January, when Parish was telephoned at home and asked if the Dia-Press could be installed without union agreements. He was told that all management wanted to do was to 'test it'. Parish had given his permission.

On Friday, 24 January overseers had been pressing composing-room members of the unions to use the Dia-Press: they wanted them to copy the already prepared pages of the *Sun* and the *News of the World*. Union officials had been resisting all day.

When Parish was told by Chapel Fathers what was happening, he rushed to Congress House. He called Tony Dubbins and Brenda Dean from the Council Chamber. He told them that he would not be able to control the situation much longer. NGA members were being pushed, he said. The Chapels were being provoked. Management was trying to reproduce everything on the Dia-Press, and, Parish said, 'The papers were being spirited away to Wapping.' He said that managers

were trying to make the Chapels walk out, but he had counselled them all not to take any action.

It was in the fifth-floor lobby, outside the TUC Council
Chamber, when Dean and Dubbins had heard what Parish
had to say, that the decision to strike was taken. Dean had
thought Sunday was the most likely time. She recalled: 'Tony
and I had a brief discussion. If one Chapel had gone out
alone, it would have been off we go. Who took control initially
was important. We did not want to come out by default.'

Arrangements would have to be made for a press conference
to announce the strike that night. Not even the Executive
Committees of each union were consulted. Dean later called it
a 'strike by *de facto*'. In the meantime they hoped the Chapels
would hold. Fathers on all four papers would be instructed
not to impede production but to do all they could to prevent
their work – the stories and pages – getting to Wapping.

In Bouverie Street the Imperial Chapel stayed until 9 p.m.,
an hour and a half after the strike was announced at a joint
NGA and Sogat press conference. It was clear to Brown that
he could no longer keep the Imperial Chapel together. His
men were beginning to drift away. Some had cleared out their
lockers – something unknown in any previous dispute. They
had earlier opened up bottles of vodka and whisky left over
from Christmas, but now there was discussion in Brown's office
about whether the remaining bottles would be safe in a locked
cupboard.

Brown left the building at 9.45. 'I was relieved. We had
been waiting for months to do this,' he said. He was optimistic:
he believed that even if Murdoch had organised another
composing room in Wapping, he would never print the *Sun*
without the machine men.

He walked to Fleet Street and went into the Printers' Pie
pub, known as the 'peanut bar'. It was solid with printers.
Brown found a surprisingly happy atmosphere. Only one of
his men showed any emotion that night.

'This is it, isn't it John?' the man asked.

'No it's not,' Brown remembered saying to him. He thought
the man was in a state because of the booze.

FOUR

Poker, not Whist

Just over half of the dozen or so senior *Times* executives who attended the morning news conference on Friday, 24 January realised it would probably be the last in Gray's Inn Road. But all knew the paper faced yet another crisis: there was every likelihood that there would be no paper that night.

Colin Webb, the Deputy Editor, took the meeting in the Editor's absence. It was a busy news day. On the home front, Leon Brittan seemed to be on the verge of resignation over the Westland affair. The results of the Northern Ireland by-elections were due. The new director of the National Gallery was to be announced. Foreign news was dominated by the successful evacuation from Aden of those in danger of being killed in the fighting in South Yemen's civil war. Webb was particularly interested in the personal message of congratulation the Queen had sent to the Captain of the Royal Yacht *Britannia* and her crew. The visit to London of the Israeli Prime Minister, Shimon Peres, was coming to an end; there was a general strike in Buenos Aires; the space shuttle *Challenger* was due for launch on Sunday.

Not very much was said about the newspaper's own crisis. The Home Editor said that Sogat had a meeting organised for 1 p.m. Webb said that if there were any inquiries from anyone about the dispute, they should be referred to the letter Rupert Murdoch had sent to all his employees, urging them to carry on working.

As the meeting was coming to an end, Webb said that the Rector of St Bride's had announced that his church would be open throughout the night for those who wanted to pray for the future of Fleet Street. The Vigil was a good story. Webb told the News Editor he wanted it well covered.

When Rupert Murdoch bought *The Times* in 1981 he described it on television as 'just another newspaper'.[1] This was indeed the paper's reputation in the Street: the 'Thunderer' had, by the early 1980s, lost much of its authority. Although still famous worldwide as a great British Institution, to Murdoch it was another of those 'sick and ailing' British newspapers whose editorial and financial ways needed an overhaul: he intended to raise its circulation and turn round its finances, something three previous owners this century had failed to achieve.

On 26 January 1981, just days after he bought the paper, Murdoch addressed the editorial staff in the *Times* newsroom. He was talking to a group of journalists who in the past few years had gone through a suspension lasting almost a year and many threats of closure. They were tired of the endless crises, wary and unsure. But they still had a sense of status, history and identity. There was still great kudos in working for *The Times* of London. 'We don't do it this way on *The Times*,' was a dated catchphrase, but was still sometimes a factor in editorial judgements. *The Times*, the journalists believed, still reflected what was good and bad about Britain. It was a paper worth protecting.

Murdoch told them he was going to make the paper viable: it would take time and money, but his promise of commercial viability was not uppermost in the journalists' minds. Clifford Longley, the Religious Affairs Correspondent, told Murdoch that not all the staff were convinced by his guarantees of editorial independence. Murdoch's reply has often been quoted since: 'I think I have locked myself in. . . . What if I found a way of tearing up all those guarantees and fired an Editor? The answer is there would be a terrible public stink and it would destroy the paper. . . .'[2]

The previous owner, Lord Thomson, had believed that a low-circulation, quality paper like *The Times* could only survive if the nineteenth-century technology of the linotype gave way to photocomposition. Although, in July 1970, *The Times* had been the first British national to publish pages produced by photocomposition – the Stock Exchange pages – 'Uncle Roy', as Lord Thomson was known in Gray's Inn Road, never realised this ambition. Shortly after Murdoch's takeover, however, the move to photocomposition was completed.

Ironically, *The Times* had been famed for an earlier printing revolution. The paper had introduced the first steam press in 1814, by smuggling it into Printing House Square piece by piece and secretly assembling it in an empty room to avoid objection from printers. Then one night John Walter II, the founder's son, Editor and Manager, asked his staff to stand by for a late foreign story. Meanwhile, the paper was being printed in secret on the new press, by steam, at 1,100 sheets an hour. When he revealed the plot to his staff, the paper was already printed.

That was not the Thomson style. Other methods were tried to compel the printers to come to terms with new technology. In the first four months of 1978, when twenty-one issues of *The Times* and nine issues of the *Sunday Times* failed to complete their print run because of industrial action, Thomson's heir, Kenneth, decided there was only one way – to impose direct inputting. The Chapels were told that if agreement could not be reached, both *The Times* and the *Sunday Times* would be suspended from publication. He wanted half the NGA jobs to go and offered generous redundancy terms. The computer equipment was already stored in Gray's Inn Road – £3 million worth. But by the time the November deadline was reached, only 19 Chapels out of 56 had agreed. The NGA had refused to negotiate unless the threat of suspension was lifted. Management refused to budge, and both papers were suspended for nearly a year.

Both titles were back on the streets in November 1979, but in the first seventeen weeks, the *Sunday Times* completed its print run only ten times.[3] Production delays were blamed for the pitifully low circulation of *The Times*, which dipped from 340,000 to 300,000.[4]

It was in late 1980 that the Thomson management's patience ran out. *The Times* journalists went on strike for a salary increase, after the management had refused to abide by an independent arbitrator's decision. Lord Kenneth Thomson, who believed he had been generous in continuing to pay their wages during the suspension, was amazed at what he perceived as a lack of loyalty. He put both papers up for sale. The company announced: 'The major reason behind this decision is the continuing troubled history of industrial relations . . . it has not been possible to operate the new technology even on a limited basis.' The company was about to lose £15 million that year.[5]

The Murdoch purchase shocked many of the staff: some left at once. The elegant and respected Washington Correspondent, Patrick Brogan, a *Times* man of the old school, was horrified. What few standards remained, he believed, would soon disappear. Brogan telexed the Foreign Desk in London, asking why his counsels of caution about Murdoch had been ignored, and then, completely out of character, he added: '. . . he will cut all your balls off, if you have any.'[6] Before the end of the year, Brogan and a few other stalwarts were gone. When the *Sunday Times* Editor, Harry Evans, whom Murdoch once described as the greatest Editor in the world, was appointed to *The Times*, fifty more went. Evans undertook a massive shake-up of staff, bringing journalists of his own across the bridge which spans the road separating the two papers. The new group was sneeringly described by the old guard as Evans's 'cronies'. Intrigue, jealousies and plummeting morale among the staff was the result.

Evans said he wanted to emulate Thomas Barnes, appointed in 1817, whom he considered 'the finest English Editor we have ever had'.[7] He said he wanted it to be like his *Sunday Times*, which had challenged and campaigned. Evans changed *The Times* considerably: he improved the layout, introduced the Information Service on the back page, used larger pictures and catchy headlines. He trebled the space given to features. Critics claimed that the paper's grammar was slipping, foreign coverage had become trivial and that it was obsessed with the Royal family. Judging from letters Evans received, some of his readers were outraged.

The rift between the pre-Evans staff and the new recruits began to cause serious problems. Losses of editions were even worse than those suffered by Thomson, and in spite of greatly increased editorial expenditure, the circulation was scarcely any better. Murdoch decided he had had enough. When he asked for Evans's resignation after just thirteen months on 9 March 1982, he told him: 'The paper's in chaos and the senior staff are in turmoil.'[8]

Evans's book, *Good Times, Bad Times*, which attempts to

vindicate his editorship, described the political pressure he was
under from Murdoch – how he had tried to bend the paper to
his will. In one telling anecdote, Murdoch 'was gouging his
ballpoint pen through a report on page 2 by Lucy Hodges'.
Hodges had written a story summarising the evidence to the
Scarman inquiry into the Brixton riots and the residents'
group's criticism of the police. 'Why do you use these
Commies?' Murdoch had asked Evans, who had replied that
Hodges was a good reporter and it was absurd to call her a
Communist.[9]

Evans's book was described by John Mortimer in the *Times*
200th Anniversary Souvenir as reading like 'a couple of dozen
riveting episodes of Dynasty'. He said it threw a 'new and un-
expected light on *The Times*'. It did just that.

Evans's portrayal of his Deputy Editor was extraordinary.
Charles Douglas-Home, 'Charlie', the nephew of former Prime
Minister, Lord Home, had been a King's Scholar at Eton,
commissioned into the Royal Scots Greys, and had served as
ADC to the Governor of Kenya. He joined *The Times* from
the *Daily Express* as Defence Correspondent when he was 27,
replacing Lord Chalfont. He covered the Arab–Israeli Six-
Day War for *The Times* and had written books on the Middle
East, Rommel and British defence. He seemed almost a car-
icature of the country gentleman. He loved foxhunting and
wore hand-me-down threadbare shirts and worn jackets in
the office.

A man who on the surface was shy and retiring, he gave the
air of standing back with statesman-like disregard for the
sordid events surrounding the Evans departure. His allegiance
was with the old *Times*.

Evans's story is that Douglas-Home, with his 'lethargic
charm', had worked subtly to get the Editor's chair from under
him. His descriptions of his deputy show him as not only a
man with glaring ambition but a loud-mouth. Evans claims
that Douglas-Home told him he did not want his job as he
could not do it and added: 'I would never work for that
monster Murdoch.' Douglas-Home, according to the book,
telephoned Evans and said: 'You little fucker, I'll come in
there and wring your neck. You've told people Larry Lamb
will be the next Editor if you go, you bastard you.' In March

1982, at the height of the unseemly row, *The Times* made
front-page headlines: 'Leaks rock *The Times*' and 'Dirty Tricks
at *The Times*'.

Douglas-Home, as the Literary Editor, Philip Howard, once
described, took over the paper 'in a raging storm, with mutiny
and panic below decks, and the ship in danger of founder-
ing.'[10] Morale was low, but he succeeded in earning the respect of many of the staff for bringing them some stability. He
brought calmness and consistency, clearly loved *The Times* and
gave it a sense of direction and strong military-style leadership.
He used his lieutenants well, was tough and fair.

He added more business stories to the paper and increased
the coverage of crime and sport. He wrote many of the editorials himself and they were strident and decisive. But there
was no doubt that the paper was changing. Senior executives
spoke of the decline in editorial standards, balance and
accuracy. Many believed that the paper's authority was
irretrievably damaged with the introduction on 25 June 1984
of the circulation-grabbing Portfolio, which office wits called
Dingo – after the Australian wild dog. The story on the first
winner, a Harrow schoolboy, which appeared on the front
page of the 26 June issue – alongside a picture of schoolboys
throwing their boaters in the air – was written by the Home
Editor, David Blake. He had been to the school to do the
interview himself: the Chapel had decided that reporting on
Portfolio winners was not a task for *Times* journalists.

Douglas-Home said that those who had opposed Portfolio
were the sort of readers who complained when news had
replaced the small ads on the front page.[11] The circulation
rose as a result of the game.

The Editor's courage during a long illness with cancer was
extraordinary. His staff were to speak later of his 'gallantry', of
how he 'led the troops' until the very last moment, of his
'aristocratic sense of responsibility'. Douglas-Home was 48 when
he died in late October 1985. His successor could not have been
from a more different background. Charles Martin Wilson
became the paper's sixteenth Editor on 5 November. The son of
a miner, he had been born in Glasgow.[12] Although his epithet in
Private Eye is 'Gorbals Wilson', he grew up in Surrey and started
his journalistic career as a 16-year-old copy boy on the *People*.

'Charlie Two', as he was known by the *Times* staff, had
worked on the *News Chronicle* as a reporter after two years'
National Service in the Royal Marines. He became Editor of
the *Glasgow Evening Times*, briefly edited the *Glasgow Herald*
and then launched the *Sunday Standard* before moving to *The
Times* in 1982 as Executive Editor. For three months in 1984
he edited the *Chicago Sun Times*, and is credited with having
taught journalists there a thing or two about news. Wilson
is said to have risen in Murdoch's estimation when he turned
down a high salary to stay in Chicago: he preferred to return
to London.

His reputation in the Street is of a man with a vicious
temper. He is a short man and looks somewhat like a boxer.
He is often satirically portrayed as a Glaswegian thug and is
said to throw telephones, bang on walls and scream. The story
which did the rounds after his appointment was about the
nickname he had given a reporter – 'fingertip man', because
'that's what you're hanging on by'. Wilson is passionate about
newspapers and when he is anywhere near the back bench
there is always tension. Few in the Street on the more popular
papers where he has worked would challenge his judgement
about the merits of news stories.

When he addressed the editorial staff on Wednesday, 6
November 1985, Wilson was obviously nervous. 'This is a very
proud day for me. It could not be anything else, having got
up this morning to find myself at what I consider to be the
pinnacle.' He promised them stability: 'There won't be any
great changes – in philosophy, strategy or personnel. *The Times*
has in the past undergone a great deal of upheaval, but I
hope that is now gone for ever. We will go on in the next
years in the same mould as we have been going in for the last
two or three years . . . I think in any case newspapers should
be the subject of evolution rather than revolution. *The Times*
has had more than enough revolution.'[13]

On *The Times*, Wilson was known for making people hit
edition times. There was no longer collegiate discussion about
the value of news stories – he would make instantaneous decisions. His criticism was harsh: he became known in the
newsroom as the 'arse-kicking machine'. Reporters said he
encouraged the use of this nickname. They recognised him as

one of the Street's typical Scottish hard-news editors – ignoring the fact that he had grown up in southern England – whom one tried not to cross. It was said that he appreciated strength: he admired those who stood up to him. He could also be surprisingly sensitive and sympathetic.

Murdoch had quickly recognised his drive and energy. Anyone who knew the close relationship between Murdoch and Wilson could have predicted the eventual appointment. It was the proprietor's way of saying thank you to a loyal, hard-working and plain-speaking man he believed was capable of waving a magic wand – whether it was in Chicago or in London. Although Wilson had been Douglas-Home's deputy, he had spent very little of 1985 on *Times* business. As Editorial Director of the proposed *London Post*, he had been busy elsewhere.

When in London, Murdoch was known to spend several hours with Wilson, longer than with other editorial executives. When the proprietor was in town, Wilson would be invited to Murdoch's St James's Place apartment for a quiet evening drink. 'It was a mutual admiration society,' said one senior executive,[14] knowing that Murdoch tended to have his 'wonderboys', who would be in favour for an unpredictable length of time. Wilson sometimes found it difficult to get away during some sessions with Murdoch. Married for the second time to Sally O'Sullivan, Editor of *Options* magazine, and with two young children, Wilson was protective of his private life. Having been single for some years, he treasured his new family, living in an elegant home in Holland Park, where J. M. Barrie had written *Peter Pan*.

Ever since he had attended a meeting in Murdoch's Fifth Avenue triplex on Sunday, 10 February 1985 – a 'brainstorming' session to discuss plans to revolutionise the Street – Wilson, the first member of Murdoch's British editorial staff to be taken into the proprietor's confidence, had been caught up in a whirlwind of organisation. In that year, although appointed Editor of *The Times* in November, Wilson would be mainly concerned with Wapping.

Wilson was in his shirt sleeves and with his tie loosened. He stood on a table to address the staff, but many journalists in

the crowded, airless room in the Times building in Gray's Inn
Road on Friday, 24 January, still could not see him properly.
Those near the front noticed he was shaking; they had never
seen him so nervous. When he started speaking, he was unusually hesitant, and he began by apologising.

He was sorry, he said, for not speaking to them as a group
earlier. 'I hope you will forgive me for that,' he said. He was
sorry too for having brought them back to the office from Red
Lion Square, only minutes after their Chapel meeting had
begun. 'But the storm has broken tonight,' he said. '*The Times*
will only survive and continue production if it can be from
Tower Hamlets.'[15] At 7.30 there had been a 'snap' story on
the Press Association tapes: the print unions had called a
strike.

It would have been easier to have taken the journalists there
first, to have shown them round, but if he had tried to engage
in any sort of 'negotiation' before the stoppage, it would have
pre-empted the printers' own negotiations, and not only encouraged but possibly guaranteed a strike.

'All of you as individuals have a very important decision to
make.' He told them of the original conception of Tower
Hamlets as a printing plant, of how the negotiations for
manning had failed. He reminded them of the *London Post*
project and told them that part of the plant had been converted with a direct-input system. It was now clear that the
print unions would not allow anyone to go to the plant, so the
company had 'expanded the editorial space and the capacity'
so that all four titles could be produced there.

'We have lost tonight's paper,' he said. 'But we do not
intend to lose any more editions of *The Times*. It is going to be
produced editorially at Wapping – on Sunday night for the
Monday paper. I am here to invite you to come along and
help us do it.' Whichever way they voted, as individuals or as
a Chapel, it was now 'inevitable' that the paper would be
produced in Tower Hamlets. The *Sun* journalists, he told them,
had just voted by an overwhelming majority to work there.

'In these circumstances, I put it to you, not working is a
pointless and most expensive gesture which helps neither you
nor those on strike.' If they thought one answer was to report
to Gray's Inn Road to 'enjoy the legal protection of contract

of employment', that was not possible. 'Our legal advice is that it is perfectly justifiable to ask you to move two and a half miles in these circumstances.' In the past, journalists had always relied on being re-hired after a dispute was over. Wilson pointed out that industrial relations law made it 'very difficult' for a company to re-hire staff dismissed during a dispute.

The journalists had three options: they could decide not to cross the picket line and join a strike which was not of their making and be dismissed for breach of contract; they could refuse to work in Wapping and lose their jobs and the years invested in *The Times*; 'or you can come to Tower Hamlets and continue to work for *The Times*.' The conditions there, he added, were 'very comfortable'.

The house agreement – which would be extended for a year – would be altered in only two ways: each member would receive an increase of £2,000 a year and there would be free family membership of a private health scheme. Someone at the back muttered that the insurance would probably be necessary 'if the printers get hold of us'.

Someone else muttered: 'He's won.'

'At a single key-stroke, this gives the journalist his birth-right,' said Wilson, referring to direct inputting. 'Those normally rostered on duty on Sunday will be expected to work. If you don't report for work you will be said to have breached your contract.' He finished his address with: 'I implore you to come with us.'

Historically, the Editor of *The Times* took little direct part in union negotiations with his journalists. His traditional duty was to protect his staff, not only from the establishment but from the owner of the paper. He was their representative and many of his journalists believed he should put them above every consideration. In a few minutes Wilson had tried to sell them the idea of Wapping and told them he would fire anyone who did not go. His journalists were stunned.

The questions which followed showed that the Editor had lost the traditional distance which stands between him and his staff. They were often ferocious and, in the words of one startled senior executive, sometimes 'impertinent'. There was some sympathy for Wilson's predicament: some felt he had been forced to behave as a management spokesman, that he had no alternative.

At 9.31 p.m. the Chapel reconvened. To be asked to go to work in Wapping was the last thing many of them had expected. Greg Neale, Chapel Father, a thoughtful and courteous news reporter in his early thirties, thanked them for the dignity with which they had behaved in the face of the 'outrageous blast' from management. It was a short and disconsolate meeting. One member pointed out that what had happened was the equivalent, in Fleet Street terms, of the invasion of Poland. The only decision they came to that night was to reconvene the following day. They had no idea where they could meet. Neale told them a notice would be pinned on the front door of *The Times* on Saturday to tell them where the committee had found a meeting place.

Most then wandered back to the newsroom. Outside the Editor's office, his assistant, screwdriver in hand, was taking from the walls the portraits of former *Times* Editors: they had been the only reminder in the editorial department's modern but drab surroundings of the paper's distinguished past.[16]

Others watched in dismay as senior management tore through the offices emptying files into packing cases and tearing maps, pictures and rotas from the wall. In the early hours of Saturday, Deputy Editor Colin Webb was wandering round the newsroom with a bottle of wine in his hand. He said it was the one from the Editor's fridge. He approached Martin Huckerby, the Assistant Foreign News Editor, who was emptying the contents of his desk and files into plastic bags. Huckerby refused to share a glass with him.

Huckerby had made up his mind. After fourteen years on the paper, he knew he would not follow it to Wapping. He said the impact of the Editor's address was 'awful'. Although he felt little sympathy with the NGA, he was to write: '. . . Murdoch's contempt of his journalists has never been more evident than on that Friday night.'[17] He spent his last hours in the building trying to get hold of foreign correspondents to tell them what had happened, and accused Wilson of having made matters worse by failing to inform people properly.

Huckerby had little time for the new Editor. He believed that the foreign correspondents provided an impressive service for a paper which had been 'debased and trivialised'. But he said that 'the stresses of trying to maintain standards amid the demands of the new Editor meant that in my last full week in Gray's Inn Road I worked 63 hours. On Friday night it dawned on me that it just was not worth it any more.' He also believed that the staff had gone through so many crises, their spirit had gone.

Greg Neale cleared out the Chapel files from his filing cabinet. He came across a bottle of champagne which the members had given him after the pay negotiations six months before.

'I would not have thought you considered this a time for champagne, Greg,' Wilson told Neale as he was passing the back bench.

'I don't,' Neale had replied. 'We'll split it when we are working together again.'

Neale also spoke to Colin Webb and told him he hoped the relationship between journalists and management would survive. 'But there was a sense,' he said later, 'we would not be seeing each other again.'[18]

Neale was respected as a Father by both journalists and management. He was forever courteous and tolerant and had always displayed a respect for the opinions of others. He had a sense of history about the paper – he could quote exact details from its historic past. And he had an extraordinary commitment to the paper. In July 1984, when *The Times* was stopped because of the Warrington dispute, he had been concerned that the paper, which should have contained the Law Society examination results, was off the streets – he knew that young lawyers always hung around the back door of the paper waiting for a first edition. Neale had taken the list from the newsroom, stood on the steps at the back entrance of the Times building and read out every single name to a large crowd of young lawyers.

He also had a sentimental link with the print unions – members of his mother's side of the family had been in print in the Street – and once he had finished packing his files in black plastic dustbin sacks, he went to the composing room to find Bob Edmead, NGA Imperial Father. Neale had always been prepared to criticise printers when he thought they were wrong, but he believed they were now in a pit that was not of their own making. Neale told Edmead and a group of NGA compositors what the Editor had said. 'We will do the best we can, Bob,' he remembers saying. 'We will try not to let you down . . .'

Before leaving the building, David Flynn, Executive Editor, went to the messengers' room. There was only one story in his pigeon-hole. It was dated 24 January and had been 'filed' – telephoned to the paper – at 19.18. The catchline was 'Vigil' and the story read: 'At the beginning of an all-night Vigil of prayer for the end of the troubles of the newspaper industry, the Director' – this should, of course, have read Rector – 'of St Bride's Church, Fleet Street, urged print workers, journalists and proprietors to try to find common ground for agreement.

'After personally inviting members of the industry to join him, Canon John Oates said last night: "It really doesn't matter if anyone comes along, but what's important is that people take five minutes to be quiet and try and understand those attitudes they don't agree with."' Flynn wrote 'last piece of copy' on the top of the story and took it home as a souvenir.

When the last printers and journalists left the Times building that night, they saw that cars had been moved from the surrounding streets and the office was ringed by police.

It took nearly seventeen hours of debate before the *Times* NUJ Chapel decided what to do about the ultimatum. During that time some of them became so distraught they could hardly speak. The debates were bitter and sometimes angry. In the past, their paper had been plagued by the print unions, whom they blamed for landing them with Murdoch in the first place. They were now being asked to take sides – the unions or the proprietor.

Both the *Sun* and the *News of the World* journalists had voted to go to Wapping. The journalists on the *Sunday Times* had not yet been addressed by their Editor. The pressure was now obviously on the *Times* Chapel: their choice would be a deciding factor in the dispute.

Wapping, with its barbed wire and search lights, twelve-foot high fence and swivelling television cameras, had become a spectre for many of them. It looked like a police station in South Armagh. A few had gone to see for themselves on Saturday morning, and they had been amazed not only by the security but at the vast and dreary plant.

On Saturday afternoon at 2 p.m. the *Times* journalists filed into the ballroom at the Royal National Hotel, Bloomsbury. As they drifted in, they were filmed by television crews. They found it strange being at the centre of media attention themselves. One news reporter was asked in the gents by someone from the *Mail on Sunday*. 'Which way will the Chapel vote?' The *Times* man was a bit put out at this approach and told him nothing.

The Chapel committee, led by Greg Neale, had decided to stick faithfully to the NUJ position. Almost all NUJ full-time officials were there with Harry Conroy, the General Secretary, whose message was the same as he had delivered at the *Sun* the night before. The union had to abide by TUC policy and have nothing to do with Wapping unless the other unions were involved – a position the *Times* Chapel had previously accepted. If the Chapel now voted to negotiate with Murdoch over the move, they risked expulsion. 'If you do go, you will be breaking an NUJ instruction . . . you will be breaking union rules and this will probably be the last time you will make a free trade union decision.' Conroy's sense of obligation and political morality was obvious: they knew he stood to lose more than he gained. But as had happened at the *Sun* meeting, his bluntness upset some members and some gave him a rough ride.

Tony Bevins, the paper's Political Correspondent, made a harsh speech. He was a powerful figure in the Chapel who commanded the respect of his colleagues for his fairness. He was already privately disillusioned over the editorial direction *The Times* was taking, but he strongly attacked the print unions. 'I want my stories to be published,' he said. 'Yesterday was typical. . . . I slogged my guts out over the Brittan resignation and there was no paper to put the story in. For twenty years the printworkers have held a pistol to the heads of newspaper managements.' But the world had changed, he said. Murdoch and News International were now the masters. He said he wanted to go to Wapping, but 'not like this'.

The anger and fear was obvious. One senior news reporter shouted: 'I want to go. But I want to go with my head up . . . not on my knees, eating Murdoch shit.' Those rostered for duty on Sunday were particularly pressured. Chris McKane, the deceptively languid Chief Sub-Editor, told the Chapel that his staff had been summoned to appear in Wapping at 8 a.m., an uncustomarily early hour, the next day.

Jake Ecclestone, the NUJ's Deputy General Secretary, was a good deal more subtle than Conroy. He had been Father of the *Times* Chapel in 1980 when they had gone on strike for more money, prompting Thomson's decision to sell. He now told his former colleagues that if they went to Wapping on the basis of the hastily amended agreement, which had been given to Neale the night before by the Editor, they would have 'the worst new technology agreement in the whole country'. The supplementary clause to the existing pay and conditions agreement committed them to working the Atex system in Wapping 'without any reservations whatsoever'.

'This Chapel is playing poker with Rupert Murdoch and I'm not sure this Chapel is good enough even to be sitting at the same table,' said Bill Johnstone, joint Deputy Father. 'We're whist players and we are up against a poker player.' Johnstone, the Technology Correspondent, was the highland terrier of the Chapel: a spry, wiry man in his late thirties with a good sense of humour, he was to deliver roughly the same speech throughout the debate. Neale and Johnstone were a good team: Johnstone was belligerent whilst Neale was forever calm.

Later that day Johnstone was to give the Chapel one of its few laughs. He had spoken on the telephone with Wilson: 'He's a worried man,' said Johnstone, and recounted Wilson asking if there was anything which was 'causing the Chapel distress'. Johnstone had suggested that the distress might be eased if he dropped the threat of dismissal. 'I can't do that,' Wilson had said. Murdoch was immovable.

No one could have predicted how any colleague or friend would feel. Cliff Longley, the paper's Religious Affairs Correspondent, said that like all of them his mind had kept changing right the way through the afternoon. 'I'm damned if I'm going,' he said. As the afternoon wore on, the meeting became more gloomy and confused. He was later to change his mind, writing a piece a few weeks later in *The Times* on why he and others had done so. The ethos of the profession, he wrote, was that news 'must get through ... it drives us now, and it is nothing to do with the character of a particular employer. Journalists believe in journalism, and are near-addicted to the daily charge of adrenalin it brings.' Those who tried to stop this, he was to write, be they 'obstructive politicians, unsympathetic judges, our management, the print unions or our own NUJ', would find journalists deploying all their ingenuity to outwit them.[19]

Some believed there had to be a way out. Lawrence Lever, a business writer who had trained as a lawyer, was insistent that they should seek the help of a leading QC. The meeting adjourned, and by 6 p.m. the Chapel committee was meeting with Alexander Irvine, a distinguished labour lawyer, in a cramped bedroom in the hotel.

After a three-hour recess, the Chapel reconvened to be told that the lawyer had little good news. He had said there was not a 'dog's chance' of getting an injunction against the company. Those who did not go to Wapping, and were dismissed, might well have a case at an industrial tribunal. But he had chosen his words carefully: 'If any of you were to be dismissed when you are aggrieved at their failure to honour your house agreement, you are advised that the dismissal is unfair.' One of the committee members remarked later that it was like calling in the U.N., and Neale thought it had diverted attention away from the important industrial and moral issues at stake.

By the time the Chapel was told of the legal advice, it was getting late. There was a keen sense of powerlessness and many members were now exhausted, with nerves stretched. Debate seemed fruitless and there was a sense of hopelessness. 'I'll strike ... I'll do anything ... but I can't stand much more of this,'[20] one member said desperately. Another suggested that although Wilson might be terrified of losing his staff, Murdoch had freelance journalists standing by, waiting for a chance to take their places. They had probably been recruited when Wilson was interviewing candidates for the *London Post*. 'Is Murdoch terrified we won't go in? I don't believe it,' said a news reporter. Pearce Wright, the veteran Science Editor, his voice choking, said he found the pressure intolerable.

The Chapel committee stood by their line of defiance. Neale did his best to persuade them that they had power. 'You are *Times* journalists and not even Murdoch, even in this political climate, could get support if he'd just sacked the entire *Times* staff.'

Nick Timmins, the Health and Social Services Correspondent, proposed an amendment against the committee's line. It was a compromise. He argued that negotiations with management should begin immediately to secure an agreement to allow all members to go. With Chapel leaders speaking against it, the amendment was put and lost by just one vote: it was 57–58.

It was nearly midnight, and the Chapel was still no nearer a formal decision. Its leaders' calls to hold firm had still not been accepted, and exhaustion was widespread in the room, now smoke-filled and littered with discarded cups and glasses.

David Nicholson-Lord, a quiet reporter and an excellent cricketer who had been on *The Times* for more than ten years, stood up. He had said nothing throughout the hours of debate. He read a motion: 'This Chapel deplores the style and content of the management ultimatum delivered to NUJ members at *The Times*, believing it is doubly injurious to good industrial relations and insulting to journalistic staff. In the long-term interests of newspaper production, however, it declares the immediate readiness of its members to move to Wapping, subject to the following conditions.'

There were five conditions. They included a call for negotiations to continue on the editorial and safety aspects of new technology, an assurance that pay levels would be negotiated from March 1986 and that the words about journalists working 'without any reservation whatsoever' be deleted from the clause on new technology. Chapel leaders spoke against it, but the Nicholson-Lord motion was passed by a hefty majority. It was nearly midnight when the Chapel broke up. The meeting had lasted ten hours.

The motion contained a caveat, passed by 62–55 votes, that the Chapel would reconvene to consider the position the next evening. It gave those who were totally opposed to the move one last chance, but it also left those due to work on Sunday in the front line. One of them, a sub-editor, approached Neale after the meeting. She was sobbing, frightened that she would be fired if she did not go. 'I put my arms round her. I assured her she wouldn't be sacked,' said Neale, privately furious at the anguish Murdoch's ultimatum was causing his colleagues.

On Sunday morning the Chapel committee met at the NUJ headquarters, Acorn House, to discuss tactics. Most now felt resigned that the Chapel would vote to go, but the committee felt that members had to hold out for the best deal. One glimmer of hope seemed the possibility of the TUC exempting the journalists from the joint union policy. As the twenty-two members of the committee were about to leave for the evening meeting, Harry Conroy put his head round the door. 'Don't exhaust yourselves today,' he warned, and advised them to get a decent meal. The committee had already decided that the meeting, due to start at 6 p.m., would be shorter and tighter.

The meeting took place in a conference room in the Marlborough Crest Hotel in Bloomsbury. When Johnstone had telephoned for a booking, he had found out that a 'Mr Webb' had already made a reservation for *Times* journalists. The Deputy Father told the Chapel that the room had been booked as a contingency plan by News International some days before in case the Editor had to address the journalists in the event of a strike. At least, Johnstone told them, to derisive laughter, they had the comfort of knowing that News International was paying for the room.

The Chapel had two motions to consider, drafted by the committee. The Chapel leaders would be recommending an appeal to the TUC to sanction negotiation – but no immediate move to Wapping. The alternative bowed to the ultimatum, seeking only further improvement to the terms. It was this later motion that was now moved by the paper's Financial Correspondent, Michael Prest.

'You may be wondering why I've remained silent throughout,' Prest said. 'For the first time I just can't agree with the Chapel committee. I believe Murdoch will sack us if we don't go in. I don't believe there is any alternative to going.' It was a lengthy, closely argued and theatrical delivery. Prest walked up and down in front of the Chapel like a university lecturer or exhorting lawyer. There was polite applause when he sat down.

It was clear by now that about fifty Chapel members had already gone to Wapping that day, including the Agriculture Correspondent, John Young, and Lucy Hodges, Education Correspondent. Most were now back and seated among their colleagues. Trembling with nerves and anger, Angela Gordon, Diary Editor, one of the paper's rising young stars, called for their resignation. She was opposed to the move anyway, but she pointed out that those who had gone had breached both the union instruction and the Chapel rules.

The second meeting soon assumed the passionate intensity of the first. One proponent of going said: 'Apart from the barbed wire, there's not much wrong with Wapping.'

Someone shouted from the back: 'That's what they said about Belsen.' Another said Murdoch had not only destroyed the unions but the Fleet Street proprietors as well.

'Murdoch is a bully boy,' a Sports sub, Simon Jones, shouted. 'You've got to stand up to him.'

By now there was news – and a revised set of proposals – from the Editor. The words 'without any reservation whatsoever' would be deleted from the proposed agreement. Further, the safeguards on new technology would be to EEC standards, he promised in a telexed message. 'There aren't any EEC standards,' NUJ National Organiser Mike Smith told the Chapel.

Chapel leaders feared that the flow of management phone calls and telexes was having a softening-up effect. Neale received a note that an 'urgent call' was waiting and hurriedly left the room, only to find that it was a reporter from *Time Out* wanting an interview. 'At a time like this?' Neale had remonstrated.

Again, discussion returned to the possibility of negotiation with the company. Conroy told them that was out of the question: the union was bound by the joint TUC agreement with the other unions. He had already tried to find a way out. He had telephoned Norman Willis, the TUC General Secretary, at his home in Ashford from a pay phone in the hotel lobby. Willis made it clear to Conroy that the Print Industries Committee of the Congress, due to meet the next day, would

consider with sympathy any request from the union to negotiate separately.

As on Saturday, one of the most remarkable speeches was
by Bevins. Neale said later that of all those who spoke in favour
of going to Wapping, the Political Correspondent's speech was
the most honest – and brave. Bevins laid out a bleak vision.
Wapping would not promise a bright future for newspapers.
But there was no alternative: 'When you are faced with
overwhelming forces and you are in a cul-de-sac like we are,
you must either fight to the death or lie down. We must not
go to Wapping with the illusion that we will go with respect.
We have a gun at our heads. I believe most of you here will
go with ashes in your mouths.'

'We are being bounced,' said Labour Editor Don Macintyre. 'You shouldn't let it happen.' Macintyre, the other
two members of the labour staff and members of the paper's
political and industrial departments, were in a particular
dilemma. They stood to lose their contacts in the labour and
trade union movement if they crossed the picket lines. If they
did not cross, they would lose their jobs. 'Every time the
Chapel stands firm, telexes start clattering with fresh concessions from management,' he said. He tried to convince them
that they had leverage with the management. If they held
out, they could force offers.

'Don't assume the *Sunday Times* will go,' he said, speaking of
the paper where he had spent two years as Labour Editor.
'They're waiting to see what we will do.'

But it was clear which way it would go once it came to the
vote. And they knew it had to be taken soon: they had already
spent nearly seventeen hours in debate. Chapel and NUJ
officials knew their battle was lost.

Industrial correspondents from Fleet Street, from radio and
television, were gathering outside the meeting room in the
lobby. Charles Rae of the *Sun* had been seen in the hotel bar.
He was carrying copies of the first edition of his paper to be
printed in Wapping. The front page headline was: 'A New
Sun is Rising Today', and underneath, 'We beat strike thugs'.
Rae had written the story, which began with 'Good Morning
Britain', and went on: 'And we're on the streets despite the
biggest print strike since the war.' The story described

Murdoch as jubilant: his two national dailies had missed only
one edition.

Rae also had a copy of *The Times*. On the front page was a
story by John Young, the Agriculture Correspondent. The first
paragraph stated: 'Mr Rupert Murdoch, Chairman of News
International, said yesterday that he was delighted with the
success of the operation to transfer production of the group's
four national newspapers to new plants in Wapping, east
London, and in Scotland.' The story went on to quote
Murdoch saying that the extent of the computer installation
had been a well-kept secret. 'I'm not quite sure how we
managed to keep it a secret.' He was 'looking relaxed and
cheerful in his office in the Wapping complex'. A paragraph
at the end said that the *Times* Chapel was meeting, but 'a
substantial number of its members pre-empted union instructions by reporting for work today'.

Neale took both papers away from the industrial correspondents. The last thing he wanted was for his Chapel to
be further dismayed by what he took to be a management
tactic.

Back in the meeting, the debate was reaching a climax.
Greg Neale made what was to be his last speech to his colleagues. He implored them not to go to Wapping. It was an
impressive speech. Neale said he was outraged at the behaviour of the Editor, who had been suborned into becoming
primarily a spokesman for the management. *Times* journalists
had a right to expect better treatment. They were being asked
to collude in the sacking of the printers – they would eventually face the same fate, he argued. 'Be under no illusions
when you go in,' he said. 'As soon as this crisis is over, the
Chapel will be under threat,' adding as an exhortation:
'Remember to cling to your sense of unity or you will have no
Chapel or organisation.' Neale said he had been proud to be
Father and proud of the Chapel. 'I have made my own personal decision.' He made it clear that he would not join them
if they voted to go.

Neale re-read the motion:

This Chapel notes the response of management to its motion
of 25 January 1986, which gives minimal assurances on new

technology, its operation and any safeguards. The Chapel repeats its belief that in delivering an ultimatum to journalists on *The Times* that they move to a new place of work, operate new technology with minimal safeguards and by doing so possibly jeopardise the employment of others on pain of dismissal, is a breach of all canons of decent management standards. Nevertheless, recognising itself to be in an impossible position, and regretting that in doing so this Chapel is forced to act in conflict with a decision of its National Executive, this Chapel resolves to work at the Wapping plant on the terms available. It will not do so if the company dismisses any member of the Chapel for not reporting to Wapping today.

The vote was a show of hands. It was an obvious three-to-one in favour of the move to Wapping. Neale stood up. He said that the committee was resigning and he could no longer continue as Father. 'Thank you, and goodnight,' he said. The meeting was over. Some members immediately rushed out of the room. Others just sat and stared. Many were crying.

On 26 January 1981, staff at *The Times* had first been addressed by Murdoch, just after he had bought the paper. He had stressed the need to make the paper viable, but recognised it would take time – 'up to five years,' he had told them.[21] Now, exactly five years to the day later, he was poised to do just that.

FIVE

Refuseniks

The Editor of the *Sunday Times*, Andrew Neil, stood in front of more than 130 journalists in a dingy room at the Mount Pleasant Hotel not far from Gray's Inn Road at 10.30 a.m. on Monday, 27 January. He told them they were the best group of journalists in the world, and, appealing to their deepest journalistic instincts, he said: 'Your paper needs you.'

In the last months, Neil's nickname had become Rambo, but this time his attitude to them was different. There was no hint of aggression or threat in what he said. They would be offered the same as the other journalists in the group: £2,000 and free family membership of a private health scheme. Wapping would be a liberating experience, free from the tyranny of the print unions.

He said that the company would have preferred an 'evolutionary approach' – this was a phrase executives and union officials had been hearing him use for some time. 'Now, revolution has been thrust upon us,' he told them. 'The crunch has come.' At no time during his speech did he say that members who did not go to Wapping would be fired. But the message was clear enough. 'We can't have people not turning up for work,' was all he said.

When Neil was appointed in the summer of 1983, he inherited a group of experienced, self-confident and committed journalists with a powerful sense of camaraderie. There was also a sense of irreverence and scepticism, and the rest of the Street saw them as a pompous lot. The *Sunday Times*, where Britain's 'new journalism' was born, was the paper where ambitious and talented journalists wanted to work. In journalistic circles it was considered the only paper which took the craft seriously, where one worked not just to pay the mortgage. 'Insight', the name of the paper's investigative team, became a by-word for quality journalism.

The *Sunday Times* had been a pioneering paper which had

enjoyed the rare luxury of editorial independence; a paper which had taken on neglected issues, attacking not only fraudsters, but institutions and executive power. It had no party line and it questioned and often opposed the government of the day. The publication in the paper of extracts from *Crossman Diaries* in 1975 had defied government attempts at suppression. The paper's campaign against Distillers had culminated not only in compensation for thalidomide victims which was ten times that originally offered, but when faced with a House of Lords injunction against publishing the story, the *Sunday Times* fought and won the case in the European Court of Human Rights.

The paper's achievements had been produced with resources rarely available in newsrooms. At the height of the Philby investigation, the paper had eighteen reporters in Britain, the United States and the Middle East working on the story. A book was produced, the first of about thirty covering major stories in the next fifteen years.[1]

Murdoch's attitude to the established *Sunday Times* journalistic team was brutal. Many former executives have testified to the fact that he considered the paper in the grip of 'Commies'. In his mind, the journalists were drunken layabouts, lazy and extravagant with the paper's expenses. But it was not until two years after the purchase, when Neil was appointed, that the winds of change were really felt. Neil, little known before his appointment, decided he would dismantle the old paper and build one of his own. He had found the paper 'a bit mired in a sixties mentality'.[2]

Neil was 34 when he became Editor – the fourth-youngest member of the editorial staff. He had first met Murdoch during his three-year stint as American Correspondent for the *Economist*. Neil had persuaded the head of a New York anti-trust consultancy, National Economic Research Associates, to allow him to set up a British counterpart to advise on and campaign for deregulation of television, and Neil had tried to sign Murdoch as a client. Neil said of that first meeting: 'He started to say to me: "What do you think of the *Sunday Times*?" I gave my opinions on it.'[3]

Neil is a man with enormous self-esteem, but who worried about his image. He read with frustration, he said, the early

Fleet Street profiles. At first he had been portrayed as a dour
Scot, and was described in gossip columns as a man who was
puritanical and known for his abstinence from drink. In fact,
Neil is a bachelor who enjoys night-life. He is a member of
Raffles, a small, members-only, drinking and dancing club,
established during the 1960s in the King's Road. He lives in a
top-floor flat in a modern block in Chelsea and has a preference for early 1960s soul music.

Coming from the *Economist*, he was viewed in the Street as
an outsider who knew very little about journalism and
printing. This attitude he blamed on the 'Hampstead drawing-
room dinner-party clique'.[4] He defended himself by saying
that he had been involved in newspaper production since
working on a student paper at Glasgow University.

His explanation for the drastic changes he made at the
Sunday Times was that the paper had become 'sloppy'. He
wanted to instil 'a bit of *New York Times* severity'.[5] 'Before I
came to the *Sunday Times*,' Neil reportedly told a gathering of
staff in the Gay Hussar restaurant shortly after his appointment, 'it was scarcely fit to be called a newspaper.'[6] He told
them he disliked almost everything about it – its staff, its
traditions and what he called '*New Society*-type journalism'. In
his first month, he disbanded the then 'Insight' team. Its failure
to produce investigative breakthroughs in recent years was
symptomatic of the paper as a whole: it was stuck in a rut.[7] In
his first two years, more than thirty talented journalists were
persuaded to resign, many accusing Neil of making the journalism reactive and not creative.

Neil forced a bias into the news coverage. The paper
adopted a strident right-wing tone which many of the journalists disliked. Neil has disputed that his views are far right:
he has said that his enthusiasm for competition, trust-busting
and deregulation is actually a radical stance – it is opposed by
big business.[8]

A watershed for some journalists had been the paper's
coverage of the largest-ever CND rally against cruise missiles,
held in London in October 1983. The headline over a *Sunday
Times* editorial the next day was 'Sunset for CND', and the
rally was described as the 'last great gasp of a campaign which
has clearly failed'.

The coverage of the 1984/5 miners' strike became symbolic for many that what had made the paper special was gone for good: the paper had unfailingly supported the government and the Coal Board. It had printed tributes to the handling of the strike by Energy Secretary Peter Walker – Neil's first job had been as research adviser when Walker was Environment Secretary and the two had remained close friends.

Neither did Neil gain popularity after the paper carried what was described as an interview by him with Ronald Reagan just before the American election in 1984. Journalists discovered that an interview as such had never taken place. Neil's sole contact with Reagan had been to submit a list of questions and receive written answers, and to spend time in the Oval office having his picture taken by the fireside.[9]

Neil is particularly obsessed with America and he is fascinated by new technology – the 'Sunrise Industries' was his term. And his attitude to the British print unions was always evident: their behaviour was a national disgrace, he said. When Eddie Shah took on the NGA in 1983, Neil became personally involved. At the height of the NGA picketing at Warrington, Neil had telephoned Leon Brittan, then Home Secretary, to ask for more police action. And it had been Neil who had first suggested to Shah that he reform Fleet Street. At a meeting at the Savoy Hotel on 7 February 1984, Neil had suggested that change could only come from an outsider. He told Shah that with the new trade union laws and new technology, there was no reason why the country could not have a non-union national paper printed on a greenfield site. Neil's encouragement made Shah's fantasy a reality. 'I knew it was possible half an hour after that meeting at the Savoy...' he said sometime later about the planning of *Today*.[10]

Shortly after he had taken over the editorship, Neil was asked to dispel a widespread rumour in the Street that Murdoch was unhappy with the Political Editor Hugo Young's authoritative column. Young was said to be on a Murdoch hit list. 'It is certainly not on the cards,' Neil had replied. 'If Hugo's happy here, then I'm happy that he's here.'[11]

When Hugo Young, who had been Political Editor since

1973, and the paper's distinguished elder statesman and
Deputy Editor, left the paper in October 1984, the old guard
knew that the *Sunday Times* would never be the same. Times
were really changing. Of Neil's *Sunday Times*, Young later
wrote: 'It makes money, but it no longer makes waves.' He
believed that the paper had ceased to do anything unique.
'The *Sunday Times* used to be a force in the land, a lamp in the
darkness. For reasons which are capricious and unnecessary,
these it has ceased to be.'[12]

In the days leading up to the crisis, Neil's bullish statements
on television about the print unions made him sound like a
member of management and not an Editor. While he parried
his journalists' questions about Wapping by claiming to have
no inside knowledge, in public he always used 'we' when
talking of the management and seemed happy to act as a
spokesman for Murdoch interests. By the time he came to
address his staff about Wapping, he was alienated from many
of them. Their worst fears about the situation, which had been
growing for weeks, were now realised. When Neil told his staff:
'I am one of you', at the Monday meeting, there were not
many in the room who believed him.

It was a seedy room with peeling wallpaper. The basement
was dingy, made worse by the cold, grey day outside. Don
Berry, Executive Features Editor, was perched on a table next
to the *Sunday Times* Chapel Father, Kim Fletcher. When the
Editor had finished speaking, Berry rose to his feet. He was
one of the few in the room who had lived through the paper's
great days, and he commanded more respect than any other
member of staff.

As Managing Editor News, Berry had been the solid rock of
the *Sunday Times* news operation. He was creative and original
at page layout and selecting stories. When he had become
Executive Editor in charge of Features, he was found to be a
brilliant commissioning editor, and a man skilled at production and organisation. He was considered to be one of the
finest editors in Fleet Street. He was also a man of honour and
principle. There was no one on the paper who had an unkind
word for him. He understood better than anyone the journalistic traditions of the *Sunday Times*. In the last years he had
become the symbol of the old regime: he had done his best to

protect the 'endangered species' of Harold Evans's staff from
the harsh realities they had faced under Murdoch ownership.
But Berry was no rebel; he had spoken in Chapel meetings
consistently favouring moderation and negotiation. His voice
was now choked with emotion as he accused the company of
ruthlessness and deception in the final stages of the campaign
against the unions. But as he had done so often in the past
with their frequently complex stories, he managed to put the
situation into some sort of perspective. Berry's talent was
turning thousands of words from several journalists into one
incisive, informative narrative. His honesty and integrity were
qualities which everyone recognised. He now spelled out for
them in no uncertain terms the moral dilemma they faced –
for many it was their most serious.

'I have never heard anything like it,' said John Lovesey,
Deputy Features Editor. Lovesey said that even though he
had spent a considerable time with Berry in the preceding few
weeks, the speech was a bombshell. 'I had never heard him
speak like that. He seemed to have gone over it all in his
mind. I was stunned.'

An articulate and graceful man, Berry held the room for
over ten minutes. He told them that once *Sunday Times*
journalists would have looked to the support and protection of
their Editor in such a crisis. Instead, Andrew Neil had publicly
taken on the role of the company's apologist.

Berry calmly accused the company of deception and ruthlessness in the final stages of the 'campaign against the unions'.
He said that some of the tactics used by the company would
be impossible to defend in the editorial columns of a serious
newspaper. 'They have compromised the paper's moral stance.
They have undermined the principles of the newspaper. How
can we urge frankness and moderation in any other dispute?'
It was not self-important, he said, for journalists to believe
that the quality and integrity of their work were essential to a
serious newspaper.

He reminded them that the print unions, in a last-minute
effort to avoid the crisis, had offered unprecedented concessions, and he accused the company of having provoked a
strike in order to sack their employees without compensation.
The journalists had been insulted and betrayed. The company

had broken the journalists' union agreement by insisting on the move to Wapping: 'But the real offence is in human terms.' And Berry had turned to the Editor and said what many would not forget: 'You have treated us with contempt.'

If the Wapping operation had been concerned with anything other than a newspaper, such moral issues would not arise. 'But we're talking about the *Sunday Times*,' he said.

Berry had not prepared a word. On the train from his neat semi-detached in Ruislip that morning, he had realised he would have to say something. By then all his fears of the past weeks were realities. The journalists had been assured by Neil that the company preferred the 'evolutionary' approach. 'I realised how stupid we had been,' Berry said. He knew he could no longer work for a company that did not treat people like human beings.

Berry had been concerned for weeks about what he had recently witnessed on the sixth floor of the *Sunday Times*, the executive editorial floor of the newspaper, and had already voiced his concern privately to the Editor two weeks before. The effect of his views in public that Monday morning was shattering: many saw it as Berry's resignation speech. He had made no attempt to pressure people into joining him in refusing to move with the *Sunday Times* to Wapping. It had been a personal statement, not a call to arms. When he sat down, he was given an ovation.

For years Berry had suffered indignity from the print unions. When he was Managing Editor News he would often work in the newsroom from eight on Saturday morning until after midnight. 'Everything I did after 5.30 p.m. was wasted because of the disruptions,' he said. 'It was as though they took my work and screwed it up and threw it away. For someone who is proud of their work, this hurts.' He said he would usually drive home to Ruislip in the early hours of Sunday morning in a fury.[13]

In 1982 *The Times* and the *Sunday Times* had at last gone one step beyond the hot-metal process. Reporters gave their copy to printers, who instead of setting it in hot metal would retype it into a computer which produced a photographic print-out, a 'bromide', to be pasted on a page. But the restrictive practices remained. Neither Berry nor any other journalist was allowed to walk down the middle of the composing room – they had to walk round the edge. No journalist was allowed to read the prepared bromides – they could only read the proofs. No journalist could ring the literals – that was the job of an NGA reader. 'We would send down perfectly clean copy,' said Berry. 'It was relogged into the computer, corrected and pasted on the page with three people watching to see it went in the right place. It was an error-producing process.' He was not even allowed to point a biro at the page. He described it as 'exhausting, gruelling and utterly unnecessary'.

Berry had been on the paper for eighteen years. In those years, he says, he had to endure everything, from the eleven-month suspension by the Thomson management to petty obstruction on the stone. He had been on the paper in 1977 when Evans had telephoned from Strasbourg to say that the paper could now publish the banned thalidomide story – the story had been attached as evidence in an appendix in the court documents. Evans wanted the print run increased. NGA machine managers wanted six more men for the bigger paper – then told management it was too late to call them in. Only eight of the nine presses had run that night – one-third of the copies with the full Thalidomide story were lost. 'I vividly recall the disbelief and despair on the face of Harry Evans,' Berry said. Evans believed 'It was then our freedoms began to be eroded from within.'

When final victory was won in Strasbourg, there was no paper at all. In November 1978, the Thomson owners suspended publication in a desperate effort to control the warfare in the press room between NGA machine managers and the Natsopa machine assistants. After a year, the paper returned to the streets. The stoppage had cost nearly £40 million and solved very little. Evans was to say he felt that no one cared any more.[14]

In 1979, Berry had become Executive Editor in the Features Department, one of the 'space barons' on the sixth floor of the paper. It was in these offices that journalists on major stories pleaded for space in the paper or for resources; where Berry, with his extraordinary ability to compromise, would tell them gently and calmly when they were found wanting or would listen to them argue under threat of the spike.

Some reporters thought Berry had suffered nothing but humiliation in the last years, as he had seen the paper become more right-wing and the old guard of the paper being pushed out. This was not strictly accurate. Berry was not one of those on the paper who dismissed Neil as a man who was responsible for having ruined a once-great newspaper. He saw the Editor as a serious journalist interested in serious issues. 'Murdoch could have chosen some flash guy who could have gone for pop-style journalism. He chose a bloke from a serious publication, interested in foreign coverage and politics.' Neil as Editor, he said, was more consistent than Evans. 'Under Harry it was journalism by orgasm. One part of the world would be ignored for a large part of the time, then, something would happen and he would throw eight journalists at it, then forget about it again.'

The *Sunday Times*, said Berry, was perhaps dull under Neil, but the operation was much more disciplined. He could remember in Evans's days two 'self-indulgent journalists' in the middle of a Saturday afternoon, right on deadline, writing a piece which had been so obviously over-long that someone from the composing room had laid the pages out on the floor and paced it out – it was 108 inches too long. 'There was no justification for some of them pursuing the truth just the way they wanted,' he said, 'when there was a paper to get out.' Some journalists would spend all Friday talking about a story, discuss it over a long supper on Friday night, start writing in the middle of Saturday afternoon – and miss the deadline.

When Neil took over, Berry said, there were feature writers on the paper who wanted to do only what they wanted, when they wanted and how they wanted. 'It was time for a shake-up,' he said. 'We were still in the sixties and seventies. With the swing to the right, the frame of reference had changed. The *Sunday Times* was stuck with the sixties syndrome of civil rights.' Neil, he felt, had taken the paper into the eighties and brought in new ideas. Berry had stuck with the *Sunday Times*, even though he had been offered the editorship of *Today* in 1985.

In his five years on the paper, a lot had happened about

which Berry was not happy. Good people had been driven
from the paper. Letting Hugo Young go was, as Charles
Wilson, Editor of *The Times* has said, 'madness'.

Neil's major defect, Berry believed, was that he was incapable of dealing with people. His bullying style undermined
his own virtues. Telling a feature writer of Ian Jack's calibre
that there was a literal on page six of his story was incredible
to Berry, who thought the piece brilliant. 'It was the only
comment he made! If he had been more able to get on with
the staff, he would be more open to their ideas.'

Berry, who describes himself as apolitical, had found Neil
tricky on certain subjects he considered 'wet and old *Sunday
Times*'. He did not like Greenham Common or CND – he
told Berry they were not important enough to write about. He
wanted new-technology stories, information on the chaos in
the trades unions. 'But I was not constantly harassed,' said
Berry. 'He just left me to get on with it and I did get a balance
and a factual account whatever the subject was. I had a good,
satisfying job. The Focus section was all mine. I worked at it
and I could always make sure my bit was all right. It was an
enclave.'

'But in the end,' said Berry of Wapping, 'I could not ignore
what happened.'[15] He had finally thrown up his hands.

On Saturday evening, Berry usually went to the Gunmakers'
Arms, a pub tucked away in a narrow street behind Gray's
Inn Road, used early in the evening by *Sunday Times* journalists
waiting for the first edition of the paper. On 11 January Berry
returned from the Gunmakers' at about 7 p.m., and minutes
after he had set foot in his office he was joined by three of the
paper's senior executives: David Robson, the Sports Editor,
John Lovesey, Deputy Features Editor, and the Deputy
Editor, Ivan Fallon.

The building was buzzing. A front-page announcement had
just been sent to the process department for the second edition
of the paper. It was headlined: 'Your bigger better *Sunday
Times*', and the story below told readers that for years the
paper had been under production restraints which had limited
the paper to a maximum of eighty pages. The last paragraph
of the story announced that the next week an additional

section would be published, 'made possible by the commissioning of News International's spectacular new printing plant at Tower Hamlets in London's docklands'.

As the story passed through each stage of the process, huddles of people had gathered. Would the front-page copy make the next stage? Surely it would not get past the volatile machine room. One Father there was said to have been held down physically by printers – but there was no disruption.

Berry felt that the announcement was an act of provocation against the unions. Earlier that week, with the crisis looming, Neil had called a Chapel meeting and had told the journalists that the company had two options. There was the revolutionary or the evolutionary path. Overall, Berry said, the impression given by Neil was that the company preferred a negotiated settlement.

This was far from the evolutionary path Neil had spoken about. The executives discussed the situation: they decided someone would have to talk to the Editor about their reservations and Berry was thought to be the best person. He walked the few yards to the end of the corridor and into the Editor's office. 'I started making small-talk,' Berry said. 'It was chit-chat and was becoming strained. I decided I had to speak and began by telling him I had no love for the unions. They had screwed the paper for years. Direct inputting was the only answer. I told him I had not been to Wapping but what I had heard concerned me. There was no library and journalists could not work without one.'

Berry had been working on a computer system installed as an experiment at the *Sunday Times* in May 1984. He had enjoyed its benefits. It was a superb aid to writing and editing, particularly on the long stories for which he was responsible every week. He knew that the same system, Atex, had been installed in Wapping, and said he believed direct inputting by journalists, which the system provided, and the freedom from the absurd restrictions imposed by print unions, was the promised land. But he told Neil that only half a dozen journalists on the *Sunday Times* were familiar with the system. 'There seems to be an assumption,' he told the Editor, 'that if you say to the journalists, "Go to Wapping," they will go. You are asking them to go out on a limb.'

If the printers went on strike over the issue, the management could sack them. 'If the journalists feel used as part of this tactic to sack people without any money, they will have bad consciences. It will undermine the moral standing of the paper.'

Berry said Neil listened and then replied: 'I am glad you have told me that. I agree with almost everything you have said. There is a danger management might push it too far,' Neil added that he would make Berry's views known and that he might have to play the 'executive card'.[16]

On Monday morning, Berry made his first and only visit to Wapping. He saw for himself how well-prepared the plant was – if a strike should ever take place. He had been told by Neil the previous week that the newsrooms in Wapping had been set up in case of 'Armageddon' – the site of the last decisive battle on the Day of Judgement. But during the tour with other heads of departments on that rainy morning, which happened to be his birthday, Berry was amazed.

'Everything was laid out,' he said. 'Prints on the walls and plants. All the computer screens were there. The detail was surprising. People were even being told where they would sit.' When he was shown the canteen, he had bumped into a former *Sunday Times* Production Overseer, an ex-NGA Father. He had not seen him since the spring, and had heard he was working for the proposed new paper, the *London Post*.

'We were old mates,' said Berry, who was glad to see him. 'I asked him if he thought we would ever come down to Wapping.'

'You will be down here,' he had replied.

The tour had been conducted by James Adams, former Foreign Desk Manager, who had risen rapidly in the ranks since Neil's appointment. He had been spending a lot of time in Wapping in the past months – he had even brought in his labrador, Souffle, walking her round the barbed wire. During Berry's visit, he asked Adams where the *London Post* offices were in the plant.

'You could look very hard,' Adams had replied. Then he had laughed. 'But you won't find them.'[17]

On Saturday, 18 January, the *Sunday Times* section was printed in Wapping. Berry heard that there had been a Chapel meeting in the Gray's Inn Road machine room but the first edition was printed, and in the right-hand column on the front page, with a graphic of a journalist sitting at a computer terminal, was: 'This week's *Sunday Times* is 104 pages – the biggest ever produced in Britain. It contains a 12-page special report on the country's most modern print plant.'

After the first edition was printed, Berry was again in the Editor's office. Neil was told that another meeting was being held in the machine room. 'Right, Joan,' Berry remembers Neil saying to his secretary. 'This is it. Get me Rupert.' Then he had turned to Berry and said: 'Don, I'm going to ask you to leave the room.' Berry said Neil spent over an hour on the telephone that evening. Later he was visited by an overseer from the machine room and was told that the Chapel had held an 'information meeting', and the print run continued.[18]

The *Sunday Times* editorial in that issue called the affairs of Fleet Street a 'national disgrace'. Readers were told that the scale of the problem was immense: production departments were overmanned by at least 50 per cent in most areas and in some cases up to 300 per cent. Three Royal Commissions and countless enquiries over the past forty years had urged Fleet Street to put its shameful house in order. Fleet Street was a conspiracy against the consumer. It was easy to understand why managements were insisting on legally binding agreements, readers were told, listing the numbers of newspaper copies lost in 1985 – 2.75 million.

Fleet Street was changing 'faster than most people think', predicted the editorial. Wapping represented the Fleet Street of the future, in which the latest technology went hand-in-hand with progressive labour practices. 'London will have the chance to re-establish itself as the printing and publishing capital of the English-speaking world by attracting back much of the printing work that has fled abroad to escape the British print unions.'

For the first time in years, the management now had the 'initiative'. But managements had to ensure that 'sudden rushes of blood to the head' did not mean they acted in an arbitrary and unfair way. The biggest challenge, however, was for the unions. 'It will be a painful process of adaptation for some of the country's most conservative unions, but it is inevitable if the print unions are to survive the coming revolution. The alternative, of course, is to use their industrial muscle to try to keep things as they are. But that way they risk losing everything.'

When commenting on the problems he faced with the British print unions, Rupert Murdoch would frequently mention one machine room. '. . . I could go to my machine room at the *Sunday Times*, 500 people employed there, I could never count more than 60 people at work at the same time. You know . . . there wasn't much work going on.'[19]

On 11 January, when the *Sunday Times* compositors saw the second-edition copy for the front page announcing that a special supplement was to be printed in Wapping a week later, a few printers paid a visit to the machine room to see Roy 'Ginger' Wilson.

Wilson, the Father of the Sogat *Sunday Times* Machine Chapel, had a legendary reputation. He had once swum across the Thames for a bet – he was so filthy when dragged out on the other side that he had been taken back to the machine room and his men had thrown buckets of water over him. An enormous, bullish man with a thick neck and huge hands, his closely cropped hair is still sandy, although he is nearing 60. His language is appalling. One avoided being on the wrong side of Wilson: he could be quite terrifying and seemed always on the verge of explosion.

'What have you done about it?' Wilson asked when he read the copy about the special section. 'You've set the fucking thing I suppose.' Wilson claimed he was getting fed up with the other Chapels in the building always relying on the machine men for action. Coming to the machine room to ask about the forthcoming section in Wapping added to his already strong contempt for the NGA. Shortly after the compositors had left his office, at around 10 p.m., his telephone had rung.

'It was Brenda. God knows how she'd found out. I told her we did not want to print that night but she told me there were certain guarantees and we should print. I was choked.' And so was his Chapel. 'I told them if we came out we would play right into his hands,' he said of Murdoch. 'Common sense took over in me. I told them if we came out we'd walk right into a trap.' His men did as he said. 'They love me.'[20]

But Wilson was not a man to leave it there. He said he had toured the building in a rage until he had found the Managing Director, Bill Gillespie, who was in a production office on the second floor with Bill O'Neill. 'I went potty,' said Wilson. He told them they were dirty bastards. 'You've taken the piss out of us.' He told them they had put back labour relations thirty years. An overseer was so frightened that he left the room. 'Who do you think you are?' he had said to O'Neill, who was wearing a sou'-wester with the words 'Boston Bears' on the front. 'You're a bully boy and you're going to fucking well come unstuck.' Gillespie, said Wilson, had told him he did not understand what was going on.

'If you do this again you won't get any movement at all,' Wilson had said as he was leaving, slamming the door behind him.

He had met O'Neill again for the first time in four years in October 1985, during negotiations for the *London Post*. O'Neill had walked into the room in a denim jacket, wearing his famous rings. 'I asked him where his hat with corks was,' Wilson said. He found that O'Neill had changed. 'Even his Australian accent had gone.' There had been a furious row. 'He'd called us "you guys",' said Wilson. 'If it's one thing I can't stand it's yankee talk like that. He said it would be like a gun-fight and when the dust settled, whoever was standing had won. I said I'd shoot him in the back.' Wilson had become so abusive during the meeting that Bill Miles from Sogat had disassociated himself from Wilson's remarks. O'Neill had simply picked up his papers and left the room. From then on, Wilson had been banned from any further meetings.

The first time Wilson had met Murdoch, the proprietor had said: 'You and me, bluey, can do business.' Wilson believed him. He now believed that most of the trouble had been caused early in the year when he had 'rattled Murdoch's cage'. He said that Murdoch, whom he knew was obsessed with the numbers employed in his Chapel, had toured the *Sunday Times* machine room 'in a pair of overalls ten times too big'. He had asked Wilson where all his men were. 'I said, "I'll educate you. Break the sheet."' Murdoch then apparently refused to break the paper. 'I said I would do it for him . . . and if I did there would be a dozen men there at once.' Wilson told him his members were like the fire brigade – there when they were needed. 'If you don't piss off,' he claims he then told Murdoch, 'I'll do you for harassment.' Laughing when he tells this story, he said that Murdoch had been appalled at his attitude.

He was equally abusive to Andrew Neil. 'Andy baby', he called him, or 'sonny'. In September 1984 Wilson had ordered the presses to be stopped because of a story about Arthur Scargill. He had demanded the right of reply. Neil told him he was censoring the paper. 'I won't forget you, Wilson,' Neil had said. 'Who do you think you are?' [21]

Wilson had a plan for Saturday, 18 January, when the special section was to be printed in Wapping. 'The management expected it to be nice and calm, didn't they?' he said. 'So I told my people they could pull it. We would put the plates on and then destroy it,' he said. But it did not quite work out that way. 'About mid-day, the phone goes,' he said. 'And it's Brenda.' She asked him to a meeting with Tony Dubbins at the Doughty Street headquarters of the NGA that afternoon. It was only two minutes' walk from Gray's Inn Road. 'Don't do fuck all before I get back,' he told his men. [22]

When he got there he found most of the senior NGA and Sogat officials, and Tony Isaacs from the *News of the World*. Dubbins told them that the situation was difficult. The unions were being provoked and before there was any action they had to await the result of the strike ballot, which they knew would be overwhelming. This was important – it could alter the public perception of the dispute. The General Secretaries were going to meet the management and things would go their way in the end.

'Ginger,' said Dubbins later, 'was vehement in his views. But it was a lot to ask them.' At one point in the meeting Wilson told Dean she had better go and talk to his Chapel herself.

Dean and Dubbins both say it was a difficult job getting Wilson back to the paper. 'They pleaded with us to print,' said Wilson. 'I told them I could not accept it. If they got the paper out with scab labour, we might as well give up the ghost.' But they did persuade him. Wilson had found it difficult to argue with Dean. 'She's a woman,' he said.

At 4 p.m. Wilson called a meeting in the reel room. About

400 of his men were there. 'There was a patter of tiny feet,' he recounted. 'In comes Bill Gillespie, who says to me, "Unless you are all back at work in five minutes you're all fired." I told him if he stayed a minute longer he'd be lynched – and he went away.' Wilson told his men to prepare the presses. But he also said: 'Be my guests, boys . . . I don't expect you to pay attention to fine detail. We will do it our way tonight.' Half the edition was lost. When Wilson left the building at 6.30 on Sunday morning, he thought he was entering a strike like any other.

When Andrew Neil walked out of the Mount Pleasant Hotel on Monday morning, 27 January, he left behind an angry, resentful and frightened staff. Ten days before, the company had been warned by the then FOC, Nigel Harris, Production Editor on Business News, that should there be any attempts to 'bully, engineer or dragoon' the journalists on the *Sunday Times* into instant cooperation with Wapping, there would be a 'swift and angry reaction'. In a letter to Bill Gillespie, Harris had written: '. . . it is, I feel, essential that the company retains the moral ascendancy in this situation. It is in grave danger of losing it by behaving badly at a time when there is available a moderate middle way – the "evolutionary" solution, as it has become known.'[23]

The letter had been shown to Murdoch. Gillespie wrote to Harris that there had always been a good working relationship with the journalists and all negotiations had been conducted in a civilised way. 'It has been no part of the policy of this company to damage, let alone destroy, this relationship. . . . There may be difficult times ahead, but there is no intention of changing this policy.'[24]

The afternoon meeting in the Mount Pleasant Hotel lasted over three hours. After the emotional speeches from journalists, all in favour of making a stand against the company, Harry Conroy spoke. His speech was remembered afterwards as long and boring. As he had done at the *Sun* and *Times* meetings, he reminded them that they were bound to a joint approach with the print unions. They were still under instruction from the National Executive and they should continue the policy they had adopted the previous week of working normally in their normal place of work. But he did not give them any concrete advice. It seemed to some that the mood of defiance ebbed away as he spoke.

The journalists were told by a lawyer that the company did appear to have broken their Chapel house agreement, as changes had been made to working conditions without negotiation. The journalists could try an injunction against the company to try to restrain breaching the contracts but he was pessimistic about their chances. The only option was a case for unfair dismissal at an industrial tribunal.

Kim Fletcher, a keen, young and able journalist, who had been Father for only one week, had spoken to Peter Roberts, Managing Editor, during the lunch break. Roberts had been on the paper almost as long as Berry. He had been Chief Sub-Editor on the *Northern Echo* when Harry Evans was Editor, had gone to the *Daily Mail* and then joined the *Sunday Times*. When he had become Managing Editor, he had dealt with the union on the management's behalf. He seemed a convenient choice when the paper was looking for a staff member for the Times Newspapers Holdings Board after Murdoch's deal with the Chapel when he had bought the paper.

Roberts was clearly identified as a management man, but he was to find he was increasingly representing management in desperate circumstances. However, he never entirely lost the sympathy of the journalists. They found him a fundamentally decent man and felt that he tried sincerely – especially when Neil was getting rid of staff – to put their cases fairly and find decent solutions. Very few would condemn him out of hand. But increasingly they could not understand how he did the job. They felt it must be pretty hellish.

Fletcher told the journalists that Roberts said the £2,000 payment was for the move to Wapping and for agreement on direct inputting. There was no clear information for him about whether staff would be dismissed if they did not go. Shuttle buses were ready and would leave from various points around London each day. The company was prepared to get an insurance policy to protect employees, families and property in the event of attacks or intimidation.

He then put a motion to the floor. There would be no recommendation from the Chapel committee. 'In view of the fact that the management refuses to negotiate on its ultimatum concerning the *Sunday Times* journalists moving to Wapping, this Chapel instructs its members not to go.' The vote would be secret – on blue cloakroom tickets. People were told they should just write 'go' or 'don't go'.

There were over a dozen speeches. Peter Murtagh, a member of 'Insight' who had not long been on the paper, said he would never go: 'My editor does not tell me I am part of the greatest team of journalists in the world and then hold a gun to my head.' One of the most powerful speeches was from Chris Nawrat, a hard-drinking sports sub-editor and a member of the Communist Party. For years, he said, the printers had treated him 'like shit'. The boot was now on the other foot and, whatever the vote, he would go to Wapping. Those who were against going were a 'bunch of liberals sitting around on their fannies not knowing what to do'. They should be aware that they lived in a real world and had to accept change. A young news reporter predicted that if they went to Wapping it was the end of the Chapel.

Some of the journalists felt that the time to make a stand against Murdoch had gone long ago. In 1981, when he was buying Times Newspapers, there had been strong grounds for referring the sale of the *Sunday Times* to the Monopolies Commission. John Biffen, Secretary for Trade, decided against referral and the journalists had decided on a law suit to force his hand. If the paper was a going concern – which most knew it was – then the referral should have been automatic and Murdoch would not have been allowed to buy the paper. Journalists were advised that they had an excellent case in law – but when the Chapel was told the possible costs, it was dropped. Only twelve members had voted at an emotional Chapel meeting to continue the action – they became known as the 'Gravedigger Club'.

At 5.15 p.m. the vote was taken. There were 68 votes in favour of going and 60 against. Berry thought the vote was desperately tight: he believed they were at the peak of opposition, which would now disintegrate. Fletcher believed that if Conroy and the other NUJ officials had not spoken at the meeting, the motion would have been carried. People started to drift away, but many of the sixty who voted not to go

gathered at the front of the room, where they decided to report
for work at Gray's Inn Road the following day.

Only twenty-seven *Sunday Times* journalists turned up for
work at Gray's Inn Road the next morning, and special entry
passes had to be obtained from the personnel department.
They spent their time in meetings in the newsroom, which
had not been cleaned since the last edition. 'It looked like a
newsroom the morning after an election,' said Peter Murtagh.
There were overflowing wastepaper baskets, desks strewn with
paper and full ashtrays. Chairs were overturned and filing
cabinets half empty, some drawers hanging open. It was
gloomy, and it was cold: the heating had already been turned
off.

There were differing views about what to do. The majority
wanted some sort of negotiated settlement which would allow
them to keep their jobs – and save face. A hard core was not
prepared to go at all. But it was decided that each should
write a letter to management stating that they were available
for work in their normal place.

The group was now called 'the refuseniks'. Berry had first
used the word during an interview with a *Guardian* reporter
and it had stuck. Their symbol became red carnations – a
bunch had been sent to one of them by a girlfriend and they
were worn as a sign of solidarity and as a means of being
recognised walking through the Sogat and NGA picket lines
into the offices at Gray's Inn Road.

On Tuesday, David Blundy, the tall, gangling and popular
Middle East Correspondent, one of the most talented and
conscientious reporters on the paper, wandered into the
newsroom. He had voted by proxy in Paris to go to Wapping
and had just returned to London. When he saw the group in
the newsroom it was simple. He changed his mind. They were
the people on the paper he wanted to be with. Anyway, his
attitude was that he worked for Berry and the *Sunday Times*,
not Murdoch.[25]

Negotiations to get the refuseniks to Wapping were organised by Murdoch. He evidently admired the Executive
Features Editor and instructed Neil to 'get Berry'. At a relaxed
lunch for senior executives in the Times building a month
earlier, Murdoch had asked Berry to sit next to him. At one

stage Berry had told the proprietor there was a danger of the *Sunday Times* becoming too big. The British were not like Americans: they did not want to throw away half the paper every Sunday. 'I think it should be twice as big,' Murdoch had replied.

Neil was to spend over two hours with Berry. The Editor told him he was needed in Wapping: his presence would boost morale. If he went to Wapping and did not like it, he could leave – and then he could get his redundancy. Murdoch would talk with him.' 'It's a rotten way to end an eighteen-year career,' Neil had said. Berry told the Editor he appreciated the offer, but that it would not work. His decision would not change.

'It would have been either a civilised chat with Murdoch or acrimonious – either way it made no difference. It was a question of our opposing attitudes to life and I think it would have been undignified for him to talk with me,' said Berry.[26]

During that week Berry had been walking along Gray's Inn Road, returning to the office after lunch, when he had bumped into Charles Wilson, Editor of *The Times*. Wilson told Berry that he thought he objected to going to Wapping because of Andrew Neil. 'I told him it was Murdoch,' said Berry.

Wilson had replied: 'Then there's nothing I can do.'

Senior Murdoch executives were beginning to realise that Berry would never go to Wapping: the proprietor was not going to get his way. From a public relations standpoint, it would be disastrous to have to sack Berry. Neil would be bearing the brunt of the proprietor's tongue.

It was certainly not support of the printers which motivated the refuseniks. All of them, like Berry, had been victims of printers' attitudes. Harry Coen, Editor of the Spectrum pages, who was refusing to go to Wapping, had been banned from the stone the year before after appearing on BBC Newsnight where he mentioned he had been tested for the Aids virus.

All week the refuseniks heard stories from their colleagues about what was happening in Wapping. There was chaos, according to some. There were not enough telephones, for a start: thirty remote telephones had been bought and snapped up within minutes. There was no darkroom for the photographers: Neil's shower had been commandeered as a temporary measure. Journalists from Wapping were seen in Gray's Inn Road retrieving stories from spikes. An executive had been dispatched to buy newspapers: there were no deliveries into Wapping.

Stories about the conditions in Wapping were exchanged at a meeting of refuseniks from all four titles in the NUJ headquarters near King's Cross. David Blundy, who had never been involved with the union – the only time he had visited the headquarters was to pay his subscription when his membership had lapsed – said it had been like going back to the thirties. 'There we were, cap in hand. We were offered a couple of late shifts on the *Guardian* and a cup of tea.' What angered him was that there had been no pre-planning. 'It was like being asked to go down a coal bunker while Murdoch's B-52's were about to launch a raid.' [27]

On Wednesday, 29 January, David Blundy and the experienced Foreign Correspondent, Isabel Hilton, had lunch with the Foreign Editor, Stephen Milligan. There would be attempts at compromise. 'What got to me,' said Blundy later, 'was that the Friday before, Peter Godwin had been sent to Uganda, which was pretty dangerous. No one had said to him, "Go, or you're fired." All we were being asked to do was go to Wapping.' On Thursday, Milligan and Peter Roberts came to Gray's Inn Road to speak to the group. Milligan opened. There was great sympathy in Wapping for the refuseniks' principled stand. As Foreign Editor, he had staff in his department who risked their lives for the paper. 'I beg you to come to Wapping this afternoon,' he said.

Peter Roberts spoke next. Negotiations for a move to Wapping had been impossible. 'I can only apologise,' he said. 'It was the speed with which things went.' They must build bridges. He conceded that their house agreement had been broken by the company insisting that they move to Wapping. It was impossible for people to leave the paper with four months' money, as per the agreement, as this would create legal difficulties for the company. No such deal had been offered to members of Sogat or the NGA. 'We need you,' he said. 'The boost to morale in Wapping would be enormous.'

Roberts left the meeting. The group decided that they would put to him a compromise, formulated by John Lovesey.

1a. The last meeting between News International and the print unions before the strike. Park Lane Hotel, Thursday 23 January 1986. (From left to right) Bill Gillespie, Managing Director, Times Newspapers Ltd; Bruce Matthews, Managing Director, News International; Rupert Murdoch, Proprietor and Chairman, News International; Bill O'Neill, Vice President, Personnel and Labor Relations, News America Publishing; Geoffrey Richards, lawyer and partner with Farrer & Co.; notetaker

1b. The first *Sunday Times* printed in Wapping – on 18 January 1986, a week before the move – with the tell-tale 'No 1' on the masthead

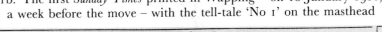

19 JANUARY 1986   No 1   Price 50p

THE SUNDAY TIMES

This week's Sunday Times is **104 pages** — the biggest paper ever produced in Britain.

Thatcher faces new rates crisis

by George Jones and Anne Jacobs

TCHER government as unrest among its ters in the wake of and affair over pro- reform the rates, ld leave more than population worse off.

It's madness," one minister said last night. "It's a gift to the Alliance in areas where we are already hard-pressed." Accord- ing to the rates green paper, 55% of the population will have to pay more under the plan to phase out the present system of domestic rates and replace them with an annual "community charge" – the government's carefully chosen term for a flat-rate poll tax to replace the rates.

cities have surfaced over both the een "plan, to be in a consultative on January 28 and ks, which take effect ministers are braced t by up to 40 Tory e Commons insoue- raic rises averaging any shire counties.

the government after Michael Heseltine's resignation as de- fence secretary and that the SDP-Liberal Alliance will pick up fresh support among angry Tory voters.

year for everyone over 18, eventually rising to £200 per person when rates are finally abolished around the turn of the century.

another 20 are considering abstaining.

Potential rebels include some of the prime minister's leading critics, including Francis Pym, Sir Ian Gilmour and Charles Morrison, a member of the executive of the 1922 back- benchers' committee.

However, the revolt goes far wider than disillusioned "wets" and includes a number of MPs normally loyal to government policy. Several protested last night that the Environment Department had not honoured earlier pledges to reward coun- cils that observed Whitehall spending targets.

Government whips are this week contacting disaffected MPs in an attempt to minimise

tomorrow's revolt. There is no extra money on offer but Kenneth Baker, the environ- ment secretary, will promise that the worst-hit counties will benefit from a redistribution of funds withheld from councils that defy Whitehall spending guidelines.

Baker plans a "robust defence" of the rates-support grant settlement that has shifted £220m into London and £200m into other inner- city areas. He will warn Tory rebels that the government cannot run away from its commitment to help deprived inner cities.

He will also argue that the next week's green paper will put forward long-term solu-

tions to the present rates mess, which ministers believe to be widely unpopular. The consultation document has been drawn up by a cabinet committee chaired by Mrs Thatcher, who is personally committed to rates abolition.

There is anxiety within the cabinet, however, that this community charge is the only option put forward in the green paper and that it is admin- istratively unwieldy.

Thatcher strongly supports the new charge on the grounds that it will increase accountability in local govern- ment by spreading the responsibility for meeting its cost to many people who do not currently pay rates.

The government had been hoping that the promise of fundamental reform of the rates would help in defus- ing growing Tory party unrest over this year's rate support gram settlement. Now it looks as if the green paper will only make matters worse.

Tory MPs representing shire counties are protesting that the government's decision to re- direct cash towards inner-city authorities will lead to sharp rate rises, well above the rate of inflation, in Tory heartlands. Some of the worst-hit counties

are Bedfordshire, Hertford- shire, Oxfordshire, Buckinghamshire and Surrey. The Association of County Councils predicts double-figure rate rises in all these areas.

The cabinet was given warn- ing last week that the govern- ment faces its worst backbench revolt tomorrow since the rebellion against top people's pay rises last July. At least 20 Tories are thinking of voting against the government and

Gartcosh, p2

It contains a 12-page special report on the country's most modern print plant

PLUS NEW CLASSIFIED SECTION 24 pages of appointments and motors

PLUS

stland iry nes in Trade

mon Freeman orge Jones larry Penrose

Hooded face of Ulster Protestant backlash

Tanks force Britannia to retreat

NMENT inquiry

2a. The 'No Go Area' housing the $10 million Atex computer after its installation in Wapping in June 1985

2b. Rupert Murdoch, with Ken Taylor, Technical Director of News International, on his left, starts the presses rolling at Wapping on the night of Saturday 25 January 1986, the day after the dispute began

3a. The Belgravia safe house at 17 Chesham Place, where 'Smylie's People' stayed in London

3b. 'The Bunker' – the code name for the South London warehouse where 'Smylie's People' secretly assembled the Atex computer system for Rupert Murdoch

4a. The *Sun* newsroom in Bouverie Street on Friday 24 January after the journalists had voted to go to Wapping

4b. Kelvin MacKenzie, Editor, the *Sun* (left) and Rupert Murdoch holding the first *Sun* to be printed in Wapping. Sunday 26 January 1986

5a. Tony Isaacs, Imperial Father, Sogat *News of the World* Machine Chapel, in the Sogat double-decker support bus parked in Wellclose Square, behind the picket line

5b. Print unions' demonstration in Trafalgar Square, 6 April 1986

MURDOCH IS BAD NEWS

6a. Brenda Dean, General Secretary, Sogat 82, at a Sogat Rally in Glasgow on 16 February 1986, putting the case for her News International members

6b. Harry Conroy, General Secretary, NUJ (left), with Tony Dubbins, General Secretary, NGA, at Congress House on 17 February 1986

7a. Eric Hammond,
General Secretary, EETPU

7b. Roy 'Ginger' Wilson, Father of the Sogat *Sunday Times* Machine
Chapel (left), with Neil Kinnock, leader of the Labour Party, at the
Wembley print union rally on 13 March 1986

8a. Charles Wilson outside the *Times* building in Gray's Inn Road on 5 November 1985, the day of his appointment as Editor

8b. Wapping: the most secure industrial site in Britain

The refuseniks would go to Wapping on four months' trial. They would not take the £2,000 or the offer of family membership of the private health scheme. If at the end of the trial period they wanted to leave, they would be given four months' money. And one proviso was that this deal would be offered to everyone else in the NUJ Chapel.

When he heard the deal, Roberts seemed enthusiastic. But he said he would have to talk with the Editor. Just after five o'clock that afternoon he returned. He said he had spent a 'bruising session' with Murdoch. The deal was on but there were two conditions. One was that the deal should be kept secret. 'Please do not go out and say the *Sunday Times* has got a special deal,' said Roberts. 'Please emphasise it is within the house agreement.' The other was that every single member of the group would have to go. The refuseniks quickly realised that this was a way of 'getting Berry'.

Literary Editor Claire Tomalin was sitting at the back of the meeting near the news desk. She had already heard about one of the provisos – that everyone would have to go – but when she heard Roberts say that news of the deal should not be released to the press, she lost her temper. She suddenly rose from her chair, pushing it back so hard that it toppled over. 'That is the most appalling thing I have ever heard,' she said. She walked backwards from him, as though from something terrible. 'I resign,' she said, and left the room. She said she had realised she could not work for a paper which would impose a condition on its journalists not to talk to the press. In her resignation letter to Neil, she wrote: 'You have become the mouthpiece for a ruthless and bullying management which regards all employees as cattle.'

Tomalin, whose husband Nick Tomalin, the *Sunday Times* foreign reporter, had been tragically killed on assignment by a rocket in the Yom Kippur war, later explained: 'I know that a great number of the journalists didn't want to do it like that. They felt horrified and appalled and they bowed their heads and went. Some of them tried to hold out. Murdoch and Neil have got the *Sunday Times* wrong.' She was later to receive a letter from Sir Hugh Trevor-Roper, one of the directors of Times Newspaper Holdings. He told her that one of his roles was to protect the Editor from the proprietor, but when the Editor had become part of management, there was not much left for the Directors to do.

On Friday, Roberts was asked to tell Murdoch he could have all but six refuseniks. The six, including Berry, decided they were never going to Wapping. The deal was rejected: the management said it had to be all of them or the deal was off.

It was in Berry's sixth-floor office that those who had resisted for nearly a week, and who had decided to go to Wapping, came to say goodbye. Berry joked at first about waiting for the company to come and take his car away. But he was shattered. 'He kept saying, "This is how the end is . . . you should always try to remember how it ends,"' one of them remembered. Wearing their red carnations, they were going together. All of them were crying. In the history of the newspaper, Berry's stand had milestone status.

SIX

Dash for Freedom

It was in the summer of 1984 that the British print unions finally pushed Murdoch to the limit of his patience. His ambitions to expand were being thwarted at every turn. His most profitable paper, the *Sun*, was stuck in the cramped and dated Bouverie Street premises and he was convinced that if only he could print more, he could sell more. He also believed that the *Sunday Times* had the potential to make more money if only he could turn it into a larger paper resembling the Sunday edition of the *New York Times*. He had invested nearly £100 million in new plants, Kinning Park in Glasgow and Tower Hamlets in East London, but they were both idle.

Early that summer, one of his executives, Brian Lawrence, Deputy Managing Director of Times Newspapers, had told the *Sunday Times* production Fathers of a plan to increase the size of the paper to 120 pages. He revealed that when the production of the *Sun* and *News of the World* eventually moved to Wapping, part of the *Sunday Times* print run would transfer to Bouverie Street. To make this possible, they would have to agree to the introduction of phase two of the new technology – polymer plates, replacing the hot-metal process with light-weight plastic sheets. The deal included an increase of £20 per man per Saturday shift.

The Chapels rejected the plan because there was not enough money on the table and they suspected that the company was trying to get round the renegotiation of their house agreements. Lawrence attempted to win the Fathers round at a meal in Fleet Street's Wig and Pen Club, when he suggested that talks on the plates could be a starting point.

Further discussions on the idea with a *Sunday Times* production manager got nowhere. Vic Dunn, NGA Father of the Machine Managers' Chapel at the *Sunday Times*, remembers being told in February 1985 that the offer had been withdrawn for the time being, as Murdoch had decided there was to be

'not a penny more invested in Gray's Inn Road'.[1] Vic
Dunn remembered: 'They told me the tap had been turned
off.'[2]

The foundry in the *Sunday Times* had always been a problem.
The machinery was old and the unions claimed that hitting
edition times was becoming increasingly difficult. A staggered
refurbishment of the machines meant that for about a year
the printers were not working to full capacity. In October
1984, repairs on the notoriously troublesome number four
plate-making automatic casting machine were almost completed when the temporary peace was broken. A typical Fleet
Street skirmish broke out. The unions said that management
wanted them to operate the auto-caster before they had had
time to test it, as had been agreed. The company said that the
Chapel had suddenly demanded more money to complete the
work on the caster, and when the claim was turned down had
refused to work the overtime to get the paper out. A total of
312,000 copies of the paper were lost.

These 'guerilla tactics'[3] were further evidence to Murdoch
that the unions would block his every move. He felt that even
personal contact with their leaders could not break their
obstinacy. On Saturday, 27 October that year, the NGA's
General Secretary, Tony Dubbins, and the union's President,
Bryn Griffiths, had a private meeting with Murdoch where
they discussed a way round one of the major stumbling blocks
to Wapping. Murdoch told them he would drop his court
proceedings against the union over secondary action in
support of print workers sacked by Eddie Shah during the
Warrington dispute. To do this, he would have to withdraw
from the Newspaper Publishers' Association, the Fleet Street
employers' body, who were jointly seeking damages against
the union. In return, the NGA would withdraw their bid to
use the Wapping move to increase the proportion of printers
they represented in the machine rooms.

It was an anomaly of history that in Bouverie Street, Sogat
printers ran the presses on the *News of the World*, and on the
Sun the two unions divided the work. In the rest of Fleet Street,
NGA members were machine supervisors with Sogat assistants.
Because of shift times, the daily maintenance of machines in
Bouverie Street was carried out by the *News of the World* Sogat
Machine Chapel. The NGA had been seeking to split the

maintenance work with Sogat when the papers moved to Wapping. This claim had infuriated Sogat and Murdoch's managers.

As with many Fleet Street talks, Murdoch believed that the meeting with Dubbins and Griffiths had ended with a deal, whereas the NGA saw it as the first step along the road to eventual agreement.

It was not only the NGA who rattled Murdoch's cage. Although he respected Brenda Dean, her union's attitude towards Wapping angered him. A member of his management said a senior Sogat official once told him that a bomb should be placed on the site to burn the plant down.[4] Sogat also had failed to reach agreement with him on staffing the publishing room, where newspapers are packed for distribution. And the negotiations on the development of Kinning Park in Glasgow, which had been going since 1978, had got nowhere.

Kinning Park was vital in Murdoch's expansion plans. His intention was to fax the *Sun* electronically to Glasgow, saving the £3 million he spent each year on airfreight. Sogat had resisted the plan because they feared he would eventually use Kinning Park to print the northern edition of the *News of the World* as well. This would put Sogat jobs in Manchester at risk. Although Sogat was still seeking an assurance that Manchester would stay open, a compromise was slowly emerging for the *Sun* to have four to six pages of Scottish news and sport set in Glasgow when the talks 'fizzled out' in 1984.[5]

By Christmas that year, Murdoch was frustrated. He had failed to reach agreement with the print unions and with 'this huge investment seemingly having to be written off, we reviewed the British newspaper market, looking as usual for an opportunity to expand out of our difficulties.'[6] Early in the New Year, it seemed as though he had made up his mind. Asked in America about *The Times* in its bicentennial year, he said, 'I'm not letting myself be trapped into thinking I'm a trustee of some historic British institution that must be kept alive at any cost. It's no good having a great name on the top of a newspaper if it's sending us into the poorhouse.'[7]

Around this time, an executive in London picked up on a phrase Murdoch had used one Saturday night in Gray's Inn Road. It was about making a 'dash for freedom'.

*

It was on Sunday, 10 February 1985, in his elegant but comfortable twelve-room New York apartment, on 88th and Fifth Avenue, where he and his wife Anna had made their home, that Rupert Murdoch outlined his 'dash for freedom' plans which were to revolutionise his British newspaper operation. A group of British executives had flown from London on Concorde the day before and the meeting, which lasted from ten in the morning until late afternoon – with a short break for lunch in a restaurant two blocks away – took place round his dining-room table. Those familiar with his style knew they would now be totally swept up by the plan – there would be nothing but work and no time for anything but what became known as the 'Post Project'.

Of them all, Bruce Matthews, the Managing Director of News International, had the most experience of Murdoch's addiction to challenge. He knew that Murdoch would now relentlessly drive them forward with his absolute commitment to the project – the Chairman was not known for looking backwards. Once he had decided he wanted something, he would throw money and energy into getting it – at almost any price. His enthusiasm was infectious. An executive has described working on a Murdoch special assignment as like 'being on a magic carpet. Suddenly you're off.'[8] In the coming months, all of them would be caught up in a whirlwind of activity.

Matthews was not popular with some members of the British management team who believed that Murdoch measured his executives on how much cash they generated. Matthews was Managing Director at Bouverie Street, in charge of the *News of the World* and the biggest money spinner, the *Sun* – he could not fail.

He had worked for Murdoch since 1971. An expert on newspaper production, he was the first Australian to complete an apprenticeship in rotogravure – the process of good colour printing on poor quality paper. He was 47, with a senior post on the *Herald and Weekly Times* in Melbourne, when Murdoch had telephoned offering him a job in England. He accepted, and later said he had decided to leave the *Herald* because 'I suspected the company wasn't thrusting forward. . . . I felt I either had to see a clear path to get to the top or I had to make a change.'[9]

Nine years after arriving from Australia, he was put on the board of News Corporation, Murdoch's main holding company, and two years later became Managing Director of News International, in charge of the British operation.[10] He was to have a strategic role in the Post Project. But towards the summer of 1985 he began calling it 'mission impossible' – though never in Murdoch's presence.[11]

Titles given to executives in the Murdoch empire were sometimes meaningless. 'When you work for Murdoch, you wear many hats,' one said. His attitude towards his employees was one of possession: people were assets. 'I've got one of those,' Murdoch would say when he needed someone for a particular task.[12] And he would have his 'wonderboys' – those who had proved themselves would be used constantly while in favour.

It was no surprise to most of them in Murdoch's apartment that day to see one of his most recent finds, Charles Wilson, Deputy Editor of *The Times*, who was now to play an even more important role in the Murdoch empire.

Wilson had impressed Murdoch when he had been sent to Chicago to sort out the *Sun Times*, a paper in the middle of a circulation war – and in trouble. Murdoch had bought the paper for $90 million in January 1984 and readers had started to defect. So had the staff – ninety had tried to join the rival *Tribune*, which outsold the *Sun Times*. Journalists had been shocked by Wilson's rapid changes in layout and content – the usual Murdoch recipe of shorter stories and bigger headlines – which had forced the paper downmarket.

No one at the meeting knew how much Murdoch had told the others. They talked about Fleet Street, about strikes and stoppages and the unions. And they also talked about Tower Hamlets. The presence in New York of Ken Taylor, Technical Director of News Group Newspapers Ltd, was indication enough that whatever Murdoch was planning, it would involve the docklands development. It was Taylor's plant: he knew every building, every screw, every rafter. By then the plant had been almost completed for production from the platemaking stage onwards for the *Sun* and the *News of the World*.[13] It was said to be Taylor's final monument to hot metal, and he had become known as the 'mausoleum curator'.

Taylor, a charming man, was well liked and respected in the company. He had joined Murdoch in 1971 after twenty years with IPC. He had also been project engineer for the *Daily Mirror* building at Holborn Circus. He was a chartered and a civil engineer and a fellow of the Institute of Mechanical Engineers.

Although trusted by Murdoch, Taylor was often at the rough end of his tongue. But, a strong, silent man, he believed that the secret with Murdoch was always to apologise, no matter what the accusation. This was to stand him in good stead. There was only one man seated at Murdoch's table in New York that day who would eventually push Taylor to his limit.

Christopher Pole-Carew was loathed by the print unions. His notoriety as a union basher dated from 1973 when he was Managing Director of T. Bailey Forman Ltd, publishers of the *Nottingham Evening Post*. He had confronted the unions during a six-week strike over the introduction of new technology. Three hundred printers lost their jobs, the unions lost their negotiating rights and less than five years later Pole-Carew had brought in direct inputting. Pole-Carew was a man who prided himself on never having lost a battle with the unions.

In 1978, when journalists on the Nottingham paper struck in support of a national pay claim, twenty-eight were sacked for disloyalty. Pole-Carew was quoted at the time: '. . . the trade unions can actually be a force for evil'.[14] Security at the *Nottingham Post* building, organised by him, included closed-circuit television, identity cards and security men.

Pole-Carew, who had attended the Dartmouth Royal Naval College, had been in the navy for eleven years. He behaved with an air of superiority. He would look directly at people when making a point: 'Do you see?' he would say, as though it should be self-evident. His clipped tones would be imitated later by the Murdoch men. He was to tell everyone, once the project was under way, that he was in charge, and during his year in Tower Hamlets was to become alienated from most of the Murdoch team.

Murdoch's operating methods were new to Pole-Carew, who a month before had abruptly left T. Bailey Forman. He had met Murdoch in his office at *The Times* in January and been given a tour of Tower Hamlets, where he had been led into the biggest press room he had ever seen. He was scathing about the printing machines bought by Ken Taylor and told Murdoch they were antiquated.

Murdoch offered him a job, which Pole-Carew later claimed he turned down because he did not want to be in charge of 'an East-End factory'.[15] Murdoch was happy with a twelve-month contract with Computer Print Consultants, a company which Pole-Carew had set up in October 1982.

Next to Pole-Carew at Murdoch's dining-room table that day was Stan Dzuiba. Pole-Carew had recruited him from school and eventually put him in charge of the first computer department in Nottingham. When Pole-Carew left T. Bailey Forman on 15 January 1985, he had taken Dzuiba with him.

Murdoch always insisted on the best possible legal advice, so sitting in on the discussion was the brilliant young lawyer from Farrer and Co., Geoffrey Richards. Educated at Corpus Christi College, Oxford, he had been admitted as a solicitor in 1972. He rose quickly; seven years later he was a partner.

The project discussed that day, one executive later revealed, concerned the idea of a new London evening paper – the *Post* – which could eventually be expanded to a 24-hour paper with national distribution. The possibility of a new evening paper had been 'loosely' discussed before. The project had not been defined prior to the meeting. One of them described it as a 'brainstorming meeting. We discussed logistics.'[16] If the company planned to produce a new paper in Tower Hamlets, using a direct-input computer – single key stroking by journalists without NGA involvement – they 'would be mad not to protect the other four titles in case the unions, objecting to the technology, halted the papers'. Murdoch 'would be out of his mind not to make damn sure the unions could not close down his other four titles. . . . If events turn out that you have pushed your luck . . . you've got a contingency plan.'[17]

This 'contingency plan' would involve a computerised photosetting system. Speed was essential: there was no time for 'state of the art'. Murdoch wanted a system which was 'dead safe' with good logistic support. He said: 'We are not taking risks.'

One month later the plans for a new paper leaked. The *Sunday Telegraph* carried an exclusive story revealing that Murdoch planned to launch a London evening paper, the *Post*, which, if successful, would become Britain's first 24-hour newspaper. These plans were at an 'advanced stage' but the launch date was unknown. News International confirmed the story.

Aimed at the 'middle market', the *Post*'s morning editions would be distributed nationally, while the afternoon and evening editions would be for London only in direct competition to the capital's only Evening, the *Standard*. The *Sunday Telegraph* revealed that it would be produced in East London, as Murdoch was keen to 'find a use for the space capacity he has at his new printing plant'.[18] Charles Wilson would become the *Post*'s Editorial Director, although he said later he would have 'the option, when the paper was launched, to become its Editor or to return to my post as Deputy Editor of *The Times*.'[19] No mention was made about technology.

Typically, Murdoch had confided in two of his senior executives based in New York six days before he had outlined the project to the British executives in his flat. Early one morning, he told them he was 'planning something for London'. He wanted a large computer system, and he wanted it quickly. He insisted that nothing was to be handled in the UK. That same morning, John Keating, his Technical Director, telephoned Atex, a Boston-based company he knew well, which was one of the major suppliers in America of computerised typesetting equipment.

John Keating, who was quietly spoken but shrewd, had the reputation of having a thorough knowledge of old and new newspaper production systems. He had been part of the American newspaper technology revolution. Born in Liverpool, where he served his six-year apprenticeship as a compositor, he had taken advantage of the International Typographic Union rule in the 1960s that allowed members to work on newspapers in the United States. He had finally settled at the *Washington Post*, rising through the ranks until by the early 1970s he was Assistant Production Manager.

At that time, the *Washington Post*'s industrial relations were a shambles. Kay Graham, the owner, who was to become a newspaper legend after Watergate was indecisive in business matters and was losing control of her production plant to powerful print unions.

At the end of 1971, Graham hired John S. Prescott Jr from one of the biggest American newspaper chains. He devised a solution to the *Washington Post*'s labour problems which he codenamed 'Project X'. Non-union, whitecollar business employees were secretly trained to run the presses at Southern Production Program Inc. in Oklahoma City.[20] In 1967, Southern Production had formed the Newspaper Production and Research Center as a training school. Newspaper companies joined the program by paying monthly subscriptions in proportion to their circulations. At that time it had two classes of membership. Full members were promised help from the others to get their papers out in the event of a strike. However, Graham, as an associate member, was only entitled to send employees to Oklahoma for training.[21]

The *Washington Post* also established its own school to teach employees how to use the newly purchased cold-type photo-composition technology. And as part of his strategy, Prescott hired a well-known tough, union negotiator, Lawrence A. Wallace.[22]

In 1974, Keating had shown two of Murdoch's executives round the *Washington Post* press room. He was hired by Murdoch within days, so he was not to witness the *Post*'s final showdown with the printers two years later when 'Project X' was finally put to the test. The machine men, negotiating a new contract, sabotaged all the press machinery. It was a fatal mistake. The resulting 139-day strike cost the *Post* only one edition: the Oklahoma-trained crews began to run the presses at the *Post*'s offices on 15th Street. For the strike's duration, the *Post*, normally prepared by 1,220 craft workers, was published with just over 300 amateurs.[23]

The Vice President of Atex's marketing operations, Ronald A. Brumback, and Harland K. LaVigne, Vice President North American Field Operations, got out of a yellow cab at the door of Murdoch's apartment two days after the 'dash for freedom' meeting. They were late, and they were also very nervous. They were there to meet with potentially the biggest client in the industry. The interview had been fixed for 5 p.m. at Murdoch's offices in the *New York Post* building on South

Street. But their flight from Boston had been delayed and when they had telephoned from Logan airport to say they were running late, they had been told to go directly to Murdoch's home – he would see them there around 6.30 p.m. As they arrived, Murdoch's limousine, which had brought him from his office, pulled up at the curb.[24]

All Brumback knew from the sketchy details he had been given by phone a few days before was that there was the possibility of a big order and that speed of installation was vital. He had been told that only Murdoch could give him further details.

Brumback, an economics graduate, was a self-effacing man. He did not seem to have the drive and personality normally associated with executives from thrusting American computer companies. But he was known as a brilliant strategist. When Murdoch asked him that evening if he could deliver the biggest ever one-off direct-input system in the industry's history within four months, Brumback did not hesitate. Murdoch told him the target date for installation in London was 1 June. Neither did Brumback baulk when Murdoch insisted on secrecy – a clause would be written into the contract. Only a select few in his company were to know about the system or where it was going. The deal was worth $10 million.[25]

Atex had cornered well over 50 per cent of the American market in new technology for newspapers. The company was set up in Boston in 1973 by two young entrepreneurs who had devised a computerised typesetting system. They hit the market at the right time: one of their first clients was the national magazine *US News and World Report*. In 1981 the company had been brought by Eastman Kodak for $80 million and by 1985 the system had been sold to 500 users around the world.[26] With Atex computers the journalists typed directly into a terminal, the story was sub-edited on screen, headlines written and a photographic print-out of the finished copy could be produced ready for page make-up. In the classified advertising department, sales staff typed the advertisement directly into the computer, which was capable of running credit checks on customers, sorting out the advertisements for the next day and printing them out in order for paste-up.

The Murdoch deal would give Atex the edge on what was becoming a fierce battle to supply the Fleet Street market.

After the Kodak takeover, Atex had opened an office in Leighton Buzzard, thirty-eight miles from central London, believing that the Fleet Street revolution could not be long in coming. Atex's competitor, Systems Integrators Inc., started by Californian Jim Lennane, an ex-IBM salesman, had also opened an office in England. SII had installed a system at the *Financial Times* operated by printers only, and provided wire service terminals for Reuters and the Press Association. Atex had a foot in the door at two national newspapers, the *Guardian* and the *Daily Mail*, who were experimenting with a partial system. A mini Atex system had been installed in the *Sunday Times* in 1982. The sub-editors gave the copy to NGA printers, who retyped it into the computer. Not one Fleet Street paper used a complete cold-type system with journalists' in-putting.

Within days of the Murdoch meeting, Brumback chose the man who would take charge of the London operation. Ben Barton Smylie, a short, stocky Texan with an infectious sense of humour, had grown up in San Antonio, where his mother was a copy-editor and his father a linotype operator. He had worked on the computer typesetting system at the *Chicago Sun Times* before joining Atex as National Accounts Manager, Sales. He was tough but fun to work with. His colleagues knew where they were with him: when Smylie took a dislike to someone, he would certainly let it show. But once set to work on a project, nothing would stand in his way. He was, one of his staff has said, a human bulldozer.[27]

When Brumback told Smylie of the Murdoch contract, he swore him to secrecy. They had to choose a small team to install the computer in London. They would need a specialist in each field – classified, editorial, systems engineers, and experts in formatting and composition. They could choose anyone from any Atex office in the United States. Each person would be bound by the secrecy clause.[28]

Brumback selected a few and reviewed Smylie's recommendations. The twelve eventually chosen came from Chicago, Atlanta, San Francisco and Boston. They were the best the company had to offer, and they became known as 'Smylie's People'. The operation was called 'Project X'. 'We had to call it something,' one remembers. They had no idea that they had chosen the same codename as that chosen by the *Washington Post* for its contingency plan ten years before.

The disappearance of Smylie's people from their offices during the next months would be explained to colleagues with the cover that they were working on a 'government contract somewhere abroad'. They would not even be allowed to talk about the operation on their office telephones. When the group had meetings in Boston, they were held at an inconspicuous hotel in Concord, just outside the city. When their first flights to London were booked, the company did not use its usual travel agents. On no account, they were told, was anyone in Atex UK to know about the plan.

It was going to be a tough assignment. Smylie's people were used to an efficient support system in America whenever they did an installation job. They were used to picking up a telephone and ordering whatever equipment they needed. In London they were to be on their own.

On Tuesday, 19 February, Ben Smylie flew to London and in a room at the Tower Hotel he signed the necessary papers to become a Director of an off-the-shelf British company called Caprilord Ltd. His home address near Boston was used on the documents and he was described as a Company Executive. His co-director and Company Secretary was John Thomas Manaras, whose home address was Brookline, Boston. Manaras was Vice President and General Counsul of Atex and had been with the company for many years. Caprilord was formed by Theodore Goddard, Times Newspapers' libel lawyers.

This anonymous company would take out the leases on the safe houses where Smylie's people were to live in London during the coming months. It would be used to purchase anything the team needed, from cables for the computer to tools.

The first planning meeting in London between Atex and their clients took place two weeks later on Tuesday, 5 March. Five people from Atex flew to London and stayed at the Tower Hotel. Among them was Joan Herring, who had been appointed Project Manager. A tall, middle-aged woman, with thick, greying, curly hair, Herring was known for remaining calm whatever the crisis. In the next months she would hold the team together. 'She has 100 per cent understanding of people,' one of them said afterwards.[29]

An expert in electronic text production, Herring had installed dozens of system throughout the States and was Atex's 'chief firefighter'. 'I suspected something was going on in Atex,' Jim Lennane from SII said months later, 'when I heard someone say Herring had disappeared somewhere.'[30]

During this visit, Herring and Smylie met Charles Wilson, Bill Gillespie, Bruce Matthews, Ken Taylor, John Keating, Christopher Pole-Carew and Stan Dzuiba. In these initial planning meetings, the *London Post* was not discussed. They planned the number of terminals needed for a complete front-end system for the editorial and advertising departments of the *Sun*, the *News of the World*, *The Times* and the *Sunday Times*.[31]

'We had to know first how many people they had. We then had to work out how much hardware was needed and how to distribute the load across the networks. There would be problems of speed. But once you know the number of terminals you get a formula,' one of the Americans explained later. 'We had to balance the system out.' The team described the operation as 'aggressive scheduling': there was not much time. The installation date was less than three months away.[32]

A major problem would arise with the *Sun* and the *News of the World* typesetting. *The Times* and the *Sunday Times* were already set in cold type, so reproduction of their typefaces was easier. Many type-characters used by the Bouverie Street papers would have to be drawn and made for a cold-type-setting system. The cold type never matched that produced with hot metal but a good enough replica could be achieved.

But first News International had to solve another problem. Smylie's people needed a hide-out in London where they could secretly assemble the computer away from the prying eyes of the print unions. The team had to find somewhere to set out and test the equipment, plan the positioning of computers and pre-cut all the wires and cables. They needed to create a plywood mock-up of the computer room which in the next two months was to be built in Wapping.

It was Matthews and Taylor who found what turned out to be the ideal spot – a corrugated iron and brick warehouse in a

cul-de-sac on a run-down industrial site in Woolwich, part of
which was used by vegetable merchants. The building was
owned by a News International company called Convoys Ltd
and had once been used to store paper. Smylie did not hesitate
when he saw it, but other were less confident. 'It was scummy,'
one of them said. 'There were holes in the roof and no heat.
It was filthy, dark and dingy. There were hundreds of pigeons
in there.' Herring was appalled.[33]

But when Smylie's people returned to London on Tuesday,
26 March, the warehouse had been 'transformed'. In the space
of a few weeks, the place was gutted, sand-blasted and painted.
The grease had been cleaned off the floor and new lights had
been fitted. It was thanks to Taylor. 'He worked his butt off,'
said one of them. 'He had got everything we needed. All England is fucked up mentally but they can move fast and perfect
if you kick arse.'[34]

At one end of the warehouse, near the mock-up floor of the
'computer room', were several trailers. One was a kitchen,
another a bathroom. There was a darkroom and offices for
each speciality – computer hardware, formatting and composition, and for the classified and editorial system. There had
been only enough power for lighting, so behind the warehouse
on a piece of wasteland Taylor had installed an electricity
generator 'as big as a box car' and a diesel tank.

They called the warehouse Bunker Hill after the famous
Boston battle in 1775 when the American militia had laid
siege to the British. The name was quickly shortened and it
became known as 'the bunker'.

The first of the twenty-seven computers, the hardware for
the Atex system, manufactured by Digital Equipment Corporation, had left Boston on Tuesday, 12 March. The
company's logo on the side of the boxes had been painted
over. At the end of February, John Manaras, Atex's lawyer,
had approached Aerload, a British company who specialised
in importing computers and electronic equipment, to handle
the shipping of the system. He had been so insistent on secrecy
that some members of the company speculated that it was a
government project. The first shipment was routed via Paris
and arrived at the bunker on the afternoon of Saturday, 30
March.[35] Smylie's people welcomed the first system and then

went to Charles Wilson's elegant house in Holland Park where they had all been invited to watch the Grand National on television.

Wilson, renowned for his enthusiasm for horse racing, won the most money that afternoon. He had bet on the winner, a horse called Last Suspect, which came in at 50-1. Smylie had bet on Rupertino at 33-1. It was not even placed.[36]

As soon as the first three computers had arrived, the team got to work. Twenty-three computers – central processing units – were eventually shipped from Boston to the bunker three and four at a time. Atex was also asked to buy about $3 million worth of additional equipment such as typesetters and graphic cameras from other American companies, which was secretly shipped the same way. The total order of computers was to reach twenty-seven: an additional two to be installed for journalists in the Houses of Parliament and two more for a newsroom which was being planned in Manchester.

Throughout April Smylie's people worked as fast as they could. The hours were long. The warehouse was only 500 yards from the Thames and it was often damp and cold, mist rising off the river. On the few sunny afternoons during April, some of the team would take sandwiches to the end of Warspite Road, where steps led down to a boat mooring. It was a depressing area but there was a good view of the Thames barrier.

Each morning a fleet of cars, organised by Smylie, would pick them up from their houses in Belgravia and Chelsea and late at night would take them back. Initially, 17 Chesham Place, Belgravia, was the team's headquarters, where they installed an Apple computer and a photocopier to cope with administration.

On the wall outside the bunker a white plastic plaque with the black lettering 'Caprilord Limited' was the only indication to visitors that they had found the right place. There was always a security guard at the door, sitting in front of a plywood partition which obscured the view inside.

There were several visitors that month. Wilson would often call in to see how it was going. They thought him a 'neat guy'. 'He was a minister plenipotentiary,' one said. They were surprised that someone from editorial took decisions which were 'way out of line with what he did for a living'.[37] Another described Wilson as 'instrumental' and said he had resolved issues 'when the management was dithering'. The Americans were to become quickly aware of the fighting and politicking among Murdoch's executives and soon worked out whom they could rely on.

Their admiration was reserved for Taylor, who could not stand the internal politics. They had seen him become sullen when harangued by other executives. His life was made particularly difficult by Christopher Pole-Carew, who considered he was in charge of the project. Smylie's people thought Taylor reacted like a true British gentleman. They considered him the best newspaper production architect they had ever met and an excellent engineer. 'That plant belonged to him . . .' one of them said. 'We came along and gerrymandered it.' One of Taylor's biggest headaches had been where to put the Atex computer room in Wapping, and he had needed their advice. 'There wasn't room in the plant – it wasn't designed for it,' one remembered. Eventually space was found on the fourth floor, where some showers had been planned. 'They were showers for his men, and we wanted to rip them out. He was upset about that.'[38]

On Saturday, 20 April, when Murdoch visited the bunker, he found them all in frantic activity. He arrived in the afternoon with Bruce Matthews, who had already made several visits. Herring showed Murdoch round the mock-up of the computer room. 'He fell in love with it all,' one said. Murdoch 'wowed' them with his enthusiasm for what they were doing. 'When a guy bigger than Time Inc. calls you by your first name,' an engineer said, 'you will do anything . . . he is a kinsman. He may be ruthless and as smart as they make them but he knew how to get through to you.' The visit was a boost for them all.[39]

Smylie's people worked well as a team. Herring and Smylie had known each other for eight years and had installed other systems together. Smylie would get wound up but Herring was never rattled. The 'odd-ball' among them was one of the youngest. Jessie Stansbury was a loud, gruff man continually questioning authority. His speciality was the hardware but he had helped to set up the bunker with the carpenters and electricians Taylor had engaged. He felt personally attached to the place, and when the project was over he unscrewed the Caprilord plaque and took it back to America as a souvenir.

Texan Brian Heston arrived in the middle of April. Described by the others as a 'wild man', he was the company's expert on software development. At the start of the project, the team were only given one paper's advertising rates. They could not manage to get the others until 'the eleventh hour'. It would normally have taken two months to devise the software; Heston did it in just two weeks.

The target date for the plant to be tested in front of 'the customer' was Wednesday, 1 May. 'These guys had laid out a lot of money and wanted to see it work,' an engineer said. 'They wanted to see it up and running.' It had been a fight to meet the deadline.[40]

Six people came to the plant test that day: Pole-Carew, Dzuiba, Matthews, Wilson, Taylor, and Ronald Brumback, who had recently been promoted to President of Atex, who flew over from America. For two hours they tested the equipment: copy was fed in through several terminals which had been put on tables in front of the mock-up. A few pieces of copy were typeset.

The only glich came when Jack Charboneau, a systems engineer from San Francisco, ripped the seat of his trousers and had to sidle out with his back against the wall. He had to rush into Woolwich to buy another pair.

Twelve executives from Atex and News International were invited to the celebration meal on 2 May. Each received an invitation which started 'Caprilord requests'. It was a black-tie affair at the East India Club, which epitomises the old world of London's gentlemen's clubs. It survives today as a merger of the original Colonial Service Club with the Sports, the Devonshire and the Public Schools clubs.

News International was represented by Sir Edward Pickering, the Vice Chairman of the company. The Americans had quickly learned that Pickering was considered to be one of Fleet Street's elder statesmen, and had invited him out of courtesy. He had started his career as a sub-editor on the *Daily Mail* in 1939, and by 1950 he had become Managing

Editor of the *Daily Express*. He was Editor in the early fifties when Murdoch had spent two years there as a sub-editor. Pickering became a director of Beaverbrook Newspapers and in 1964 joined the *Daily Mirror* group, becoming Chairman in 1968. In 1981 he had been appointed by Murdoch as a National Director of *The Times*.

'He would pop up at pivotal meetings from time to time,' said one of the American team. The other representatives of News International that night were Bill Gillespie, Managing Director of Times Newspapers, Wilson, Matthews and Pole-Carew. John Keating was there from New York.

Brumback, Manaras and Atex Vice President Dick Bowen came from Boston. Atex executives in Leighton Buzzard had by now been let in on the secret project. Alec Hollingworth, Managing Director of the British subsidiary, and Max Coebergh from the Dutch office, which in the weeks to come would be helping with personnel, both received an invitation.

A photographer had been organised through the club to take a picture. Caprilord sent a copy to each of the guests afterwards. In the middle of the group, standing next to Wilson, is Smylie, who framed his copy and hung it on his office wall when he got back to Boston.

One person refused the Caprilord invitation. Ken Taylor had made his excuses. 'He wouldn't break bread with Pole-Carew if someone had a gun to his wife's head,' one of the twelve explained. Earlier, Taylor had threatened resignation after being told that Pole-Carew wanted to receive progress reports from Smylie.[41]

The booking at the East India Club had been made by Smylie through the club's reciprocal arrangement with the Harvard Club, to which Manaras belonged. He had hired a dining-room on the ground floor overlooking St James's Square. They ate well that night. It was a classic early summer menu of poached Scotch salmon and new potatoes. The *canapés* were smoked salmon, asparagus and caviar. For dessert there were fresh strawberries and cream. They drank Chassagne Montrachet. It was a formal occasion. The toast was to the Queen.

'We tried to do it with class,' one said. 'We tried to do it the British way. We had one celebration for the workers and one for the chiefs.'

Herring hosted the dinner for the 'workers' that night, at Verbanella, an Italian restaurant in Beauchamp Place not far from the Chesham Place safe house. The restaurant had become one of her favourites.

On Tuesday, 21 May, Herring attended a top-secret meeting in Wapping. They would now have to smuggle the computer into Wapping. She told Pole-Carew, Gillespie, Wilson, Taylor and the lawyer, Richards, that 'all the hardware was functioning'. The team was awaiting instructions to move the system. 'CPC stated that nothing should be moved into TH at the present time due to security problems,' the minutes record. There was some discussion: it was agreed to wait two days for 'KRM' – Murdoch – to arrive. Herring told them there would be a 'computer response time test at the Bunker on Friday 24th May at 9.30 a.m.'.[42]

All four 'APS-5 photosetters are in this country at the Bunker', they were told. The typesetter is the high-tech equivalent of the linotype machine. Each of the four APS-5 machines waiting in the bunker was capable, after receiving signals from the Atex system, of producing four thousand newspaper lines a minute. The type set was 'phototype' ready for page make-up. The American manufacturer, Autologic, had sent engineers to London who had also worked against the clock to assemble their equipment in the bunker. The APS-5 machines had come from America in late April through a shipper organised by Atex.

Taylor reported that there was no danger in bringing the computer in. But the contractors on site who were in trade unions were a problem and there would be a danger in the 'wiring to remote places'. He said that 'false floors, ceilings, partitions . . . can be done but the cable run represents a huge problem'. He said this would be discussed with Murdoch when he arrived the next day. But everything else was going to plan. The computer room would be ready by the end of the week.

Pole-Carew reported that security was satisfactory, although there was only one person at the bunker. The minutes reveal how security-conscious the group was. 'As instructed by BM, the meeting room had been debugged prior to this meeting and was being checked to see whether anyone was listening in from long range.'[43]

Wilson told them that the Editors of the *Sun* and the *News of the World* were concerned about 'the look' of their newspapers being reproduced accurately. 'CW has a whole day's copy which will be produced at the Bunker to reassure them.'[44]

Smylie was in America when the computer was finally moved during the last weekend in May. He had gone home the weekend before for the Memorial Day holiday. The operation was organised by Herring. Contractors had been banned from Tower Hamlets two days before.

At 11 p.m. on Friday, 31 May, three 40-foot lorries, each with the distinctive red and blue logo of Concorde Transport, drew up outside the bunker. The nine-man crew took just four hours to complete what was for them a routine job. The system did not have to be packed up or crated, but was moved to Wapping 'naked' in Concorde's custom-built trucks.[45] There was only one moment of apprehension: a helicopter flew low over the Tower Hamlets plant. 'No one panicked,' Herring said later.

The computer room in Wapping, on the fourth floor of the main block, was patrolled by a security guard. Access to the computer room was restricted to a select few. It was to remain the most secure part of the building. Within a few months, an electronic security door had been installed, which could only be unlocked with a combination number punched into a small panel and a plastic card inserted through the top of the panel. Only then would the door click open.

A control room ran the length of the computer room, separated from it by a glass panel. Lined against the panel were desks with nine Atex terminals. With the terminals the systems engineers would carry out daily maintenance tasks.

Behind the engineers was a small ante-room which contained the switch panel, which looked like an old-fashioned telephone switchboard, where wires from the 540 terminals which were to be installed in the building would eventually be connected. Any terminal could be connected to any computer in the network. This would take forty miles of cable.

From the control room, double doors led to the air-conditioned computer room itself. There were three networks, consisting of rows of central processing units – the computers – and in front of them banks of disc drives – one for each computer. Each network was labelled: C for classified, which had eight CPUs, T for *The Times* and the *Sunday Times* with ten, and S for the *Sun* and the *News of the World* with six.

Every terminal in the building would be connected to two computers within the appropriate network. One was 'on line' and the other was 'listening', making an exact copy of each file. Each network had one spare computer and drive. They were on stand-by, ready to take over if any computer 'went down'. Each disc drive had a memory capacity of approximately 300 million characters or commands.

On the back wall of the computer room was a head-high shelf with modems connecting the networks to the news wires – the Press Association and Reuters – and the House of Commons, where News International planned to install an Atex system based on two computers and four terminals.

There was also a connection for a system which was to be installed in a newsroom in Manchester. The idea was abandoned when the company dropped plans to publish separate editions of the *Sun* and the *News of the World* there. The computers were later moved back to London and added to the classified network.

The installation test was several days late. On 1 June the weather was hot and the air-conditioning failed to work properly. On 2 June the group fired up two of the computers, but it was not until 5 June that the test was completed.

It was when they arrived in Wapping that things started to go wrong for Smylie's people. News International had recruited a few production people from Gray's Inn Road to learn how to programme the system. There were thousands of operational problems and Herring, according to some members of the team, found herself running up against 'ingrained Fleet Street sexism'.

Murdoch was said to see Herring as 'some sort of heroine', and on each visit to the computer room he would ask, 'How are you, Joan?' And he would always thank her for what she had done. But she was being treated badly by his second-tier management. 'She built the thing and was now being told how to run it,' one of the Americans explained. 'Not only was she American, but she was a woman. She knew far more than any of them.'

Many problems arose because the News International people felt that Smylie's team were determined to set up the system in the same way as they would for an American paper. 'That's not the way British journalists work,' one remembers saying, trying to explain that copy prepared in Fleet Street newsrooms was much more heavily sub-edited than in America. Eventually staff were brought in from Atex's Leighton Buzzard office and Smylie's people were being eased out.

'Joan and Jessie Stansbury would keep things to themselves,' a senior member of the News International computer staff remembers. 'We were treated like hicks. We did not speak the same language. They were always taking short cuts because of the rush and they were hyped up. They thought we were delaying matters, but after all, we were the ones who were going to have to live with the system.'

In early September, Smylie had the unenviable task of telling Herring that she would have to return to the States. He broke the news in the house which had become their second London headquarters, 57 Park Walk, a three-storey, mock-Georgian terrace in Chelsea. She was said to have understood professionally but not emotionally and Smylie remarked to someone months later that he was not sure whether she would ever forgive him for sending her home before her system was 'up and running'. Herring thought long and hard about the project once she was back in Atlanta. 'I had seen it happen in the States in 1975,' she said, confessing she had had a moral dilemma about what eventually happened. But she added that she believed Murdoch had 'really wanted to negotiate'.

When Smylie talked about 'Project X' afterwards, he would dismiss it. 'I'm nothing but a typewriter installer – it just happens they are faster, that's all. And I know where to put them.' He laughed. 'I was the right guy in the right place at the right time.'

Murdoch's new printing plant stood on nearly thirteen acres of reclaimed dockland two miles from Fleet Street. Part of the site had been a morass of mud, all that remained there of what had once been one of the busiest ports in the world.

The contractors had had to bore down forty metres until they hit Thanet sand for the test piles. Five warehouses dating from the beginning of the nineteenth century were demolished to make way for a red-brick building which was almost as long as three football pitches.

The GLC Ancient Buildings Department had insisted on the preservation of a long, low warehouse, with beautiful fan arches in the basement, which had been used to store rum. It was a listed building and had formed part of the dockyard wall, running along Pennington Street on the north side of the site. The company was told to retain the ornate rainwater heads on the guttering, the old hoists and pulley and the cast-iron security bars on the ground floor. It originally planned to use the warehouse for boilers, chillers for air-conditioning and general stores, and the basement for oil, ink and paraffin tanks.

To the workers in all production areas in Bouverie Street, used to cramped, crowded and dirty conditions, Wapping would have been a paradise. The printing plant had a huge press hall with plenty of space between the machines and devices to reduce ink spray and paper dust. The reel store was 35,000 square feet and could hold six days' supply of newsprint. A two-way, 22-foot-wide ramp built to motorway standards led to the split-level publishing area where there was ample room for stacking bundles. The seven-storey services block at the eastern end of the site housed the foundry, platemaking area, workshops, canteen and production offices. When building work started in July 1979, Wimpey Construction (UK) Ltd, who had been given a design-construction deal by News International, had even submitted plans to Tower Hamlets Council for a swimming-pool.

After the *London Post* announcement in March 1985, the plant went through a rapid transformation. Not only had space to be found by Taylor for the Atex computer room, but the plant also had to be prepared to accommodate the editorial staff of Murdoch's four Fleet Street newspapers.

In the spring, meetings began to coordinate the strategic planning of the project. These were attended by those who had gone to the 'dash for freedom' meeting in New York and others from Murdoch's British and Australian companies, who by then knew of the project. Bill Gillespie, Managing Director of Times Newspapers Ltd, was now more involved. John Cowley, brother of Murdoch's Managing Director of News Ltd in Australia, had arrived to help organise the production areas and John Allwood, chief accountant at Bouverie Street, had joined the group. The minutes and agendas of these meetings, which identified people by initials only, were usually collected up afterwards and destroyed in one of the plant's three shredders. They tell a fascinating story of how Wapping was transformed.

By Tuesday, 21 May, Taylor was able to report that the platemaking area was ready, the editorial areas were on schedule for the end of June, and the press room for the third week in July. Only the preparation of the composing room was causing a problem. Space in Wapping was tight. John Allwood told them extra premises were needed for the Accounts Department.[46]

Charles Wilson was responsible for Editorial. At that meeting he reported he had 'identified the people he wants to undertake training and is holding them in readiness but their names cannot be released at the present time'. There was a need for key staff to be appointed in the composing area. Gillespie told them he knew 'some people who will probably come across (about ten)'. Geoffrey Richards requested any ideas for points to be included in contracts of employment.

Murdoch was keeping a close watch on what was going on. 'The phone just did not stop ringing,' said one of those involved. 'In June he asked us all to carry radio pagers so he could get to us at a moment's notice.'[47]

All of them were made aware that security for the project was a priority. One of Pole-Carew's first decisions had been to erect the high steel fence around the plant. He planned to add the spikes later. The razor wire (4,000 metres), known as Barrier Z, bought from Germany, was in Wapping by June. The theory behind the fortifications was that, if the plant was ever stormed, they would need ten minutes to allow the police to arrive, and the rows of razor wire were eventually laid to try to cause this ten-minute delay.

Colour-coded security passes were issued to everyone who came on site. In the space for 'Dept/Title' most people were described as 'Consultant'. Each pass was numbered and dated. Taylor's number was 001. Pole-Carew's was 007.[48]

By August, as a constant stream of contractors came on site, security was increased. Their Security Consultant, Bob O'Hagan, insisted his department needed to know who was coming on site and 'their level of knowledge of the project'. He asked for an approved list of personnel who could gain entry to the computer room as it was considered that too many people had access.

Every attempt was made to keep their activities a secret. They discussed window-film and blinds for sensitive areas, 'in order to avoid the possibility of telescopic photos being taken of the rooms at T.H. to identify people'. O'Hagan was investigating the purchase of one-way film to cover the windows of the computer room and the training area, although they would still have to use window blinds when the lights were on.

O'Hagan was also looking into personal security for key executives and their families. On 28 August he produced a report with an introduction which announced: 'This document contains some items obtained from an unauthorised classified source.' It was not for general distribution. 'Inform your local police of who you are, and of the project in which you are involved, in order that they can make their contingency plans for your protection,' he wrote.[49]

O'Hagan considered that 'there are amongst us people who may be regarded as targets for terrorism', so he warned: 'Be sensitive to persons behaving in a suspicious or unaccountable fashion.' His report told those at risk not to maintain regular patterns of behaviour. At home they should fit locks and chains to doors and windows, remove or trim trees and shrubs near the house to minimise the possibility of concealment and keep dustbins in an enclosed yard. He also suggested they should consider keeping a dog.

'If you believe that you are a possible target for a car bomb attack, I list below the types of devices used and where to look for them,' he wrote. He told them to look carefully round the outside of vehicles: '. . . get a mirror set at an angle on the end of a stick. Look under the car, check wheel arches. . . .' He also advised about letter bombs. 'It is my view that all mail and parcels directed to this plant should be subject to positive screening; however, in the absence of that the points to look for ... are', and O'Hagan described the tell-tale signs of a parcel bomb.

They were warned about discussing confidential matters on the telephone. 'Remember that British Telecom is able to transmit your call by radio signal to many UK destinations when land lines become congested.' As for office security, they were told that all documents and letters, even shorthand notes, were to be shredded, and instructed: 'Do not hold contentious discussions in public places, i.e., corridors, toilets, canteens.' The phrase 'the need to know', he wrote, was being bandied about all too readily. 'Is it absolutely essential that they need to know? ... If you tell someone half the story, he may tell someone else who only knows the other half.' To identify visitors, a new pass had been introduced which 'will instantly warn you to be guarded in your conversations. Do not assume that because the visitor has some knowledge of our project that he/she is privy to it in total.'

Through the summer, more and more people came to Tower Hamlets. At the beginning of August, Matthews told them that ten Australian girls were available to be trained in editorial/advertising inputting on the computer terminals. Pole-Carew reported that mechanical technicians were needed and electronics people to train on the Atex system. The minutes record that from the end of the month 'a selected group of people (editors) will come to T.H. to train under the Atex editorial trainer – Ben Smylie to organise'.

Premises for the Accounts Department had been found in Peterborough but it was going to take three to five weeks to get telephone lines installed. A computer system would be ready for installation in a week. 'Data base of sales ledger from T and ST has been obtained and is being tested on the equipment,' according to the minutes of a meeting held at Tower Hamlets on 8 August. But by the middle of that month there was still no electricity supply and they thought the offices would not be ready until the second week of September. Twenty-five clerical staff for the new offices were being interviewed.

John Keating, who was spending his time travelling between the offices of the *New York Post* and Wapping, was organising recruitment of some overseas personnel. He called on the services of Southern Production Program, the Oklahoma company which had trained people for the *Washington Post*'s contingency plan, 'Project X', ten years before. Jim Stuckey, the Executive Director and General Manager of Southern, and his press instructor, Frank Bourlon, started training new recruits on the presses on 27 August. They stayed two weeks and trained thirty people. They were impressed with their students' mechanical knowledge, even though they had no experience of printing presses. 'We removed the mystery and mystique of this gigantic piece of iron,' said Stuckey.[50]

Training for the platemaking and composing areas, where equipment was installed and tested, started on the same day. In platemaking there was also to be a two-week course. Matthews wanted the paper store and ink tanks to be full by the end of August.

He had informed the executives that 'go-day' would probably be 1 October. He 'updated them on the union situation'. 'It was to make people aware,' one of them explained, 'from now on it would be dangerous and we might have to go live.'[51] The expression 'go live' was becoming a catchphrase they all used.

There were four newsrooms being prepared in Wapping. The two that were to go in the old warehouse – the *Sunday Times* and *The Times* – were causing problems. They had wanted to reinforce the roof and skylights in case petrol bombs were ever thrown. In May, the company had asked for planning permission to convert the warehouse into offices. Matthews stressed that they must avoid contravening the Planning Acts. As it was a listed building, Richards stated that it was vital to get the change-of-use certificate before anything was done.

By Thursday, 8 August, it was reported that the 'Sun and NOW areas will be ready within 2–3 weeks. T and ST still behind.' The *Sun* and *News of the World* composing areas were 'looking good and should be ready by 19 August with T/ST composing ready by the end of August. By the middle of August, dial-up trials to test the Reuters link had been arranged, but the wire service from the Press Association had not been organised.

The warehouse continued to worry them. Taylor told them

at a meeting on 19 September that the old building was 'at the half-way stage'. They had problems with 'various different authorities' over planning permissions, but they now had a change-of-use certificate and GLC approval had been received. But he told them he was still waiting for 'GLC consent for the job as a whole'.

There was some argument about when the computer terminals could be installed in the building. Wilson felt that 'in view of the current level of knowledge known by the NUJ . . . that the terminals should not be put in yet'. He had been told they could be connected very quickly when necessary. Rod Hunt, who was Computer Manager at *The Times* and had been brought into the project at the end of May, did not think that was possible. Taylor told them the problem would be overcome 'at the appropriate time'. Six operators were being trained on terminals and were becoming competent. There would be a team of twelve eventually. Wilson reported that 'training is on-going in the USA and in Leighton Buzzard for limited editorial staff'. Hunt reported that the 'editorial side as regards Atex is now stable and will work satisfactorily'. He told them that Reuters was installed and the Press Association lines were now in.

By mid-September there were fifty-nine staff in the press room. Four more were expected from Australia and two from America. The plant was full of newsprint and ink and there had been successful test-runs on the presses.

They were now preparing for Murdoch's forthcoming visit on 29 September. Matthews told them a report had to be ready for him on the progress at Tower Hamlets: they would have to define clearly the availability of 'equipment and competent labour to operate it'. Matthews told them that Murdoch would be discussing the *London Post* with the unions on 30 September.

Minutes taken at that meeting record Matthews saying: '. . . it is most important that the *London Post* only is discussed with suppliers etc. at the present time, and that the other publications are not mentioned at all. The printing of the other publications at TH should not be discussed outside the Group, and the contingency plans being made are for a state of emergency only.'

Three days before Murdoch was due to arrive, it was reported that there were now eighty people in the press room, and they were expecting four more trainees from Australia and the States. There were sixty people in photocomposition, thirty-one in the publishing area and eleven technicians. Numbers would increase in all areas during October.

There were continuing fears about security. O'Hagan was 'looking into the list of plumbers on site'. One of them had been reported by Gillespie as being a 'mole'. That day they had been obliged to take the security coverings off the windows of the Atex and training areas for the benefit of the District Surveyor who was visiting, although they felt 'this does make us vulnerable as regards the Atex equipment, from a security point of view'.

During the last weekend in September, Murdoch held two strategic meetings. The first was with Pole-Carew, Taylor, Keating, Wilson, Gillespie and Cowley, to ensure he was thoroughly acquainted with the progress in every department in the building. On the Sunday he had a smaller meeting with Wilson, Gillespie, Matthews and Richards. Together in Murdoch's London flat, they devised the statement Murdoch was to make when he met the print unions the next day.

When the General Secretaries of the five print unions – the AUEW, EETPU, NGA, Sogat and the NUJ – arrived at the Inn on the Park on Monday, 30 September, they were desperate for information. Their suspicions were growing about what was happening in the plant. They knew that the presses had been rolling in Wapping and 'dummy' newspapers had been printed there.

But when Murdoch entered the room there was no time to ask him anything. He immediately started reading from a four-page statement which made it quite clear that he was at the end of his tether. He told them Fleet Street's working practices were a disgrace to them all. Disruptions had led to the loss of several tens of millions of pounds, 'sometimes nearly bringing our whole company down'. In spite of that, he had undertaken a major and expensive building programme at Tower Hamlets. 'When the costs of our plant in Glasgow are added, there will be little change from £100 million. . . . At Tower Hamlets, when negotiations were opened with the unions, News Group was presented with claims for manning levels and work practices which would have meant an actual financial penalty for moving into this great new plant,' he said.[52]

They had satisfied themselves that there was an opportunity for another evening newspaper in London which might quickly become a 24-hour daily, and so in the spring he had hired an independent company, Computer Print Consultants, to help make Tower Hamlets an economic and efficient base for publishing the *London Post*.

'These decisions and actions coincided with the announcement of another new daily newspaper to be launched by Eddie Shah,' he said. That paper was not yet a 'major threat', but it demonstrated clearly that other publishers and companies were willing to move into their markets. 'They will be competing with the overwhelming advantages of modern technology and one-union, no-strike agreements.'

No one spoke. Without pausing in his quiet delivery, Murdoch continued: 'We cannot stand aside and allow our markets to be captured.' They recognised an obsessive newspaper proprietor. '. . . If we cannot compete with our present titles, as seems the case, we must start new ones. And be first. We will be in a position to launch the *Post* by spring of the next year. We have started to test some of the equipment and that process will continue throughout the coming months. The presses have to be made operational, as does the new and highly advanced publishing equipment.'

As he finished his speech, Murdoch softened his approach. 'Because many of us have known each other for many years and have learnt to appreciate each other's difficulties, I have told you where we stand. I wish that our earlier negotiations had been more fruitful. It is a tragedy for your members that they were not.'

Murdoch told them he still wanted to move the *Sun* and *News of the World* to Tower Hamlets as well as produce the *Post* in 'one integrated operation'. But it was 'difficult to see any point in going through another series of long, unpleasant and emotionally draining negotiations with so little prospect of success.'

Murdoch told them that if talks on manning the *London Post* made good progress, they would be extended to include the transfer of the *Sun* and the *News of the World* to the new plant as well. 'The music has changed,' he told Brenda Dean at one point, 'but the dance has not.'[53] Murdoch insisted on a tight deadline for the talks. He said it had been set by Eddie Shah, not him, and gave them three months – until Christmas.

When the print union General Secretaries left the Inn on the Park that day, they felt reassured. They believed there would now be some serious negotiating about the *London Post* in the coming months. They thought it was a new beginning.[54]

It was not only the General Secretaries who believed that the *London Post* was a reality. Murdoch's senior executives from Britain and America knew how cleverly he had kept all his options open. He was now ready for any eventuality. Whatever happened, it seemed he could not lose. 'We could now respond to any threat,' an executive explained. 'They'd always had the ultimate weapon – now we had it.'[55]

It is a feature of Murdoch management that he does not tell his executives his overall plan. On the surface, he treated men like Matthews, Gillespie, Taylor, Wilson and Keating like chums. And the people who ran his companies around the world called him 'Rupert'. But this did not mean they knew him well. It was Japanese-style open-door management.

'I think he made his mind up as he went along,' said one executive who was involved from the beginning. 'He just saw it developing. I don't believe there was a master plan.' Another disagreed. Murdoch's fall-back position had become his prime purpose. From the first day he had talked of the *Post*, he had always intended moving the four papers to Wapping.

'Of that,' he said, 'there is no doubt at all.'[56] He had heard Murdoch call Wapping the 'bear trap'.

There was discussion among these senior Murdoch men in the last months about what would happen if the unions did not go on strike. *The Times* and *Sunday Times* would have stayed in Gray's Inn Road and 'we would have ended up with the *London Post*,' one said. 'He would have ended up with too much computer equipment but that would have been small change to him. There's plenty of other Murdoch companies throughout the world who could use the equipment.'

Bill O'Neill was convinced from the outset that the unions would strike. So was Gillespie.[57] They believed it was the only response the unions knew. But Matthews always talked about producing the *London Post*. 'From February and March 1985 onward,' he was to affirm later, 'the priorities so far as the *London Post* was concerned were editorial and the physical preparation of the Wapping plant.'[58]

Charles Wilson said he believed in the *London Post* and that most of his time in 1985 had been taken up as Editorial Director of the paper until his appointment as *The Times*'s Editor in November that year. 'From the beginning,' he later claimed, 'the plan was to produce the newspaper on an editorial direct-input system similar to the Atex system that I had used in Chicago. . . . I was very conscious of how sensitive would be the revelation of such plans to our workforce at *The Times* and the *Sunday Times*.'

He had planned the character and the market targeting of the paper, which, he said, 'had been a fascinating exercise because it was the first time that the 24-hour concept had been attempted in Britain . . .'. He had drawn up a staff list and had appointed three assistants: Mike Hoy, an Australian who worked on Murdoch's *Daily Post* in New York; Richard Williams, Deputy Sports Editor of *The Times*, and Tim Austin from *The Times*'s Foreign Desk.

Wilson said the first projected launch date of the evening paper was in autumn 1985, and the 24-hour paper in spring 1986. But by the summer of 1985 it was clear that the plant would not be ready, so they had announced that the *Post*'s launch would be postponed.

Wilson affirmed: 'We also began work on preparing "dummies" of the new paper, first single pages, then sections and on to whole editions of the proposed paper.' He had appointed David Banks, Executive Features Editor of the *Sun*, as Systems Editor, responsible for the direct-input equipment and training.

'I have to say that I never had any doubt that it was the Group's intention to produce the *Post* as I have outlined. I conceived a newspaper that I thought would be successful and it was real to me in every sense.'

The journalists who had secretly come from the four papers,

and the handful of senior production men who had decided to take up discreet offers, had been told different stories. Some, sent away for training, were told they were working for the *London Post*. When they were finally allowed back from training and went to Wapping, they believed the plan was to move all four papers. Others were told at the outset that the printing of all four titles had been the plan after all.

It was Murdoch's middle management who thought there had been a master plan. In the last three months of 1985, they came to expect that his four Fleet Street papers would eventually end up in Tower Hamlets. They dreaded it. The pressure to prepare the plant was intense and they worked sixteen hours a day, almost seven days a week. What they all came to dread was 'going live' on four papers. 'During the highs we thought we could do it. During the lows we thought we couldn't,' one manager said.[59]

What amazed them was Murdoch's level of involvement in the project. 'It was a very personal thing for him,' one of the managers later recalled. 'He had a phenomenal memory and would come through my department and remember a problem I'd had days before . . . always calling me by my first name.' Murdoch was sometimes humorous. 'He'd laugh when I said we just weren't ready and make a joke about overmanning.' Sometimes he would encourage, saying, 'Bloody exciting, ain't it. Bloody exciting.' They took to repeating this to each other in a mock Australian accent.[60]

Murdoch was changeable. If he found disaster, he could be ferocious. He would start hammering on a table and shouting. 'Fix it,' he would yell.[61] A manager remembers him in the composing room, shouting, 'You're bloody incompetent. You've let me down,' and walking away without waiting for an explanation.

In early December the word was that they would have to be ready by the end of the month. But on 19 December they were given Christmas and the New Year off. For many journalists it was the longest Christmas break for years.

In early January a team of twenty Atex employees from America, who had been selected to train journalists, came to London. Simultaneously, a group of journalists from Murdoch's papers in Chicago and New York arrived. The rumour went round Wapping that Murdoch had reserved five weeks for London. It was an unheard-of length of time. 'This is it,' they said to each other.

On Saturday, 11 January, Murdoch took a few people to lunch at the Savoy.[62] Bill O'Neill was on one side of him and on the other an American typesetter, Marlene Rae, who was nicknamed the 'fastest typesetter in the West'. A forceful, highly competent and determined woman, she had been a linotype operator from a small newspaper outside Chicago. She could type 40,000 characters an hour and had been instrumental in keyboard training.

There was a good cross-section of the people whom Murdoch had needed – and found – for Wapping. Bill Dell, a former NGA Father, who had been head printer at *The Times* and had suddenly resigned in the summer, was now in charge of the composing room in Wapping. Adam Conrad, an Australian and expert in telecommunications, was there, as was Charles 'Charlie' McNeil, who had been one of the best machinists on the *Daily Mirror*, an afternoon tabloid in Sydney; he was in charge of the Wapping press room.

It was a relaxed and informal occasion lasting two hours. Murdoch was wearing an old-fashioned blue suit with turnups. A notebook was sticking out of his pocket. He had put it on the table and made notes throughout, mostly about problems they were having in their departments. He had told them 'D-day' was approaching and asked if their departments were ready. Some of them found it hard to believe how charming he was, how relaxed they could become in his presence.

They thought they would definitely 'go live' on Saturday, 18 January, when the *Sunday Times* special section, already printed in Wapping, was due to be distributed. They thought it would be the final straw for the unions. So they prepared for a strike: they shadowed the entire paper.

Sunday Times stories had been 'spirited away' from Gray's Inn Road. Some stories had arrived at Wapping technically, through a system nicknamed the Green Box, which was capable of electronically transferring the cold type set by NGA printers to a disc which was brought into the plant. Page layouts were smuggled out of the *Sunday Times* newsroom by executives – James Adams, the Assistant Editor who had just been put in charge of systems development, Editor Andrew Neil and Peter Roberts, Managing Editor – and then smuggled back again.[63]

They began shadowing the edition on Friday, 17 January. There were a dozen journalists and production managers putting the paper together with the inexperienced new recruits, who were pasting the copy onto page layouts. No one but Peter Roberts from the *Sunday Times* was directly involved. Graham Courtenay, who had been the *Sun*'s Assistant Night Editor and had disappeared from Bouverie Street in October, was feeding copy into the Atex system. David Banks, who had mysteriously left the *Sun* that summer and had been made Assistant Editor (Production) of the *London Post*, was doing the same. Tony Norbury, former Production Editor of *The Times*, who had been taken on as Production Editor of the *London Post*, was organising the typesetting and page layout. Also from the *Sun* there were Peter Pace, Sports Editor; Kelvin Holland, an Assistant Chief sub-editor; and Roy Pittilla, Assistant Editor.

They worked almost non-stop through the night and all day Saturday. Gillespie kept them informed of the union situation, but they did not believe that Roy 'Ginger' Wilson would allow the presses to roll that night. From time to time one of them would raise his head from a terminal or the drawing-boards where copy was pasted on the page to be told about what was happening in Gray's Inn Road.

When they had done all but the last six pages, Gillespie came to the composing room. 'They're printing,' he said. They were bitterly disappointed. An hour later they were told that the presses had stopped. A Chapel meeting was being held in the machine room. They were told to keep going and finish the paper and be ready to print.

There was only the front page left to do when the news came through that the presses in Gray's Inn Road were running again. They could pack it in. But they had worked hard and long and there had been a build-up of steam. They decided to carry on. Someone set 'No. 1' above the masthead and about 1,000 copies were printed. Many were shredded later for security reasons.

They finally went 'live' a week later. On Friday, 24 January, the night the strike started, Murdoch lost *The Times* and the

Sun. He did not intend losing editions of the *News of the World* or the *Sunday Times*.

Murdoch was everywhere. 'He was into everything,' a manager said. He remembers Murdoch raising his voice at James Adams, in the middle of the *Sunday Times* newsroom, after discovering that no one had efficiently organised inputting copy into the computer. The *Sunday Times* newsroom was a particular problem. Adams, who had helped to set it up, had been known to the production staff as the 'plant director'. All he had seemed to do in the last few weeks was to order potted plants and prints for the *Sunday Times* newsroom walls.[64]

The journalists had started arriving from Bouverie Street and a few came from *The Times* and the *Sunday Times*. Murdoch said later that he had never doubted that the journalists would come to Wapping. He had reservations about *The Times* Chapel, where he believed there was an element of traditional trade unionism, caused by the younger, lower-paid journalists who worked on the *Times Literary* and *Educational Supplements*. He thought the *Sunday Times* journalists were pragmatic and the majority would come. He had once walked through the *Sunday Times* newsroom in Wapping and said there were too many desks. 'We might not need all these.'

When the first journalists arrived, they found their new world amazing. They entered the most secure industrial site ever built in Britain. It was picket-proof. The plant was surrounded by searchlights and a twelve-foot-high spiked metal fence behind which were triple rolls of razor wire. The double front gates were electronically controlled from an adjacent guard-house. Uniformed security guards were everywhere: they monitored the pictures from a series of infra-red rotating remote-control cameras.

Inside, the security was as tight. All employees were photographed and issued with colour-coded, numbered passes. For instance, a white pass allowed access to the *News of the World* but not to the other newsrooms.

The newsrooms were spotless: open-plan areas with row upon row of new desks each with a computer terminal. They looked like factories. There were no partitions, no room for privacy under the bright fluorescent lights. 'It looked like the

Starship Enterprise,' one *Sun* journalist remarked. Another said it looked like the Ministry of Truth.

They were welcomed by American Atex staff. 'Hi!' they would say, introducing themselves by their christian names, showing the manual needed to master the technology and saying they were there to help with any problem. 'Just call.' Each journalist had been given a code-word with which they would access their particular files in the computer.

Once they had written their story on screen, they were told which code would send it to the sub-editors, who would edit it on screen and eventually key it to be typeset. The sub-editors put on type instructions which would be understood by the computerised typesetter. After it was printed out it would be pasted up on a page.

They met the new printers pasting up the pages. They were young, enthusiastic and inexperienced. None of the journalists had ever seen women working on 'the stone' before. They chatted and joked with them. They found out that some had been hairdressers, hotel receptionists, plumbers and carpenters. Some had been unemployed. These people had jumped at the chance of £15,000 a year.

The journalists saw many familiar faces. Those already working in Wapping had gone through a most strenuous week. Many had slept in dormitories in the Portakabins near the *Times* end of the old warehouse. None of the systems installed in the last months had been fully tested. The news that they were finally going live had thrilled them.

At around 8 p.m. on Saturday, 25 January, Murdoch stood at the panel in the press room which controlled the 48 Goss headliner presses. His plastic security pass with his photograph and the word 'Chairman' hung from his trouser pocket. Bill O'Neill and John Cowley were at his side, other executives and Editors behind. Murdoch paused. Ken Taylor was missing, and for about three minutes the group waited while someone went to find him. When Taylor arrived, Murdoch gestured for him to stand by his side. Only then did Murdoch press the red button for line one, and started the presses rolling. There was a whine as the motors were picking up and a metallic thud from the folders. Then they all clapped and cheered. Murdoch simply smiled. Two hundred years of Fleet Street history were over.

There was just one tradition Murdoch kept to that night. Like any new proprietor who had just taken over a Fleet Street paper and had watched the first edition come off the presses, he toured his plant and thanked his staff. One of his managers remembers him being like a kid that night. 'He was dancing,' he said. 'I'd never seen him like that, I don't think he really believed they would strike.'[65]

The first lorries came down the floodlit ramp shortly after 9 p.m. There were technical hitches, but three million copies of the *News of the World* were printed in Wapping and 750,000 in Kinning Park, two million down on the Bouverie Street print run. Wapping produced 1.2 million copies of the *Sunday Times*, which was only 150,000 down.[66]

Murdoch had to overcome one more hurdle in his 'dash for freedom' – getting the papers to the readers. He had prepared one last contingency plan. Throughout the strategy meetings in 1985, an independent distribution system had been seen as the final key to unshackling the company from the traditional print unions. The plan was audacious.

Newspaper distribution was traditionally done through 250 wholesale houses in Britain – all Sogat closed shops – servicing 40,000 newsagents. Murdoch's whole operation risked falling at the last fence if the Sogat packers and distributors were to refuse to handle his papers. It was a risk he was not prepared to take.

To achieve a nationwide distribution of his titles uninterrupted by industrial action, he also had to outflank the rail unions. Newspapers had always been taken to provincial centres by special trains, some sorted *en route* by Sogat members into newsagents' bundles. Wholesalers collected their consignments, which were divided and packed at their depots or at the railway station and taken by fleets of vans to the retailers.

To both British Rail and the wholesalers, News International's distribution contracts were valuable. To BR alone, the News International business was worth £9 million a year. The wholesaler's cut was between 7 and 13 per cent of the newspaper's cover price, which for the two largest wholesale houses, W. H. Smith and John Menzies, represented £22

million and £14 million worth of business each year. To the
nineteen wholesale houses in London, eleven of which belong
to either Smiths or Menzies, the company's titles accounted for
more than a third of their trade.[67]

No national newspaper proprietor had ever managed to
extricate himself from Sogat's grip on distribution. Eddie Shah
had considered by-passing the system by distributing his
proposed new paper, *Today*, using local road transport
companies and groups instead of existing wholesalers. He later
announced 'a partial retreat from that position', which Sogat
said 'never seemed very credible anyway'.[68]

At the end of March 1985, Murdoch decided to ask 'my
friends and partners in Australia, the TNT Transport Group,
to investigate the possibilities of an independent distribution
system'.[69]

Thomas Nationwide Transport had been set up by an
Austrian-born refugee, Sir Peter Abeles, in Australia. Murdoch
had already had dealings with the company through their
joint ownership of Ansett Transport Industries, Australia's
leading private domestic airline, and a major communications
company. In 1978 TNT had established a British subsidiary
in Lancashire, and by 1985 it had achieved a turnover of
£100 million. The company claimed to be the biggest parcels
operator in the UK.[70] They attributed their success to their
thrusting business philosophy: 'provided there are profits to be
made we will meet the needs of the customer'.[71]

On 16 April 1985 TNT's Project General Manager, Tom
Bell, presented News International with a 45-page Operational Proposal, in line with information supplied by Pole-
Carew. Its terms of reference were 'the distribution of the
following News International newspapers: the *Sun*, *The Times*,
the *News of the World*, the *Sunday Times*, the *News of the World
Colour Magazine*, the *Sunday Times Magazine*, the *Times Supplements* (4 titles)'. These newspapers could be delivered to
'39,765 retailers in the United Kingdom' from Tower Hamlets
and Kinning Park in Glasgow, using TNT's network of
depots.[72]

The company had twenty-eight centres throughout the
country, four of them in London. It also had the use of more
than 400 'dispatch posts', the premises of companies with a

TNT franchise used for the collection and delivery of parcels. They told News International they would need an extra 908 vehicles to make the deliveries, including 780 4.5 ton delivery vans. It would be a logistically complex operation, but Bell said their proposal offered clear advantages: 'complete control'; 'improved service – "middlemen" will be eliminated and retailers will enjoy direct contact with News International'; and 'continuity of service – TNT enjoys excellent industrial relations'.[73] TNT's fee for the service would be £1,067,000 per week.

On 30 May the company's General Manager, Alan Jones, met Murdoch to discuss the tender at Murdoch's St James's Place flat. A week later, he wrote to him confirming that TNT could deliver 5,000,000 daily newspapers to retailers by 6.30 each morning in all but the most remote parts of the country and would distribute 6,625,000 Sunday papers.

Pole-Carew had taken charge of the distribution problem. While Managing Director of T. Bailey Forman, he had organised the distribution of the *Nottingham Evening Post* and had computerised the home deliveries. Bruce Matthews affirmed later that 'much of the effort and research which went into the question of distribution of the *London Post*, and into the contingency plans to distribute the existing titles by road, in the period from February 1985 onwards was made by CPCL staff' because News International had relatively little experience of distribution by road.[74]

Following detailed discussions with TNT, John Hayden from Computer Print Consultants Ltd had produced on unheaded paper an eight-page, undated document entitled 'The Post'.[75] Based on a Monday to Friday, 48-page tabloid with five editions totalling 650,000 copies per day, he anticipated needing 140 vans to deliver direct to the 7,000 newsagents in the capital, which he had divided into three areas: Outer London, London Post Codes and Central London. Bruce Matthews affirmed later that the document was produced 'in or about late June 1985' along with 'many other working papers' which could not 'immediately be located'.[76]

In the absence of a formal contract, a Deed of Indemnity between News International Plc and TNT Roadfreight (UK) Ltd was signed on 28 June. News International would underwrite £7.17 million for vehicles and equipment, and £332,000 for staff and premises. They promised to meet all interest charges on cash borrowed by TNT for the project; to pay for recruitment; and to cover all expenses until the intended start-up date, 1 October. News International also agreed to reimburse TNT if the project did not go ahead. A five-year contract was eventually signed.[77]

TNT had also offered to handle the administrative work: invoicing, delivery notes and 'returns' – unsold newspapers. However, News International intended to keep control of this vital area.

That summer, the company's circulation reps were asked to update their records on retailers' addresses and supplies. They were told to get the information discreetly from the wholesalers, but were not told why it was needed. 'The whisper soon went round that they were doing an exercise to see if they could get their papers out without the wholesalers,' one rep said later.[78] Some provincial wholesalers became increasingly concerned after reports from drivers that they were being followed on their delivery rounds by 'mystery vans'.[79]

Many were made suspicious by the reps' questions and refused to cooperate, saying it was against company policy. But it was too late. News International had sufficient information to provide the data-base for a distribution system. They used contacts who used to work in the newspaper industry to do the spadework, verified figures by telephone and revamped their old records.[80] The information was keyed into their computer by a Derby-based bureau during October and November.

In June 1985, Murdoch's Australian 'computer guru', Ross Wood, and his two assistants, came in on the project. He had suggested they buy a £2 million Fujitsu 7.800 machine, the most powerful mainframe computer in the world. Similar to the system News Corp Ltd used in Sydney, it was the first of its kind in Britain.[81] It was IBM compatible and could be linked to their terminals in the administrative offices in Peterborough.

Wood placed the order through Siemens Germany, the European agents, at the beginning of 1985. The computer arrived from Munich in early August and was stored at

Aerload's Slough warehouse for nearly two months because the air-conditioning in Wapping still was not working properly.[82] By the end of September the computer had been transported to the plant and was up and running.

The plans had been laid for a completely independent national news distribution system. It would take a while to shake down. All who attended the strategy meetings in 1985 knew there would be chaos for weeks if it were ever tried. 'We hoped we'd never have to put it into operation,' one of them said.[83]

SEVEN

Recognition

'Mr Murdoch may have his plans... but we have ours,' Brenda Dean confidently told reporters at the first press conference after the strike call. She had already briefed branch officials, in no uncertain terms, about those plans. They were told that their task now was to gain and keep trade union and public support. No other national newspapers would be hit. There was no point in concealing union funds in case of court actions: that had proved futile and costly for the National Union of Mineworkers. There would be non-violent picketing, controlled by the union nationally – no repeat of the scenes on the miners' picket lines. Dean had been determined from the start to set the tone of the dispute.

Sogat's 4,300 Fleet Street members were called out on strike at 6 p.m. on Friday, 24 January. Dean had stood in front of London officials and Fathers, crammed into the seedy Britannia Street basement, the 'call room' – Sogat's labour exchange – where the casual employees went each day to get work. She had made a brief statement. To her amazement, when she had finished speaking, they had all clapped and cheered.

The union's first General Secretary ever elected from the provinces and not London had been in office for barely ten months, and she was still learning Fleet Street ways. In her twenty-four years in the union in Manchester – seven years as Branch Secretary – she had never heard anyone applaud after a strike-call. 'I called that strike with a heavy heart,' she was to say later. 'We were entering the like of which we had never seen before.'

As the first lorries with the *Sunday Times* and *News of the World* moved down the floodlit ramp at Wapping, there were no problems from pickets. The closure of roads was strategically planned. Side roads in Wapping had been sealed by police – the notification, 'Commissioner's Directions', under the Metropolitan Police Act, 1839, signed by Sir Kenneth Newman two days before the strike had begun.[1] Under police guard, the lorries, jeered by about 100 pickets, sped down The Highway. In Glasgow's Kinning Park the first lorry, loaded with copies of the *News of the World*, left soon after 10 p.m.

Murdoch's biggest problem now, Dean knew, would be distribution. She believed he was about to attempt to move newspapers by road, replacing the century-old rail and road system, and would try to circumvent the traditional union-controlled distribution outlets. In London he could deliver papers directly to newsagents, by-passing Sogat wholesale workers and putting at risk a further 1,500 Sogat jobs.

But she believed that in the provinces the lorries would deliver to the established networks of wholesalers. This would provide the unions with their strongest card. Branch officials were told that the TNT drivers, members of the TGWU, would be instructed not to cross picket lines. And in spite of possible court action under new labour laws, Dean and her National Executive Committee had instructed Sogat drivers and warehouse workers up and down the country not to handle News International papers.

In those first weeks many papers were late and there were shortfalls in some areas – but there was little disruption in the provinces by Sogat wholesale members. In London, the complicated plan for delivery by small vans to newsagents did not work that well, but it improved as the days went by. It looked as though Murdoch's plans were going to succeed.

Dean worked hard, travelling the country, telling provincial members that the London dispute could be won if only they would black Murdoch's titles. She went to her home base, Manchester, to urge members there not to handle the titles. They were her people: she had worked hard for them for twenty years. At a packed meeting of 300 Sogat officials, she pleaded: 'If you walk away from your colleagues dismissed in London and their families you don't deserve to be called trade unionists.'[2] But walk away they did.

In the few areas where members did refuse to handle the papers – Merseyside and Glasgow – wholesale managements turned out to get at least partial distribution to newsagents. Dean said that in some areas her members had been intimidated: in Coventry some were fired for blacking the titles, but later reinstated.

It was not just fear of dismissal which held her provincial members back. Dean knew that they had refused to support their fellow trade unionists because of the London Branch's reputation – the 'London People', or 'the Mob' as they were sometimes known. There were just 30,000 Fleet Street workers in Sogat's 203,000 membership. They were notorious for wild-cat strikes, over-manning and practising Luddite protectionism. They earned fabulous wages for ridiculously short hours.

By the end of the first week, with delivery times improving, the unions could no longer pretend that any action would bring News International to its knees. The electricians behind the wire seemed indifferent to threats of suspension from the TUC. Members of the TGWU, driving the hated TNT lorries, continued to cross the picket lines. Sogat and NGA members carried on printing the Sunday colour magazines and the *Times Literary* and *Educational Supplements*. There was no longer any possibility of real pressure. News International was winning: Murdoch's year of planning was beginning to pay off.

Murdoch had deployed every legal weapon in the labour law created by the Thatcher governments. The dispute was not just to be fought on the streets of Wapping but in the courts. No sooner had he transferred production and sacked the workforce – using the full power of a law which had been on the statute books for decades – than he was taking out writs to curb the effectiveness of any industrial action. In the space of three weeks, he launched a dozen legal actions, the majority against Sogat. Just over two weeks into the dispute, Sogat's £17 million assets were sequestrated. The High Court judge also fined the union £25,000 for contempt of an injunction banning them from instructing wholesale newspaper distribution members not to handle the four titles.

Dean fought for public sympathy. Her statements on the day of sequestration were designed to appeal. 'We want to be lawful people, but the laws are so loaded against us that we either have to choose between them or walking away from our people. Mr Murdoch has ditched them. The laws have ditched them. Their trade union is the only friend they've got.'[3] On 'News at Ten', Dean, who had turned out to be a television natural, gave an impressive performance. She said the dispute was about 'destroying trade unions',[4] but she made sure the viewers knew that her two convalescent homes were under threat. She knew she had to change the view that her members were Fleet Street fat cats who had deserved all they had got; half of those thrown out of work were low-paid telephonists, secretaries, cleaners and librarians.

Gradually she began to win the developing propaganda war with News International. The pretty General Secretary of Sogat, demure and reasonable, had Murdoch crouched behind his barbed wire claiming it to be the future. News International executives kept hoping a few of the militant Fathers would appear on television, but Dean's tactic of deliberately keeping them out of the limelight was paying off.

What did not help Murdoch's image, and was a significant early breakthrough for the unions in the propaganda war, was the leaking of a lawyer's letter from Wapping. It was from Geoffrey Richards of Farrer and Co.

The leaked letter from Richards to Bruce Matthews was written on 20 December 1985, the day after talks with the union on the *London Post* had broken down. Copies were sent to Murdoch and eight senior executives, including Bill Gillespie, Managing Director of Times Newspapers, Bill O'Neill and *The Times*'s Editor, Charles Wilson. Richards gave detailed advice on the most expedient and cost-saving method of getting rid of the work force. 'Dear Bruce,' the letter started: 'Since the very first day I was involved in the *London Post* project I have advised that, if a moment came when it was necessary to dispense with the present workforces at TNL and NGN, the cheapest way of doing so would be to dismiss employees while participating in a strike or other industrial action.'

Richards advised that a strike would be better, 'either because it was easier to identify a striker or because only one or two people may black a particular piece of equipment . . .'. A striker would be in breach of contract, he wrote, and 'can thus be dismissed instantly'. A striker would not be entitled to redundancy and would have no claim in the event of unfair dismissal 'provided all the strikers have been dismissed and none selectively re-engaged'. The words 'all' and 'none' were underlined.

The letter went on: 'Given that we are now much nearer the date of a possible explosion – although I appreciate that a more "evolutionist" approach may still (necessarily) be adopted – I thought it would be sensible (not least because some of these points came up only on Wednesday) if I reiterated the advice already given. It will be useful if the key people in the project have the main principles of law firmly in their heads at all times.'

But it was the last paragraph of the letter which the unions claimed showed the true extent of the company's contempt and cynicism towards their workforce. Richards noted that the managements operated complicated rota systems, 'and many of the Sunday employees are different to the weekday employees'. The idea, he wrote, 'is to catch as many employees in the net as possible, and it seems to me likely that that will be done best if the dismissals take place at the weekend rather than near the beginning of a week'.[5]

Dean's accusation of a 'conspiracy of deceit' had become believable. 'I'm accusing Mr Murdoch of deceiving me when I met him, and of deceiving his workforce,' she said on television, with the air of someone who had been personally outraged.[6] Dean said that while she had been negotiating with News International in good faith, they had conspired behind her back.

Dean was increasingly portrayed as the standard-bearer of trade union realism. It seemed at times as though Murdoch had made trade unions respectable again, and although Sogat and the NGA never made a policy decision that Dean should have a high profile, she said: 'Tony always told me to go first.' Tony Dubbins had quickly realised how Dean would be best employed on television. Her general attitude was more likely to appeal; Dubbins's demeanour and rhetoric were unlikely to gain much public support. She had been quick to learn to take advantage of the considerable and sudden media attention she attracted. And she enjoyed appearing on television. People were beginning to listen, and Dean, the first woman to head a major industrial trade union, had enormous appeal with journalists. She became popular and famous.

In most interviews, she referred not to strikers but to the 'four and a half thousand families of our members . . . in this dispute that is weighing most heavily on me'. She seemed honest about her feelings and caring about her members. '. . . I started off the day feeling, I suppose, a little bit down . . .'.[7] In one interview, a week after the dispute started, she was seen sitting with her parents in their small bungalow just outside Blackpool. She told viewers that apart from the bonus of seeing her parents, her father, a life-time supporter of the Labour Party, was useful in giving 'local background . . . the way that local people are reacting to the dispute and that's very good because when you're involved in something like that you very soon lose contact with the world at large. . . .'[8]

Dean led the first mass demonstration in Wapping on Saturday, 8 February. She marched in front of 1,000 women, sacked workers and wives, who joined the 2,000 pickets at the gates. The rally did not stop the papers, but it had been a good way of making the point that many of the sacked employees were clerical workers – at the bottom end of the Fleet Street pay-scale. There were teenage girls – secretaries, telephonists – voluble tea-ladies, and cleaners. Dean wanted attention for those she considered to be the real casualties of the Wapping War.

Continually, she stressed that the picketing should be peaceful. She blamed outsiders for the violence that flared during this first rally. Of the sixty-two people arrested that night, the majority were unconnected with Fleet Street. 'Don't they have the basic intelligence,' she said, 'to see that Rupert Murdoch wants some incident to justify his coils of barbed wire, video cameras and oppressive security?'[9]

Murdoch was not so much troubled by the sudden outbreaks of violence during demonstrations as by the effect that constant picketing was having on his staff. The pickets were steadfast: it was a cold winter, but with the Chapel structure still intact, the Fathers threw themselves into organising the picketing. Members had to sign on when they went on duty: the traditional disciplines remained. It was not just their jeering and insults outside the gates which demoralised Murdoch's staff. Employees were followed home and cars were vandalised. A *Times* journalist, Chris Warman, had his throat slashed by a broken glass. There were anonymous telephone calls, abusive letters and death threats.

Murdoch gave his senior executives bodyguards.

When the then Employment Minister, Kenneth Clarke, criticised Murdoch, the company realised it had serious problems. Clarke told a lunch in the Commons: 'Rupert Murdoch's public relations could do with a little improvement.' He said that Murdoch was not 'an instantly popular figure'. Clarke said he sensed 'some lingering sympathy for the thousands of men now out of work, even if their own folly led them to this end'. He described Dean as 'the most persuasive spokesman the left in the trade union movement has found for some time'.[10]

By February, Murdoch was talking to his senior executives about the threat Dean posed. A poll commissioned by the company on the public perception of the dispute showed that Dean was a popular figure. The company realised it was losing the propaganda war. Dean had turned out to be a formidable weapon, and although the unions had not succeeded in stopping Murdoch, they managed to get him back to the negotiating table.

On Friday, 4 April, the General Secretaries were asked to an afternoon meeting with News International at the Mayfair Hotel, Berkeley Street. Both sides had agreed that the meeting would be better kept secret – they wanted no press interest. Brenda Dean's tactics at this meeting would be the same as those she had adopted for others: she would try to steer all negotiators away from recrimination and anger. 'If it got too bitter, it would only last twenty minutes,' she said, knowing how volatile members of both sides could become. This was to be the third meeting since the dispute began, organised through the shuttle diplomacy of the TUC. There had been no progress. Rupert Murdoch had not yet made an appearance, and Dean hoped he would not be at this one: she believed that if he was brought in too soon there would be 'another fiasco'. 'He's not a detail man,' she said. 'He makes the major decisions.'[11]

That morning Dean had heard from a journalist who told her Channel Four News had just received a call from Wapping: the company had requested a crew for the evening programme. Murdoch would be making an announcement. Harry Conroy had heard the same from one of his contacts as he was leaving a NUJ Executive meeting. They knew they could expect an offer that day.

But from the start of the meeting it seemed that an offer was the last thing they should expect. Rupert Murdoch was not there and the talks, opened by Bruce Matthews, quickly descended to recriminations. Matthews took delight in telling them how well the company was doing in Wapping and that their picketing was futile. He complained that his secretary had been obscenely abused by a picket. Alf Parish, National Secretary for the NGA, was determined to argue. He reminded Matthews of the lorry 'which had ploughed into the crowd' on 12 March. He had been on the picket line that evening and had sat waiting for an ambulance with the Sogat printer whose leg had been broken during the incident.

Conroy was bored. 'We were going round and round in circles,' he said. He was playing hangman and noughts and crosses with NUJ National Organiser Mike Smith on hotel notepaper. Dean knew they were getting nowhere fast. After nearly an hour, the company negotiators asked for an adjournment.

The General Secretaries stayed behind in the conference room. 'We've got to say something,' Dean told them, when Matthews and his team left the room. 'We'll be sitting here talking and he'll be announcing a deal on television to our members telling them something we don't even know.'[12]

When Matthews and his team came back into the room after a twenty-minute break, Dean immediately said: 'I have to tell you that we know Mr Murdoch is going on Channel Four News tonight. What's going on?'

Matthews was taken aback. 'I've just spoken with Mr Murdoch,' he replied, 'and we do have an offer to make to you.'[13]

It was an offer Murdoch had been thinking about since Thursday, 27 February, when he had walked into one of his director's offices in Wapping at 8.30 a.m. He had been holding a copy of *The Times*, folded to the letters page. 'What do you think of this?' he had said.[14]

The letter, headed 'Wapping Dispute', had been written by Duncan Forbes, a reader from Croydon, Financial Controller of a computer company. He had written: 'News International

currently have printing plant that is surplus to their requirements. Sogat, either alone or with assistance from other
unions, could commit its considerable assets to obtain this.....
With the workers in possession of the means of production, the
way is then open for the launch of a truly left-of-centre popular
daily newspaper, one that the Labour Party has consistently
maintained does not exist.' The letter ended: 'Surely there
exists here something worthy of consideration, something
better than 5,000 people unemployed.'

The Forbes letter suggested that Sogat lease or purchase
the plant at Gray's Inn Road and that News International
could 'hardly ask an exorbitant price as they claim the machinery is yesterday's technology.'[15] Murdoch had immediately spotted the public relations possibilities of such an idea:
he decided that instead of selling the union his excess printing
plant, he would give it away to the Labour movement.

When Matthews told the General Secretaries of Murdoch's
idea, they were amazed. Conroy immediately wrote a note
to Mike Smith, and smiled when he saw him read it. 'Clever
bastards,' he had written. It was also disconcerting.

Matthews began reading from a list. The company would
not just hand over the back end of their Gray's Inn Road
building, but also the two-year contract to print the London
editions of the *Guardian* on the presses there – worth £1 million
a year. They would get the Atex photocomposition setting
equipment, furniture, fittings and sixty press units which could
produce a million copies a night. He would even give them
management help. But there were conditions: the unions
would not be able to sell the building for five years. No paper
could be printed there which would be in direct competition
with any News International titles. If they rejected the offer,
the plant would be closed down or offered for sale to somebody
else and the presses put into store. They realised why Murdoch
had stayed behind in Wapping and asked for a Channel Four
crew.

Dean's first reaction was to tell Matthews that she objected
to the management of news in such a way. 'We've been set
up,' she told him. 'You would have announced that offer on
television while we were sitting here, wouldn't you?'

Matthews replied: 'You'll be making a statement too.' He

was right. Dean had already told Channel Four News that she would be in their London studio ready for the programme.[16]

At 5.45 p.m. ITN trailed the item. There had been a major development in the Wapping dispute: 'secret negotiations' had taken place that afternoon, and full details would be given on Channel Four News at 7 p.m. The scoop could not have been better timed. It was the first time Channel Four News's Friday programme had been extended to a full hour.

'Why,' Alastair Stewart asked when he introduced Murdoch 'live' from Wapping, 'would a successful businessman give away these buildings?'

Murdoch, as laconic as ever, explained: 'We feel they have been misled and gave us a bad time . . . this gives them the opportunity for jobs and addresses the question of whether or not the Labour movement gets its own paper . . . we have no use for it . . . and,' he smiled wryly, 'we will risk the competition.'

Murdoch said that the union members stood no chance of ever getting into Wapping but a new paper would give them jobs. He gave another wry smile. 'I will also give them advice on manning levels.'

Stewart turned to Dean, sitting next to him in the Channel Four studio. 'This is no alternative to compensation,' she told him. But they would look at the offer carefully in a 'constructive way'.

It was the tenth week of the strike and Wapping was back in the news. Dubbins openly accused Murdoch of trying to recoup some of the ground he had lost in public relations. 'The general impression the British public has is that Mr Murdoch did not handle this very well, to say the least.'[17] He told the newspapers the offer was 'dangerous'.[18]

But all the General Secretaries knew that the offer had to be given careful consideration. It appeared generous: it was said to be worth between £50 and £60 million. The Labour movement had wanted a paper ever since the TUC sold its 49 per cent holding in the *Daily Herald* to IPC in 1960: the stumbling block had always been finance. The movement wanted a paper more committed to the Labour Party than the *Daily Mirror* or the *Guardian*, but less party political than the *Morning Star* or *Labour Weekly*.

At a Trafalgar Square rally on Sunday, 6 April, Norman Willis, TUC General Secretary, told a crowd of 7,000 that the Gray's Inn Road offer did not 'lessen our obligation to the sacked workers'. Much as the Labour movement wanted its own paper, he told them, and much as the dispute showed they needed one, the priority was people and not property. But he said: 'There will still need to be a detailed study of the feasibility. I have to say I would start such a process seriously, genuinely, but with some scepticism.'[19]

The General Secretaries and their officials had their doubts about Gray's Inn Road from the start, and they found themselves suddenly faced with the changed newspaper economics demonstrated by Eddie Shah. Drawbacks to the deal were spotted almost immediately: a Labour movement paper, selling one million copies, would not employ more than 1,000 staff, and those who did get a job could not expect a launch within a year; the capacity of the presses was way beyond a Labour paper's needs and the typesetting equipment, in the words of one NGA composing room official, was 'clapped out'. A new direct-entry typesetting system would be needed.[20] There was still the problem of finance: Eddie Shah had needed over £20 million and the proposed new quality daily, the *Independent*, needed £18 million for a contracted print run of 300,000.

Twelve days after the Gray's Inn Road offer was made, the company and unions met again. News International increased the offer: the company was willing to throw in £15 million redundancy for those who would not get a job on the new paper. Murdoch wanted a speedy resolution: if the offer was not taken up in three weeks, the Gray's Inn Road building would be sold 'lock, stock and barrel'.[21]

The Unions now had a radical idea of their own, which would fall in line with the company's oft-stated wish for an orderly and stable bargaining relationship. They proposed the establishment of what they called the 'News International National Joint Committee', which would involve four production unions and all the company's printing plants. The body would have sole negotiation and recognition rights, which meant there would be no more Chapels. ACAS would be used for conciliation and there would be binding arbitration which could be triggered unilaterally by one party. The print unions had almost conceded O'Neill's union conditions for the *London Post* – all but having legally binding contracts and abandoning closed shops.

The company waited a month before reacting. In talks between Bruce Matthews and the General Secretary of the EETPU, Eric Hammond, and the electricians' National Secretary, Tom Rice, Matthews called the committee idea a 'nongoer'.[22] The EETPU, representing the bulk of the Wapping workforce, had been asked by the print unions, via the TUC, to try to conciliate and persuade the company of the wisdom of the idea. Matthews also told them that the deadline the company had imposed for a response on the Gray's Inn Road offer would not change from 7 May – the increasingly violent picketing outside had made Murdoch dig in his heels.

Violence during the Saturday demonstrations outside Wapping was getting worse: on 3 May it was appalling. Over 250 were injured. Ray James, Sogat *Sun* Machine Chapel Father, who had led the machine branch march, was one of more than 80 arrested. Police in full riot gear and mounted police had charged the crowds in Wellclose Square. The officer commanding, Deputy Assistant Commissioner Wyn Jones, who had been in charge of policing Greenham Common, had a squad armed with plastic bullets on standby.[23] Dean was badly shaken by what she saw that night. 'They just came and pushed and hit anything in their way. The police conducted a riot. . . . There was no warning.'[24]

The pickets believed that the police put the safe passage of the TNT lorries above all other considerations. Roads were closed to local residents and traffic lights were synchronised on green to give the lorries a straight run out of the area. The pickets nicknamed the police 'Murdoch's paperboys'.

Matthews telephoned the TUC to say that the picketing was going to harden attitudes and make concessions less likely. There would be no further talks with the print unions until they gave some sort of response to the Gray's Inn Road offer and the £15 million compensation. He was critical that they had been so slow in coming back: 'We handed them a rosy apple, they looked at it, put it down, picked it up and then handed it to the professionals to see if it was worth eating,' he said.[25] He let it be known that the new Wapping workforce had just voted by a 95 per cent majority to set up its own internal consultative committee on Japanese lines.

Matthews was becoming increasingly bullish in his statements: 'If you go to a casino and play the numbers game, as they did, and you lose, you don't go back to the casino the next day and ask for your money back.'[26]

News International was now on the offensive. Full-page newspaper advertisements were used to put their case. 'We wanted to run our business one way. The printworkers wanted to run it another. To settle matters, we're offering them a business of their own.' The advertisements described the offer as a 'gift of a £60 million printing plant' and 'up to £15 million cash'. It was 'unparalleled in the history of industrial relations . . . we believe that this offer is far-sighted, fair and imaginative . . .'.

The job of investigating the unparalleled offer was given to the Unity Trust, a bank funded by money from the trades unions. When Trust representatives met Matthews, he told them: 'The offer is not a game.' The company wanted the right to get on with its business 'without the taint at present attached to it'. Matthews said they wanted the 'Wapping problem' resolved.[27] The idea had been to create jobs, although he agreed that a new publication was not something to rush into. There was a danger that 'people can fall easily into the trap of putting what they want in newspapers rather than what the market needs'. If a new paper at Gray's Inn Road was to work, it would need very strong and able management: a newspaper could not be run on a committee basis. He extended the deadline for acceptance to the end of the month. If they did not receive a 'reaction indicating a genuine effort' to investigate the project, News International would probably try to sell the building.

Matthews told Unity Trust that if the new paper was not Labour and trade union orientated, the company would not include the freehold of the land and buildings. They wanted to prevent the building and plant coming under the control of an existing newspaper proprietor, who would simply transfer part of his production. And he gave them his views of what sort of newspaper would be viable: it should be aimed at the right wing of the Labour Party.

The Executive Director of Unity Trust, Michael Marsden, reported back to the unions. He said he had assessed the offer on a 'pessimistic basis': a surveyor had estimated the value of the freehold building at only £1 million. A feasibility study for a new paper would take nine months and cost around £250,000.[28] The Chief Executive of the *Financial Times*, Frank Barlow, who had been asked to do a technical study of the offer, told the unions that a Labour movement newspaper printed in Gray's Inn Road might require as few as 300 staff to be viable, and half the jobs would be for journalists working on a direct-input system: a paper in Gray's Inn Road would never break-even on traditional manning levels.

Brenda Dean apologised to Mr Justice Hirst in the High Court on Thursday, 8 May, purging contempt and winning back the union's £17 million sequestrated asssets. She had delayed for as long as possible. Bill Miles and the provincial members on the National Executive Council had urged her to do it sooner. Miles said they had everything to lose and nothing to gain. More than a quarter of the union's full-time officials were no longer being paid, their cars had been seized – Tony Dubbins had let Dean have an NGA car – and some branch phones were being cut off. Pensions could not be paid to retired members and there were 1,300 claims outstanding for accident benefit. There was an increasing possibility that Sogat would have to abandon the biennial conference in June. Dean commented: 'It is only a fool who would continue in a sequestrated position for an instruction that is just not working.'[29]

The Audit Bureau of Circulation figures published in March had showed that the reason for the sequestration – the instruction to wholesale members not to handle News International titles – was having little effect. 'If our wholesale people throughout the UK had swung in with full support, this dispute would have been over by now,' Dean said. She said she would never forgive them, particularly in Manchester, where as Branch Secretary she had been trusted and respected by her members. She had earned that popularity not only through hard work negotiating deals but also for the care she took of her members. She was remembered for taking brandy and bags of chips to frozen pickets, sending flowers to secretaries who had worked overtime. 'They will rue the day,' she said bitterly.[30]

Dean was now in serious trouble with her London members. The statement issued by Sogat's London District Council the day of the purge registered 'disgust and abhorrence' at the action. The purging was seen as a retreat – her London members felt abandoned. 'She's lost her bottle,' *News of the World* Imperial Father, Tony Isaacs said. 'What we want is leadership from the front, not from behind.'

Dean expected the reaction. Bill Miles, the experienced Fleet Street negotiator who had guided her through its industrial maze in the past months, did not have to spell it out. She knew all too well the militant attitudes of the 'London People' and the problems they had caused for her predecessor, Bill Keys, like her, an enthusiastic supporter of reform.

In the mid-seventies Keys and other print union General Secretaries got together with the proprietors to try to sort out once and for all the Street's industrial problems. The resulting Programme for Action proposed flexibility on the union side in return for assurances of no compulsory redundancies. When it was put to ballot in 1976, recommended by officers from all the print unions, Chapels were warned that rejection of the Programme would lead to titles failing and compulsory redundancies.

In Manchester, Dean had recommended the plan for her newspaper employees, believing it was the best deal London would get – it was certainly favourable compared with the agreements she had negotiated over the years for the low-paid provincial members in the general trade.

But the Programme for Action was resoundingly rejected by the shop floor – it was a crushing defeat for the national officials and showed that the leaders of print unions had little control over the Chapels. There was further illustration of this in 1978, when the entire London Central Branch delegation marched out of Sogat's conference over a long-running dispute in a small South London printing company which they felt had not been properly handled by the union nationally. 'Shut the door,' Sogat's lay President for Manchester had shouted at them from the platform as they filed out.[31] Dean knew that the majority of Sogat's members regarded the Wapping dispute as nothing more than a re-run under another name of the same old problem.

For years, the Street's Chapels had demonstrated their independence from the union leadership. Dean, who prided herself on her negotiating skills, found the level of negotiation in the Street abysmal. 'My job is to secure agreement by persuasion, cajoling, logic and sometimes force of personality based on other people's belief in my honesty and sincerity,' she said.[32] 'A skilled negotiator does not say to management: "Pay up or you've got no paper tonight".' The first time she had attended London negotiations was at Times Newspapers just after the year's suspension: there had been fifty-six Chapel Fathers in the room. 'It was,' she said, 'negotiation with mob instincts.'[33]

In her short time in London, she had realised that some of the Fleet Street stories she had heard over the years were not apocryphal. 'Have you ever seen a Fleet Street funeral?' she once asked. 'It's like the Mafia.' She described the Street as a 'little world . . . it's introverted'.[34] She would never forget being told that a television cameraman who had wanted to film her standing in a machine room when she had first become General President in August 1983 had to pay a Chapel Father £25 for the privilege. And the salaries some earned had amazed her. 'I don't know what they spend it on,' she said. 'They all live in council houses.'[35]

Bill Miles, General Officer, had been invaluable when Dean first became General Secretary. 'Before meetings, she would ask me everything I knew about the management we were seeing and about the Fathers – who to trust and who to watch for.'[36]

But Dean believed that the Street was changing: membership in London Central Branch was dropping. From 25,000 in the mid-sixties, it was now 13,000. And for the first time, Sogat had a General Secretary from the provinces who was unsentimental about the Street and its archaic ways.

On Monday, 19 May, at a meeting in Central Hall, Westminster, Dean faced the wrath of the London branches. For over three hours she was insulted, sworn at, jeered and slow-hand-clapped. 'It was awful,' she said later. 'It was the worst meeting I have ever attended in twenty years in Sogat.'[37]

To have turned down the invitation, as had been suggested by some officials, would have been 'cowardice'. Dean believed in her own infallibility: she said she was quite capable of answering all the questions the militants could put to her. 'I was sad,' she said. 'I did not feel I had anything to be ashamed of. A lot of it had been orchestrated.' Her members were in 'culture shock'. It was the first time Fleet Street had gone on strike and the papers had still got out.

Sitting next to the Chairman of the London District Council, George Holmes, with Bill Miles close to her, she remained calm throughout, although sometimes strident and sometimes hurt. Her opening seemed designed to infuriate. 'I felt I should be here,' she said.[38] There was immediate raucous shouting. 'I know feelings are running high,' she continued. 'But any differences we have should be in this room today. The press is just waiting for a divided situation.' She then gave a lengthy report on the negotiations. Sogat's claim in order of priority was still jobs, recognition and compensation. If either Bouverie Street or Gray's Inn Road should re-open the members would have jobs there, as they would in Manchester if Murdoch ever decided to print the *News of the World* there again. She ended her report by saying that the members would make decisions in the dispute – they would be balloted on any offer.

Members complained that the Fathers had not been consulted over negotiating concessions during the 'secret' talks; they had not been asked about the News International National Joint Committee – which if accepted would wipe out the Chapels – neither had they been consulted on the purging of contempt. They believed the only way forward was to continue with sequestration, which would lead to the seizure of Sogat's buildings. There would then be a resurgence of support from the labour movement and immediate escalation of the dispute.

'She understood the Chapel structure all right,' said Tony Isaacs, Imperial Father of the Sogat *News of the World* Machine Chapel, later. 'What she was trying to do was to have her Executive Committee run our dispute. They wanted to make all the decisions and then just give us an ultimatum. A London General Secretary would have understood the mood . . . we wanted recognition.'[39]

Dean was bombarded with questions but retaliated calmly. She explained the decision on sequestration – it had 'prevented the full and normal running of the branch offices'. The union, in some areas, was in danger of breaking up. In any case, the union had been sequestered for an 'NEC instruction which was clearly not working'. But her answers were often lost in the noise of heckling.

'There will be no change in policy,' Dean emphasised to the press after the meeting. 'We are on line.' She left for Northampton, where she was due to meet about twenty members, staff of a small warehouse supplying stationery, who were just about to enter pay negotiations. She arrived two hours late: 'They waited for me . . . they were wonderful,' she said. 'They knew what had happened and they said they were glad I had arrived in one piece.' In the next few days Dean described the union offices as being 'inundated' with letters and phone calls of support. The message from the provinces was – 'We're not having this.'[40]

It was Bank Holiday in late May. Only a handful of pickets were standing at the police barriers in Wellclose Street in the warm evening. Some were further back in Wellclose Square getting tea from the NGA caravan parked behind the now well-worn patch of grass where from the speaker's platform there was a good view of the ramp where every evening for the past eighteen weeks Murdoch's papers had left the plant.

Printers were standing in small groups talking uneasily about the news which had just been announced on the radio. They were desperate for details. A 'Final Offer' had been announced after talks between Murdoch and the General Secretaries at a Heathrow airport hotel. None of them had known that talks were taking place. The money on the table had apparently more than trebled to £50 million. None was too impressed. Ray James, Father of the Sogat *Sun* Machine Chapel, had brought a moment of light relief when he quipped that he did not think £50 million was that bad – 'until I realised I had to share it with everyone else'. These steadfast pickets wanted jobs and recognition.

Sitting on the Sogat double-decker bus, Tony Isaacs was constantly on the telephone. He was getting tired. At times he would stare out towards the plant, the view now partly obscured by spring leaves. The bus looked seedy. The log book was now dog-eared, with its columns of information on every movement of every lorry and every hated wire-grilled bus that had gone into and come out of the plant. Sogat 'Murdoch News is Bad News' leaflets were piled on a table alongside issues of 'The Picket' newsletter and the *Wapping Post*, a newspaper produced by 'refuseniks' – the journalists who had refused to go in – and striking print workers. In the kitchen end of the converted bus, the water in the kettle was simmering for tea – there had never once been a shortage of tea on the picket line.

Isaacs had been on the phone for two hours. Over a dozen times that evening he had said the same thing to different people. No sooner had he finished one telephone call than he was dialling another. He was cajoling, he was angry and at times he was blunt. Surprisingly for Isaacs, he sometimes sounded desperate. The news of a Final Offer had really upset him. He had calculated that the £50 million would not benefit his members, but was geared towards the union's lower paid and older members. But worse, there was nothing about recognition or jobs.

Isaacs was on the phone frantically trying to organise opposition. It was not easy. There were few people readily available on a Bank Holiday – Isaacs was convinced that the timing of the offer was another Murdoch public relations ploy to get muted initial reaction. Isaacs wanted a few of the Fathers on television saying what they thought. The offer, as far as he was concerned, was not worth even putting to ballot. But he was predicting that it would be. 'It's evil,' he said. 'If we don't do something about this, we've lost this dispute.' To the London branches, Dean was no longer out of step, she was completely out of line.

Dean had been told of the Heathrow meeting, another organised through the TUC, two days before. This time, the company insisted on secrecy and the print union officials agreed that meetings were easier without reporters chasing them down hotel corridors. News International had booked rooms at the Sheraton Skyline and the first meeting would begin at 6.30 p.m. on Sunday, 25 May. They had been told that negotiations would continue until Monday.

Bruce Matthews, Managing Director of News International, opened the first session and led throughout on Sunday night. Murdoch, he said, was flying into London from New York early on Monday morning – only then would there be replies to many of their questions. He reminded them that they were still being held to the 30 May deadline for their reply on Gray's Inn Road.[41]

Dean told him of the Unity Trust findings: the offer had turned out to be worth only £1 million, but she said if he gave them the front part of the building as well, the value would increase to £5 million: offering just the back part was neither 'viable or serious'. Matthews replied that if this was a 'stumbling block', the company would 'pass over the front'. Dean asked if they could have Bouverie Street.

'Mr Murdoch wishes to sell the building,' he replied. It was 'obsolete for modern newspapers'.

Dubbins asked if the company would consider printing part of the *Sunday Times* and *The Times* in Gray's Inn Road. 'We're not expanding in London,' said Matthews. The company was planning a new plant 'somewhere between Watford and Glasgow'. And anyway, they were now using polymer plates and the reel size on the machines had been changed.

Matthews would not talk money. When Dean told him that the £15 million offer was not enough, he said they would have to wait for Murdoch's arrival. She asked him about her London wholesale members – some 300 were being made redundant because of News International's change to direct distribution. He would not talk about them. She changed tack. What was the company's reaction to their idea of a joint negotiating committee? 'It must be looked at seriously,' she insisted. 'Please look at it again.'

Dubbins took over. What about recognition? 'Recognition,' Matthews told him, 'will be determined by a ballot among people in the plant.' Dubbins said that was 'nonsensical'. It would be a 'fixed ballot'. The NGA General Secretary now believed there would be no serious negotiation until Murdoch arrived, that Gray's Inn Road was a side issue and this initial meeting had been held by the company to identify the main stumbling blocks.

After a break for supper, News International told them a suite had been organised so they could watch BBC's 'Heart of the Matter' report on the dispute. Harry Conroy of the NUJ and Mike Smith, National Organiser, thought that a total waste of time – they had not cancelled their Bank Holiday plans to watch television with News International negotiators – and they went to the bar, joined shortly afterwards by Tony Dubbins and Alf Parish, NGA National Secretary.

The talks resumed at 11.20 p.m. and went on for an hour and a half. They were acrimonious. Matthews wanted to talk about Gray's Inn Road, the unions about recognition. 'I don't see how people on the outside should have any influence on the people inside,' Matthews told them crossly.

'That workforce took jobs on the basis of a new newspaper . . . it never appeared,' Dubbins instantly retorted.

'Your people went on strike to win, you have now lost,' Matthews countered.

'The *London Post* was a blind,' Parish said, adding that the company had no intention of negotiating. Bill O'Neill reacted at once. It was the worst moment of the evening. Parish later described O'Neill as 'getting out of his pram'. They had rarely seen him quite so angry.

'That's your contention,' he shouted, denying the accusation.

Parish replied: 'If you are telling me you were serious about negotiating in September, you are living in cloud cuckoo land.'

Parish and the other General Secretaries were by now convinced there had been no serious negotiations. Five weeks after the strike began, the company had announced that Murdoch had decided to postpone the *London Post*, blaming the unions. 'If it had not been for the union action, the paper that would be coming out of Wapping would have been the *London Post*,' said Mike Hoy, acting Editor of the paper.[42]

Matthews was to give his reasons for the postponement in a court affidavit later in the year. 'It was clear to me from the beginning of the strike that the Group's resources would be fully stretched for the time being in producing the existing titles.' He affirmed: 'There would have been problems in find-ing suitable accommodation for editorial, advertising and other staff. The computerised editorial systems would not have sufficient capacity to cope both with the existing titles and the *London Post*. The Wapping plant was not conceived or built for its present purposes and, despite the measures we had taken as part of our contingency plans, it was obvious to me and to my Board colleagues that to add another newspaper at that stage would only have exacerbated the problem.'[43]

On the second day of the secret Heathrow talks, Murdoch led the News International team. At his request, Norman Willis, General Secretary of the TUC, had arrived. Murdoch told them he wanted to end the 'long and unpleasant dispute'. He was flying back to New York on Concorde later that day and wanted a speedy resolution. 'The same things were said,' Dubbins remembered. 'It was nastier, that's all.' He said Murdoch was 'snide', and it was difficult to get him into reasoned argument. There was a particularly heated exchange between Dubbins and Murdoch.

'You, Mr Dubbins, and your people have been spitting at my staff,' Murdoch said at one stage. Dean had never seen him so angry. She said afterwards it was like waiting for a volcano to explode.

Dubbins had lost his temper: 'You had better withdraw that . . . I have never been at your gate.' Dean wanted to stop them. Since her first meeting with Murdoch in late 1983, she had realised that his attitude to the NGA was particularly aggressive. She quickly tried to interject, thinking that if she did not succeed, the meeting would soon be over.

Dean asked him if he would ever revert to the traditional wholesale and distribution network. Murdoch simply said: 'No.' When Dubbins asked if he would put some printing back into Gray's Inn Road, Murdoch said: 'I have just been released from that nightmare. I don't intend going back.' Parish suggested that if the *London Post* had been a reality, would it not be possible for the sacked printers to produce it for News International in Gray's Inn Road. 'I will never let you guys produce that,' Murdoch had replied.

He rejected their idea of a News International National Joint Committee. 'The people crossing those picket lines don't want to be represented by you,' he said. What he wanted were legally binding agreements. He suggested a twelve-month cooling-off period on recognition. 'But I am not having Chapels and I'm certainly not going to have a closed shop,' he said. As for jobs, there would be more available if the company expanded. Jobs would be open to union members who would not be 'punished' or 'victimised' for the strike.

'How will we know about them?' asked Willis. Murdoch told him that when the company advertised, they would send copies to the unions, but there were no jobs available at Wapping at the moment.

When the meeting re-convened after a forty-minute adjournment, Murdoch said that as there appeared to be nothing more to say on other matters, they might as well all get down to compensation. The dispute was a 'tragic conclusion' to years of bad Fleet Street practices and a dispute the company had not wanted. But he was prepared to increase the money on the table on condition it went to ballot with the recommendation of acceptance from the General Secretaries. There would be three weeks' money for every year of service, with a maximum of £155 a week. There would be a minimum of £2,000 for each employee, but an age limit of 65.

Calculations on how much the offer was worth were quickly done on hotel notepaper during the adjournment. They reckoned Murdoch would be paying in the region of £30 million. Conroy and Mike Smith thought that offering three weeks' money was strange, and that, if pushed, Murdoch would increase the offer. Tony Dubbins said he would not be able to sell such an offer to his members.

At one point during the adjournment, Dean met Murdoch in the centre courtyard of the hotel, and with the experienced and elderly Ken Graham, head of the TUC's Industrial Relations Department at her side, talked to him for some minutes about her London wholesale members who had been made redundant because of the changes in the traditional distribution network.[44]

When they re-convened, it was Norman Willis who told Murdoch that the money was not enough. Other Fleet Street employees before and after the Wapping move had been given much more by other proprietors, he pointed out. 'Think again,'

Murdoch said. If other proprietors had offered more, they had 'bought efficiency and peace'. He was under no obligation to offer anything at all. But the General Secretaries, and particularly Willis, tried to get him to increase still further.

It was Dean who managed to get a concession. She had raised the problem of her wholesale members again. Although they were employed directly by wholesalers, Dean told Murdoch he owed them something as they had handled his titles for years. Now all they had been offered was statutory redundancy pay. Murdoch agreed to pay each one £5,000. But then he said: 'This company is not a money fountain ... now is the time for leadership and for you to tell your people this is it. It must be clear it is final and if it is not put to ballot in a week, it is off the table.' Again, he led his negotiators out of the room.

Willis told them he had a feeling they could get just a bit more. But he repeated Murdoch's caution: 'You do know it's final.' Dean said there was no doubt in her mind about that. The attitude of Dubbins and Alf Parish was different: they had agreed earlier that they would only 'push on' to see what could be achieved. They were firm with Willis: they told him that the money was 'discriminatory', that it was geared to Sogat members and was nowhere near the redundancy levels in their Times Newspapers Agreements.

When company and unions sat down together again late that afternoon, Murdoch increased the offer from three weeks' to four: from a total of £30 million to £50 million. He gave them two documents. One was entitled 'Final Offer'. Five points had been clearly drafted. There would be four weeks' pay, with the same limits as before for each worker; the redundancy would not exclude any worker from future employment with the company; pending legal actions against the unions would be dropped; union recognition in Wapping and the Glasgow plant would be reviewed in a year; and the unions would be given both the front and rear of Gray's Inn Road. There was another page of supplementary points. The unions would have to agree to take no disciplinary action against those members who had not gone on strike. As for the journalists who had refused to cross the picket lines and work in Wapping, their cases would be 'determined by the Editors of their respective titles'. There would also have to be a cessation of 'official picketing . . . and other forms of industrial action'.[45]

The General Secretaries managed to get an important concession that evening. Murdoch threw in the front end of Gray's Inn Road – the editorial and administrative offices – pushing the offer up by another £4 million.

At 6.15 p.m., the Final Offer was announced. Murdoch appeared at a press conference in his shirt-sleeves, Bruce Matthews on one side of him and Bill Gillespie on the other. 'We are under no obligation to pay any money at all and we are putting this forward in an attempt to close down the picketing,' he said. It was an 'extremely high price for bringing the dispute to an end.'[46]

Sogat's National Executive decided by 15 votes to 9 to put the Final Offer to ballot. Although Dean made no recommendation, the message was clear. Members had to 'make the decision they individually wanted to make . . . in the quietness of their own homes'. She believed the offer was final and she also believed the company would stick to the 6 June deadline imposed for a decision. Asked by a reporter about accusations that she had let her members down, she replied: 'There is no river to sell people down any more in Fleet Street . . . the place is in turmoil.' She added: 'I had people who had been made redundant who had been lucky to get two weeks.'[47]

The ballot was the last straw for the leaders of the London Machine Branch. They applied to the High Court for an injunction against Dean and the National Executive to prevent the ballot taking place on the grounds that the union's general rules had been contravened – ballot papers had been sent straight to members' homes, not distributed through their branch officials and Chapels. They also claimed that the ballot form was misleading and one-sided: the activists argued that nothing was final in industrial relations.

Bill Miles remembers waiting for the High Court result with Dean. 'It was the one time,' he said later, 'when I saw her showing her feelings. She was frightened.'

'What are we going to do if they win?' she had asked him. He told her not to worry but to wait for the result. Mr Justice Saville accepted that the Machine Branch did have a technical case but, given the company's deadline for a ballot response, the court held that under a 'balance of convenience', it would be improper to grant the injunction.

Brenda Dean went to Scarborough two days before the Sogat '82 biennial conference was due to open. It was her first conference as General Secretary and, true to her reputation, she was giving herself plenty of time to prepare. On Friday, 6 June, she spent the whole day in her hotel room with coffee and sandwiches, writing what she called her 'State of the Union' speech and poring over conference paperwork.

In Manchester she was known for her careful preparation, said to date from her days as a secretary. Someone who had known her well was Brian Redhead, BBC Radio Four presenter, who had been Editor of the *Manchester Evening News*. 'She doesn't take a step forward unless she knows where that foot is going to land,' he said. She had always organised her life with great care. It was the same with her appearance: Dean was always immaculate with perfectly painted nails, careful make-up and neat hair. Redhead remembers her having what she called 'Brenda time' – time to herself to prepare to face the world.[48]

Dean was in the hotel room working on her speech when she heard that the London Branches had turned down Rupert Murdoch's Final Offer. As each of the five London branch ballots had been counted at Sogat's headquarters in Hadleigh, near Southend-on-Sea, she was telephoned the result. When the final result was known, she telephoned Norman Willis's office at the TUC, spoke to Alf Parish, and then drafted a press statement.

She would not admit to surprise. 'I never said which way I thought it would go. It was a reasonable offer and I knew it was final.' But she admitted later that from that moment she had no idea where the dispute was going. 'I was now faced with the task of getting the union to support a dispute with finance diminishing very fast.' There was, she knew, no support in the provinces for the 'London people'. 'I was mentally gearing myself for another long slog,' she said.[49]

On television that evening, Bruce Matthews said he had spoken with Murdoch. The offer 'will be withdrawn finally tonight'.[50] In a *Sunday Times* Focus feature that weekend he was quoted: 'It's a second suicide.' He was described in Wapping 'slumped into his chair' and was 'surprised and somewhat depressed'. The first suicide, he had told the *Sunday Times* reporter, was when the unions had decided to go on strike in the first place. The printers were now left with nothing, 'no jobs, no recognition, and now no money'.[51]

Tony Dubbins's immediate response was to say that the dispute now had to be stepped up: there had to be help from the TUC and from the labour movement. But the spotlight was on Dean, who now faced her most serious crisis. She had all but endorsed the offer and the London militants – many already in Scarborough to lobby the conference – were after her blood. She had 'sold out'. Dean knew she would face pressure to return to secondary picketing, and the London members were talking of a vote of no confidence. There was even speculation that she might resign and seek immediate re-election to demonstrate the strength of the union's support. There was a rumour that the London Branches would declare UDI.

The 'state of the Union' speech, which Dean had taken such care over, was her opening offensive. It was a scathing attack on her critics. 'There are some branches in this union who seem to be taking the view that they are not part of Sogat, and that they have a federal rather than integral relationship with the rest of the union. . . . Any talk of or attempt at a breakaway in this union will do nothing for the members that the wreckers purport to represent.' She was not interested in 'machismo breast-thumping' or 'street corner chants about selling people down the river'.[52]

But by the end of the week, the union's executive and the militant London Branches seemed to have publicly patched up their differences. Dean told the conference in one of her last speeches that she accepted without equivocation that the dispute was about jobs and union recognition in Wapping. The London members had not heard her say that for weeks. In return, they supported a National Executive motion that the dispute would be controlled by the Executive and there would be no activity which could lead to the re-sequestration of assets.

Her friends in the Labour Party and trade union movement

had rallied round. Norman Willis's speech in Scarborough gave no 'unrealistic pledges'. He told delegates: '. . . as the National Union of Journalists and others have found in this dispute, it's not just a question of issuing instructions. It's a question of winning support from those concerned and getting them on your side.'[53] Neil Kinnock praised the steadfastness of the Sogat members in the dispute, who at 'various sites' had done their best to resist and reject those who had come from outside the mainstream of trade unionism to try to defame the movement with violence. He was full of praise for Dean, for her role in winning public understanding of the cause, and called her a 'valued asset to the movement'.[54]

Bill Miles, the Fleet Street veteran, due for retirement in 1987, in his farewell speech to Conference, said: 'I have worked with five General Secretaries – Brenda Dean is the most devoted and sincere. Her handling of this dispute is without blemish . . . anyone in my last 15 months who thinks they can rubbish Brenda as they have in the last 6 months should be warned you can get a terrible sting from a dying bee.'[55]

Dean herself said of the conference: 'It was very successful for me. London lost more that week. London people were being told to push off. They were alarming the delegates with their lobbying.' She said that by the end of the week the 'London people' had actually become alienated. 'It was very sad.'[56]

The dispute could only be won, she had said in a hopeful and rousing speech just before the end of the conference, with the union intact, working, functioning and seeking support up and down the country. Some weeks later she confided that she felt the dispute was in fact lost 'when the very first newspaper lorry left the plant'.[57] All she hoped for now was an honourable settlement.

EIGHT

'The enemy within'

The 1,400 members of the London Press Branch of the EETPU – the Electrical Electronic Telecommunications and Plumbing Union – were marked by the union's leadership as trouble-makers. And they revelled in the reputation. They regularly financed disputes frowned on by the National Executive and they took into the branch members blacklisted by employers. The leadership hit back at them by ordering investigations into the branch every time they stepped too far out of line.

The fourth investigation into the branch in twelve years was prompted by yet another dispute they had joined without the national leadership's backing. In July 1982, eighteen EETPU members had come out in support of Sogat at Robert Maxwell's Park Royal printing works in West London, disrupting production of the *Radio Times* and other BBC publications. The strike lasted nearly nine months. On 20 January 1983 an inquiry was launched. The first thing the union's National Secretary, Tom Rice, wanted explained was why a Sogat official had attended their branch meeting in August the previous year.[1]

In the spring of 1982, the London Press Branch secretary, Sean Geraghty, had heard a disturbing story. Two senior union officials, he was told, one from the NGA and the other from the EETPU, had been overheard talking about his branch. They were fogbound in Glasgow airport, and during the rumoured conversation the EETPU man offered his companion the London Press Branch for a sum of money. It might have been the drink talking, it may never have happened, but when Geraghty heard the story he decided that if the branch was to be married off, it would choose its own partner.[2]

The story was never substantiated but rumours gained ground. In August of that year a speculative article appeared in the *New Statesman* which seemed to confirm that the elec-

tricians' leaders were looking for bids from the print unions
for the branch's members.[3]

The EETPU London Press Branch officials decided to take
matters into their own hands. At the TUC conference in
Brighton, Geraghty spoke informally to Joe Wade, the then
NGA General Secretary. Geraghty arranged to go to the NGA
headquarters in Bedford to 'explore the possibilities further'.
At around the same time, national officials from Sogat got in
touch to arrange discussions on a possible merger. It was to be
this partnership that developed over the coming months.

By March 1983 the General Secretary of the EETPU, Frank
Chapple, moved to block the breakaway. He wrote to Len
Murray, who was General Secretary of the TUC, to tell him
what was going on.[4] Under the TUC's Bridlington rules,
codified in 1939 to settle demarcation disputes between unions,
no one from one trade union can join another unless freed by
the first. If that does not happen, both parties have to present
their case to a TUC disputes committee who rule against one
of them.

Two months later, on 20 May, a mass meeting of the electricians' press branch voted by three to one to tear up their
EETPU membership cards.[5] Just over half of them did. With
the branch now split, the rebels' leaders were faced with two
further problems: could the employers be persuaded to negotiate with them when the companies had agreements with the
union they had left; and could the members be kept together
while the TUC was wheeled into action to adjudicate?

At first, Geraghty was confident that the TUC would rule
in Sogat's favour because of their preference for single-union
industries. But by now the breakaway movement had gained
its own momentum and could not be kept to the pace of the
TUC's disciplinary procedure.

Letters from the London Machine Branch of Sogat to the
EETPU asking them to set into motion the transfer of the
Fleet Street electricians under Bridlington procedure received
sarcastic replies. Enclosing a copy of the booklet *TUC Disputes
Principles and Procedures*, for 'your guidance', the EETPU
National Officer, Tom Rice, said the people referred to were
still members of his union. The union had not accepted its
members' resignations.[6]

Despite pleas from Sogat's General Secretary, Bill Keys, to keep to the rules the London Machine Branch defied the national officers and took in the rebel electricians in July 1983. 'We knew we would not get away with it,' Geraghty said, 'but by then we had to keep the breakaway people together.' Once Chapple had made it clear he would not let them go, the merger was doomed anyway, he added.[7]

When the TUC's disputes committee finally met on 26 August, its ruling against Sogat came as no surprise. The union was told to exclude the members already taken and to cease recruiting. Delaying until 2 November, the date after which they would face suspension from the TUC, Sogat complied. But the EETPU was never to forget or forgive. Eric Hammond, who took over from Chapple, was later to describe the incident as 'an unprovoked attack' by Sogat.[8]

This skirmish with Sogat was seen with some irony by those who considered the EETPU as ruthless and unprincipled in the cut-throat trade-union membership wars. In the changed industrial relations' climate since the new labour laws and mass unemployment, it was the EETPU, more than any other union, which was to embrace what was known as the 'New Realism' needed to prosper in a Thatcherite world.

To Eric Hammond, its General Secretary, the EETPU was the model union of the future. He talked about profits, productivity and technological change. 'We believe the class war is obsolete,' he said.[9] He also believed in low rates for apprentices, flexibility of labour, joint training with management. The union produced glossy recruitment brochures and provided technological training, teaching members skills to get them or keep them employed. But the EETPU did not stop there. It also offered life insurance, mortgages and even a cheap towing service if members' cars broke down.

The electricians' union also believed in strike-free deals. It devised what proved to be an attractive package to offer companies. Such agreements traded a single-union, single-status workplace and some worker participation in the running of the company with the promise of a flexible workforce and binding arbitration to settle disputes. The EETPU did not insist on a closed shop and the workforce's flexibility allowed the company to respond quickly to changing market demands without risking constant 'who-does-what' rows. Most trade union leaders objected on the grounds that this type of deal effectively eliminated the strike option – the workers' only real weapon.

The philosophical and political objections of other unions to the electricians' approach were played out in the TUC in 1984 after the EETPU struck a deal with Hitachi in South Wales. The television and video company in Hirwaun, which had been run jointly with the giant General Electric Company, had hit hard times. GEC pulled out in 1984, leaving Hitachi with the option of closing the factory or restructuring the business. Hitachi chose the second option, to 'take control of the business and install Hitachi conditions and standards as quickly as possible.'

Six unions had been recognised at the plant. The largest was the EETPU, which represented two-thirds of the workforce. When the company decided they wanted only one union, they chose the electricians' and announced that they were signing a deal with them. The other unions objected under the Bridlington principles and took their case to the TUC. The case against the EETPU was strong but the electricians argued self-defence: if they had refused a single-union agreement, it would have led to a non-union plant.

The TUC ruled that the electricians' union should not have signed their own agreement with Hitachi until the dispute had been resolved, 'if necessary by TUC adjudication'. But it let the deal stand on condition that the EETPU make certain concessions, such as advising new employees that they could join one of the other unions. The aggrieved unions were outraged by the TUC's verdict, which they viewed as totally contradictory. If the deal remained, the conditions were meaningless. In an unprecedented move, they challenged the disciplinary committee's ruling. But the TUC reaffirmed that its decision was binding and not open to appeal. Hammond welcomed the ruling as a vindication of his union's position.[10] To right-wing General Secretaries, he had become the voice of reason; to the left he was introducing American-style, non-political trade unionism.

Writing in the *Sun* in July 1985, Hammond had defended the strike-free agreements. Under the headline 'We reach the

parts other unions can't', he explained that the agreements
provided effective machinery to minimise conflict and enabled
disputes to be settled around the table. There were a dozen
such deals which worked successfully. The country, he said,
was bogged down with 'archaic industrial practices'.[11]

The General Secretary kept himself in the spotlight and
became a hate-figure for the left. He defied the TUC over
government money for ballots. There were some who thought
he actively sought expulsion, which would free him to form a
right-wing breakaway group which could then poach members
from other TUC affiliates. He indignantly denied this. He
believed that the TUC was changing and was becoming a
more moderate body.[12]

Hammond proudly claimed that the EETPU was the most
democratic union in Britain and that he was more in touch
with what his rank-and-file members wanted than other union
leaders. Following the court battles twenty-five years before
when the corrupt, Communist leadership was routed, the new
right-wing leadership had set about branch reform and the
EETPU had become a centralised body. In the eighties, it
had a computer-based directory of all its members.

The EETPU would always take action when the cause was
right, he said. His members would act if the government
sacked trade unionists at GCHQ – the Government Communications Headquarters – and he said he would have
supported the miners if they had held a ballot.

Hammond seemed positively to enjoy baiting left-wingers.
He always adopted a belligerent attitude when confronting
activists. At the TUC in 1983, he denounced 'terrorists, les-
bians and other queer people in the GLC Labour party',[13]
and the following year described members of the National
Union of Mineworkers as 'lions led by donkeys'.[14]

That year Hammond astounded his critics when he applied
to join the Confederation of British Industry, the employers'
group. He argued that as an employer who provided training,
he was entitled to membership. In the event, the application
was turned down.[15] He also invited Norman Tebbit, then
Secretary of State for Trade and Industry, hated by the left as
the architect of the anti-union laws, to open the union's new
high technology training centre in Cudham, Kent. In the

battle over Wapping, Hammond was to enrage his left-wing colleagues on the TUC even more.

In the summer of 1985 the word quickly went round the pubs in Southampton. 'There's a job up in London and the money's good.' The rumour soon spread through Fawley's oil refinery and Vospers Thorneycroft Shipbuilders. Queues started forming at the EETPU's office in the city's Bedford Place. Their contact was the Area Secretary's assistant, Vivian Seaman.

Area 22 office was a clearing-house for local unemployed EETPU members. It was unique in keeping a permanent register of jobless electricians who were informed when a vacancy came up.[16] Southampton was a good recruiting ground: the shipyards were making redundancies and Fawley's, one of the largest employers, gave their workers short-term contracts.

Bert Brown, who had been on the branch committee in Southampton and was a shop steward at Vospers, was one of the first to start following up the rumours. At the EETPU's biennial conference in Blackpool in July, he had heard that Vivian Seaman's son, Stephen, who had been out of work after his cleaning business folded, was now working in the area as a recruitment officer for the union. Brown was furious. He believed that the union had side-stepped the proper proce- dure in not giving the unemployed members on their register the opportunity to apply for the job.

Before he had a chance to raise the matter at his next branch meeting, he was asked by two young apprentices at Vospers if he had any forms for 'this press job in London'. He was mys- tified. Determined to find out more, he rang the Area Secre- tary, Mick Scanlon.

As Scanlon was not in the office, Brown spoke to Seaman. At first she was evasive. He was beginning to lose his temper. 'I've been in this union for forty years,' he said, 'and I want to know what is going on.' She told him they were recruiting for jobs in London. The area office was finding suitable ap- plicants who would then go on for interviews with a London employment agency. Four hundred had already been taken on, Brown remembers her saying. When he pressed her for more information, she had warned him: 'I don't want people making waves over this.'[17]

Brown's initial concern – the appointment of Seaman's son to a union job – was raised at the next branch meeting, held as usual in the Southampton Labour club. The branch decided to write to the National Executive for an explanation. A reply from the EETPU's head office was read out at the August branch meeting, which was unusually well-attended. The hardcore of ten was boosted to eighteen because of the growing interest in the 'London job'. They heard that Seaman had been appointed for a specific task and that task was now completed. No further details were given.[18]

Brown was still not satisfied. He suspected that recruitment for London was not as straightforward as he was being led to believe. There was talk of a 'new concept' which meant that the electricians would not only install the equipment and maintain it, but that they would also operate it. To Brown, a good trade unionist, this meant only one thing – poaching. He believed that the EETPU recruits were being trained to do printers' work. In September he rang an NGA Father, Mick Plumbley, in the composing room at the *Southern Evening Echo* in Southampton and told him his fears.

By then, interviewing was well under way. Candidates had received a letter from the Area Secretary, Mick Scanlon, giving them the date and time of their interview with Charles Paterson employment agency in London. John Fraser, who had taken voluntary redundancy from his labouring job at Vospers, was greeted by Scanlon when he arrived for his interview at the agency's Black Prince Road office on 16 September. He was told they were recruiting for the *London Post* and he would be working in the publishing room where the printed papers are stacked. There would be three months' training, the company would pay for coaches to bring them to London each day, and he was asked whether he wanted another interview. It took less than five minutes.

His second interview was in the Tower Hotel, next to Tower Bridge. As Fraser entered the twelfth-floor room, he was shown from the window an industrial site; that was where he would be working, he was told. At this interview the questions were more pointed. Was he prepared to work if there was any trouble? Did he belong to any left-wing groups? Would he consider moving up to London? He was also given more information about the job.

Fraser did not ask any questions. He was unemployed and the job was worth £12,000 a year. He could not believe his luck when his interviewers concluded by asking him whether he could start on the 23 or 30 September. He was given an application form to complete and bring with him on his first day.[19] A News International executive later explained the cursory interviews. They needed to staff the plant quickly. 'If they could walk and talk at the same time they were taken on!'[20]

At around the same time, trade-union circles in Glasgow were buzzing with rumours that dummy copies of News International papers were being produced at Kinning Park by electricians who had been recruited in a similar way.

Jimmy Hay had worked at the plant for less than forty-eight hours when he decided he could not square it with his trade-union conscience. Although he was a maintenance engineer and a member of the AUEW, it struck him that he had been employed to do print work. He was also disturbed by the high level of security and talk of having to be bussed through picket lines. When he resigned on 19 November, he rang his union District Secretary to tell him what was going on.

He said he had been given a job application form by an electrician friend who had picked it up while on an EETPU training course. He had filled it in and sent it to a Mr P. O'Hanlon at a private address in Lanarkshire. Hay's interview on 29 October in a Glasgow hotel had been arranged by the Charles Paterson agency. At the time it had seemed to him that the interviewer was more interested in his background than his skills.

The following day he had been invited to the Kinning Park plant by Magnathena, a company he had not heard of before. Sitting in on the interview was O'Hanlon, whom he recognised as an EETPU official. Hay claimed he had been asked if he would mind joining the electricians' union, as it would be a single-union plant, and whether he objected to crossing picket lines. He badly needed the job, and had tried to give the answers he thought they wanted to hear. He told them he would be guided by his union's line.[21]

By the autumn, the two main print unions' head offices had begun receiving reports of News International's recruitment drive. Sogat had heard from its Glasgow office that three of the union's members had applied for jobs at Kinning Park. They had gone through the interview procedure, during which they had met O'Hanlon and had been told that the EETPU 'would be the only union recognised by the company'.[22]

In Southampton, two men in particular were digging. Mick Plumbley, the NGA Father who had first heard the stories from Bert Brown, was collecting information from members of the EETPU Chapel at the *Southern Evening Echo*. Six electricians gave him anecdotal evidence from their neighbours, families and drinking companions of people who had gone to work in Wapping. He also interested a local reporter in the story who, in the early hours of Friday, 1 November, organised the first pictures of coaches taking Southampton men to London.

Plumbley's report went via his branch officials to the NGA headquarters at Bedford. Officials there had also been contacted by the EETPU's branch president in Southampton, Arthur 'Ginger' Pearse. That August, Pearse had seen men lining up at his union's office. He was delighted, thinking it meant new work in the area. When he asked what the job was, Seaman had put her finger to her lips, indicating she did not want him to know. Pearse then made it his business to find out.[23]

In late September, Pearse had addressed a public meeting in London organised by a local left-wing group within the print unions, and had revealed the Southampton connection in the Wapping plant. Two weeks later he was invited by NGA General Secretary Tony Dubbins to the union's regional office in London. Pearse passed on all he knew about the number of people going to London, the jobs they were doing and the way they had been recruited.[24]

With the evidence amassed from Southampton and Glasgow, the print unions – the NGA and Sogat – with the AUEW prepared a formal complaint for the TUC against the

EETPU. It was lodged on 17 December. By then, the electricians had provoked them further. The EETPU's National Executive had decided on 10 December not to be part of the joint approach in News International negotiations. After a meeting of the TUC's Printing Industry Committee on 16 December failed to force inter-union cooperation, Norman Willis summoned all General Secretaries concerned to Congress House under the TUC's Rule 11.

He had already written to them to try to persuade them to tackle the News International problem together, but following the TUC's General Council meeting on 18 December, Willis had said: 'I decided that this was of such importance that I should intervene.'[25] Rule 11 held the threat of disciplinary action and even suspension. Three days after the General Secretaries met at the TUC, Willis wrote to them with formal advice that 'it was imperative and urgent that the five unions seek a common approach'.[26]

In early January, Eric Hammond, General Secretary of EETPU, wrote to Willis for 'clarification'. Did his advice preclude any negotiation with News International without the consent of the other unions? The General Secretary's reply conceded that separate talks had not been ruled out, but stressed again that no agreement or arrangement should be reached with the company without the consent of all the unions involved.[27]

The print unions' complaint was finally investigated by the TUC General Council on 30 January. They had requested a hearing under Rule 13, the TUC's catch-all disciplinary rule which comes into force if a union has not complied with advice given under Rule 11. Hammond, a member of the General Council, did not attend that day. He wrote to Norman Willis saying he would be absent because he 'feared for his safety' after being mobbed by protestors two days before when he had arrived for a meeting at Congress House.[28]

The TUC investigation lasted six hours. The print unions had prepared a 30-page confidential submission detailing their evidence against the EETPU. They sought to prove that the electricians' union had, or should have, known what their members were doing in Wapping and Kinning Park, charging officials with doing nothing to stop them.

Armed with the evidence of the Southampton coaches and Jimmy Hay's story, they told the General Council that they had learned in July and August that the presses in Wapping were being tested. On 6 September they had been given a dummy of a paper printed there and were told there had been a full print run. They pointed out that the usual printing practice was for the machines to be tested by the people who are going to operate them. They believed that a dummy run at Kinning Park in October had been undertaken by electricians, although the EETPU officials maintained that they were only there to install equipment.

Their evidence included manning lists leaked from Wapping, which they said pointed to the electricians' union being less than candid about the number of people working at the plant. There were considerably more people on the lists than the fifty the EETPU had consistently maintained had been contracted to set up the machinery.

The print-union General Secretaries were also concerned at the apparent failure of the EETPU to stop the recruitment by their local secretaries after the other print unions had told officials of their suspicions. On 30 September they said they had been assured by the EETPU's National Officer, Tom Rice, that recruitment had now ceased. They presented the General Council with what they saw as damning evidence – a compliment slip from the Area 22 office, signed by Vivian Seaman and dated 7 January 1986. They said it had been attached to a Charles Paterson application form for Wapping sent to an NGA member in Southampton.

Having heard the evidence, the General Council ruled that the EETPU's activities could be construed as 'detrimental to the interests of the trade union movement' and contrary to the principles and policies of the TUC. There were seven specific charges for them to answer. The first was that the EETPU had jeopardised the prospect of the other unions reaching agreement with News International by refusing to adopt a joint approach to the company despite formal advice from the TUC General Secretary.

The other charges against the EETPU amounted to an accusation of an 'arrangement' between the EETPU and News International, against the interests of the traditional print unions. The EETPU members in the two plants had 'imperilled' the jobs of Gray's Inn Road and Bouverie Street workers; the union had assisted in the recruitment of a new workforce for the company, with the understanding that the EETPU would have a single-union deal at the new plants; their members had produced the special section of the 19 January *Sunday Times* in breach of existing agreements other unions had with the company; and recruitment in Southampton had continued despite assurances from Tom Rice that officials had been told to stop.

On the morning of Wednesday, 5 February, the TUC held one of its most crucial meetings in recent history. Eric Hammond, the General Secretary of the EETPU, was to answer the accusations of the print unions that his union, the TUC's eighth-largest affiliate, with 350,000 members, had played an instrumental part in the secret recruitment for Wapping and Kinning Park.

At this meeting, Eric Hammond had to respond to the charges. If he failed to satisfy the TUC General Council, he would be directed to offer undertakings for the future: failure to do that would lead to banishment from the TUC and that possibility, which he now faced, was seen as the most damaging threat to the unity of the trade-union movement for decades.

In the days leading up to the meeting, Hammond had been anything but repentant. He had already threatened to take the TUC to court to defend his union's right to remain a member. He had said that the instruction from the TUC that his members in Wapping stop work was asking them to act illegally.

The EETPU had been edging towards suspension for weeks: before the dispute started, the union's National Executive had decided not to follow Willis's formal advice for a common approach with the other unions to News International. Hammond had argued that this had represented an extension of the TUC's authority. He had said that a common front was impossible because, unlike the others, his union had no objection to legally binding deals. Thirdly, Hammond claimed that a recent issue of the Sogat journal incited violence against

him. Charges levelled at him, he insisted, were motivated by
political prejudice and membership ambitions.

On the eve of the TUC meeting, Hammond had issued a
circular to all his union's Executive and to branches, in which
he claimed that the union was an important force for change
in the newspaper industry. He had written: 'We believe that
our members have a right to develop their skills and opportunities as the impact of electronics advances.'[29]

Outside Congress House, sacked printers stood waiting.
'Hammond, The Enemy Within' was written on one of the
many placards they carried. The General Council, already in
session on the fifth floor, could hear their angry shouts from
below. Suddenly, the shouts turned to a roar. 'I think they
might have arrived,' Brian Stanley, the Post Office Engineers'
leader, remarked.

Stanley, a prominent member of the TUC's right-wing
faction, had been among Hammond's most ardent supporters.
During the TUC row the year before about whether unions
should accept government money to conduct postal ballots,
Hammond had been supported by Stanley and all his natural
allies on the right. This time it was different.

At a secret meeting a week before the Wapping dispute
started, in the offices of the Iron and Steel Trades Confederation in Gray's Inn Road, about 100 yards from the *Times*
and *Sunday Times* building, the right-wing group on the General Council had told the electricians' union that they could
not count on support if faced with TUC disciplinary action.[30]

Hammond had not attended that meeting. He had sent
along John Spellar, the bearded former MP for Birmingham
Northfield and an EETPU research officer, known as a tough
and skilled political fixer. The message Spellar was to pass on
to Hammond was unequivocal: however much they supported
the EETPU's approach on policy issues, they could not con-
done the electricians taking the work of other unions. The
members of this caucus believed that the EETPU had connived
in the Wapping operation.

When he entered the Council Chamber that day,
Hammond knew he had no supporters in the room. He had
brought with him two of his closest advisers: Tom Rice, his
National Officer, responsible for Fleet Street, and Tom

Breakell, the union's President, a blunt-spoken Lancastrian. Also at Hammond's side was Michael Short, a good-looking young lawyer from Lawford and Co., the company which had been acting for the union since 1960, reputed to have a thorough grasp of TUC regulations and practice.

The four men passed through the heavy, green, hide-covered doors and were immediately ushered to places round the large mahogany table opposite Norman Willis, TUC General Secretary; Ken Graham, his deputy; and Ken Gill, Chairman of the meeting and General Secretary of the white-collar union TASS. A former member of the Communist party, Gill was an arch opponent of Hammond's.

The Council Chamber at Congress House is a monument to fifties architectural design. It is the lightest and airiest room in the building, with two huge net-curtained windows running its length and a Canadian pine slatted ceiling supported by four white columns. It is in this room that the most crucial decisions affecting Britain's labour movement are taken.

As Hammond and his men took their places, there was a scraping and shuffling of chairs as those sitting near them closed up to make room. 'We are in session,' announced Gill. 'First of all, welcome to Eric and his colleagues.'[31]

Hammond told them he had a document to present which was a detailed and complete refutation of the charges against his union. If the Council members approached this submission with an open mind, they could only conclude that the charges were groundless.

But first it was essential, he said, that the members had a proper understanding of the background, not one based on 'speculation, rumour and carefully nurtured half-truths which have typified much of the public comment and media coverage'.

'The Fleet Street industrial relations jungle has enjoyed a notoriety over the last twenty-five years which cannot have escaped the attention of any of the members of the General Council,' he said. The damage done by this 'notoriety' was not the subject of the complaint, but the Council members should bear it in mind when considering what was 'detrimental to the interests of the trade-union movement'.

He went on to cite damning official reports into the newspaper industry: the Royal Commissions in 1962 and 1977, the 1970 Report of the National Board for Prices and Incomes and the Joint Standing Committee of publishers and unions which had recommended a Programme for Action, rejected by the membership in 1976.

'Other industries have not been able to resist technological change,' Hammond said. But if change could be postponed, he added, it could not be resisted indefinitely. It was better to negotiate for change rather than have it abruptly imposed.

'The newspaper industries in America, Europe and Japan have not stood still. . . . Fleet Street proprietors are now pressing to introduce the sort of radical changes which in other countries would have, and have been, spread out over twenty-five years.'

Hammond then turned to the specific allegations about recruitment in Southampton. In September 1985, he said, National Secretary Tom Rice had been told by Sogat officials that they had heard rumours that electricians were being recruited by the area office to work in Wapping. 'Mr Rice told those who spoke to him that he knew nothing of this matter and that he would look into it.'

Hammond told them that the area official, Mick Scanlon, who handled the employment register there – unique in the union – did not normally vet employers to establish if they recognised the EETPU or any other union. It was not unusual for Scanlon to receive inquiries from employers outside his area, 'nor for employers to recruit outside London for work in the London area'.

When Scanlon had received a request for labour from the Charles Paterson Agency, he had 'merely processed it in the normal way'. He had not seen any reason to obtain clearance from the head office and he had not discussed the matter 'with anyone from head office before Mr Rice contacted him in September to inquire about the rumours'.

Hammond told them that Rice had reported to the EETPU's Executive Council on 29 September when it had been decided that all requests for labour from London employers should first be referred to the union's head office. Scanlon was told formally of this decision by Hammond on 10 October and, said Hammond, all contact with the agency ceased. '. . . Neither he nor his office gave any further assistance in the recruitment of labour to work at Wapping.'

As for the famous compliments slip, Hammond told them that Vivian Seaman denied that it had been attached to an application form for work through Charles Paterson. Seaman had pointed out that she sent many items from her office and believed one of the slips may have been attached to an application form to 'create a misleading impression'. The date, she had said, had been added by someone else.

Rice had informed the print-union leaders on 30 September at the Inn on the Park Hotel, while waiting for talks to begin with Rupert Murdoch, that he had made inquiries into the Southampton recruitment rumours and had established that the area office there had assisted with some labour – estimated at fifty or so members. Rice had told them that to the best of his knowledge the members were engaged on normal contracting work, installing and commissioning equipment. He had told them that the Southampton area office was instructed not to assist further.

Hammond then hit out at Sogat. When the 30 September meeting with News International had ended, the print-union negotiators had got together for a meeting. Rice, Hammond claimed, had been told that Sogat wanted separate negotiations with the company.

'We can only speculate on the reason for Sogat's insistence on separate negotiations,' said Hammond. But he said that some clue about the union's attitude could be obtained from comments made by Bill Miles, General Officer, on Channel Four on 20 November. Hammond had the interview to hand. Miles was quoted as saying that Sogat would look at a single-union agreement if another union failed to come to terms with new technology, risking job opportunities for his members. If the NGA, Miles had said, or any other union put his members at risk, then 'I think seriously we would have to think about crossing their picket lines and getting the newspapers back on the street'.

Hammond then dismissed the charges about Glasgow. O'Hanlon, the EETPU Motherwell Area Official, had been told by Rice to refer any requests for labour from the printing industry to head office. O'Hanlon said he had been approached by

Charles Paterson in October 1985 to recruit electricians and that he had sent application forms to a 'number of companies where he knew redundancies were imminent'. He had allowed his home to be used as the return address.

'The EETPU does not approve of Mr O'Hanlon's use of his home address in this fashion,' said Hammond. But by no stretch of the imagination, he argued, could anyone believe that O'Hanlon was trying to hide his own involvement in the recruitment.

O'Hanlon, Hammond told them, had been worried about the secrecy that the Paterson agency's client insisted on, so he had attended the second interviews arranged with candidates. 'Mr O'Hanlon ... says that some of those interviewed at the same time were members of other unions and in particular Sogat.' O'Hanlon had said that although it was clear the applicants were being recruited to work in a printing works, there had been no indication of the duties they would be carrying out.

Hammond told the TUC: 'Mr O'Hanlon's activities were carried out on his own initiative and without any consultation with or encouragement from the union's head office.'

As for the EETPU members already in Wapping, Hammond told the TUC that he had no idea how many there were. He had asked Rice on 23 January, when he had first received the TUC complaint, to go to Wapping to find out, but the dispute had started the next day and such a visit would have been 'misunderstood'.

However, the EETPU had made some 'informal enquiries' and in addition to the 'approximately 80 members' from Southampton, he believed that about 100 electricians were in the plant, employed by sub-contractors 'who had carried out installation and commissioning work who may have been recruited by London Post (Printers) Ltd'. This, he said, had not involved the EETPU in any way.

'There is no way of knowing ... whether all of those 180 are members of the union or indeed whether there are other employees at Wapping who may, for example, have been recruited by word of mouth.' Hammond added that the press had reported 500 employees in Wapping, including 'substantial numbers of Sogat, NGA and AUEW members'.

'Since that strike began,' Hammond said, 'the EETPU now understands that there are a large number of Sogat members working at Wapping together with a much larger number of members of the NUJ.'

As for the TUC asking him to stop EETPU members working there, Hammond told them his union had received a letter from London Post (Printers) Ltd's solicitors informing them that if the union did so, they would apply to the courts for damages and an injunction. 'The EETPU does not issue calls for industrial action so lightly.' If the EETPU was to be held responsible for the actions of its members, then so should Sogat, the NGA and the·AUEW for the action of their members employed at Wapping.

Hammond paused. He was now, he said, going to answer the allegation which he believed was at the heart of the matter: 'The EETPU wishes to state . . . as categorically as possible that it has not entered into or continued any agreement, arrangement or understanding with News International covering all or part of the operation or groups of employees at Wapping.' The complaint against them, he said, contained no evidence other than the complaining unions' expressions of suspicions.

He then threw down a challenge. 'If . . . the General Council still wishes to persist with these charges, the EETPU calls upon the General Council to consider precisely what it can reasonably and lawfully ask the EETPU to stop doing.'

Hammond had been speaking for almost an hour. He was now in the last stage of his opening defence. The interpretation which the complaining print unions put on the facts was that the EETPU had been in 'collusion with News International' and were responsible for the unemployment of Fleet Street workers.

'We totally and emphatically reject that construction,' he said. 'The immediate responsibility for that unemployment lies with the bad judgement – and yes, I must say, for the matters at stake demand plain speaking – with the incompetent leadership of Sogat and the NGA.'

Hammond became more and more aggressive. He said: 'If we are totally to accept their version of events, it involves a plot by Murdoch in some way aided by the EETPU to create a situation whereby their existing members would be provoked

into strike action and Murdoch would then claim justification
to transferring to Wapping.'

He went on: 'Perhaps there was a plot: but I tell you un-
equivocally that we had no part of it, no knowledge of it. But,
I must say this, there was widespread speculation that
Murdoch was planning to switch existing titles to Wapping. If
it was a secret, it was abysmally kept. So why, with suspicion
running rife, did they walk into this trap?' No one spoke.

Hammond, many of them then realised, had really done his
homework. He went on to quote a speech made by one of his
main accusers, Tony Dubbins, NGA General Secretary, at his
union's conference in 1978. Dubbins had said that it seemed
to be the desire of members to look back to the days when
entry to the union was solely through a craft apprenticeship.
'If we do that, it will not be a case, like King Canute, of
getting your feet wet; it will be a case of a massive tidal wave
of changing techniques sweeping over this industry, with the
creation of an alternative non-union industry or an industry
organised by alternative unions.'

There was silence. The EETPU General Secretary had
another quote for them. It was from an editorial in the
Guardian a week before which had predicted that the electricians could find themselves isolated, exposed and ultimately
expelled. The problem, the editorial had pointed out, was that
unions on both sides were spoiling for a fight.

'You have decided,' he told them, 'regardless of our answer,
to rid yourself of the EETPU.' Some member unions had calculated on taking his members, he said, some were under pressure from the 'several factions of the left who are making their
cause the destruction of the EETPU'. This, he said, did not
inspire confidence that everyone in the room would deal with
the complaint fairly. 'You are probably outraged that I should
doubt your integrity or political backbone,' he told them.

Hammond had almost finished. He told them that there
were over 700 NUJ members in Wapping and 700 TGWU
drivers for the distribution of the papers. 'Yet we alone are in
the dock,' he said. The charges defied both common sense and
natural justice.

It was 11.55 a.m. and time for an adjournment. The
Chairman asked the EETPU officials and lawyer to leave the

room but told Hammond that as a General Councillor he had
a right to stay. 'I understand that,' Hammond told them, 'but
I feel I am here as the leader of our delegation.' He left with
the other members of his team, telling the Chairman he would
be available outside.

After the doors had shut behind him, the Chairman, Gill,
thanked them for their discipline throughout. Before they
asked questions, Gill said, they would have to study the 32-
page document with 16 appendices which Hammond had
submitted in his union's defence. They would have to stay in
the room and read through lunch. 'We will do our best to get
as wide a variety of sandwiches as possible.'

The meeting resumed at 2.25 p.m. It was now time to cross-
examine Hammond. 'Can we get the EETPU in?' Gill asked.

Norman Willis, General Secretary, started the questioning.
He homed in on the EETPU's decision not to join the common
negotiating position he had insisted the other unions adopt.
Hammond told him: 'We would have just been part of the
general attitude of the printing industry's unions. We would
not have been separate or distinct. We would just have been
drawn in to endorse what the other unions say is the way to
proceed.'

Quickly, the questions returned to recruitment for Wapping, and it was a few right-wing General Secretaries who
hammered at what they thought were the weakest parts of the
EETPU's defence. At one stage, Hammond, getting tetchy,
told them that the print industry was not his number-one priority.
'It is a piddling industry as far as we are concerned and the
sooner we can get distanced from it the happier we will be.'

Roy Grantham, the balding, mild-mannered General Secretary of the white-collar union Apex, Association of Professional, Executive, Clerical and Computer Staff, said: '. . . we
have been told by you today about the four officials who were
party to such recruitment by two plants owned by the same
company. Were you saying you had no understanding or
agreement in prospect of any kind? It seems very strange.'

Hammond replied testily: 'You can put what description
you like on it; that is the fact of the matter. We have no
arrangement, no understanding, and nor are we seeking one
at this moment.'

Ron Todd, General Secretary of the TGWU, was one of Hammond's most persistent interrogators about the role of the EETPU in the recruitment for Kinning Park, Glasgow: 'The question I would like to know is in August, September, October of 1985, whilst there may have been no agreement or no joint understanding, was there knowledge that people were involved in the knowledge of News International intentions . . .?'

'I have already answered this in a number of ways,' replied Hammond. 'I have already given my reply and I do not want to add to it, but it does get a bit tiresome.'

Todd took exception to this. 'What is tiresome?' he asked. 'I have raised a question and all I have posed is this. We have a statement and the TUC must listen to all the parties. If we were to rush them because Eric thinks it is tiresome we would then be accused of accelerating it and having made up our minds already. I want to know exactly what transpired . . .'

Without pausing, Todd pushed the questioning. 'All I am saying is, yes, maybe you can put on paper "I have no agreement or understanding with them", but I ask the question and I am sorry if Eric thinks it is tiresome: was there knowledge in August, September of what News International intended to do?'

'No,' said Hammond. 'There was not.' And looking round the table at the other General Secretaries, he said: 'All I am asking him to do is to accept the same thing from us about our knowledge of what happened with Mr O'Hanlon and what happened with Scotland. There are things that happen in big organisations which you do not know about. What we are making clear is that as soon as they were complained of, we took steps that were necessary to put a stop to it. I will keep repeating that, even though it is tiresome, Ron, but that is the fact of the matter.'

It was Brenda Dean, General Secretary of Sogat, who then took up the cross-examination. She felt like responding, she said, to the personal insults in the EETPU's submission, but she knew that would not help. 'This is not going to be resolved by rhetoric,' she said.

'We did not start along the insult trail,' said Hammond. 'We have put our view as we see it and we see a situation being manipulated because there is no other way out but to make us the scapegoats of other people's decisions in Southampton.'

Dean wanted to talk specifics. Using as evidence lists of staff who were employed in the plant, she queried why there were relatives of Mick Scanlon, the Southampton official, named: '... the lists of staffing levels that we had for September included three Mr Scanlons working on the press line. There may well be a relative link there in the relationship. There was a Miss Ann Scanlon in the photocomposing area. Surely there must be some link. Surely you cannot say no members have had contact with the EETPU?'

It was Rice who answered her: 'It is not unusual, I think, for families to follow each other with jobs, in fact it is a tradition. I would like to have a look at lists from any of the newspapers and see all the brothers, but not so many sisters, although plenty of brothers, who are on those lists ... when there are job opportunities made available to the kind of workers they are, they follow them,' he said of the electricians. 'That really is the root of the current controversy – understanding that situation.'

Tony Dubbins, General Secretary of the NGA, took up the questioning. He, too, latched on to specifics. He spoke of the secrecy which surrounded the 'movement of large numbers of people from Southampton to Wapping'. Rice told him that the EETPU had not organised any bussing. 'We have told you,' Rice added crossly, 'that the recruitment stopped following our decision that it should cease in September.'

The cross-examination lasted until well past five in the afternoon. The Chairman wound up the session by telling them he wanted to record the fact that the EETPU – setting a precedent – had been allowed to have a lawyer present. Hammond quickly retorted: 'Well, we are used to making firsts. We hardly saw this as an inquiry but a trial, and it underlines, I say again, the importance we attach to TUC membership.'

Hammond and his team left the room. The Council had to consider the next step. Virtually everybody was agreed that the EETPU had acted against the interests of the movement. But they now had to consider, one by one, the seven specific charges levelled against the electricians, and vote on each. It was charge seven which was to cause problems. It dealt with whether or not there had been an 'arrangement' – in defiance of TUC policy – between the EETPU and News International.

On this particular accusation, Dubbins was adamant. No one had contested, he said, that the EETPU from Southampton – and certainly in Glasgow – had an arrangement with News International. Dean supported him. If they rejected that particular accusation, she said, they would be saying, 'anything goes as long as head office don't know about it'.

Ken Graham, Deputy General Secretary of the TUC, told them he was uneasy about the charge as it stood. 'It is saying that there has been a carefully worked out, over a period of time, conspiracy as far as Wapping is concerned.' He considered the TUC on firm ground concerning the other charges of imperilling jobs and recruitment. 'I get slightly uneasy,' he said, 'when you are saying there has been a conspiracy. I do think we need some solid evidence to support a proposition like that . . . I don't think you can move just on suspicion . . . you have had very firm consistent denials against this theory.' Graham said that he had his own suspicions, but he would vote against this particular accusation. He was only one of eight. Charge seven was carried.

The EETPU was found guilty of five of the seven charges. The General Council decided that they were not guilty of the charge that they had helped in recruitment in exchange for a single-union deal. The dated compliment slip had not swayed the Council, who also found the EETPU not guilty of breaking Tom Rice's assurances to the other unions by continuing to recruit after 30 September. As TUC rules dictated, the General Secretary had to produce a paper recommending the directions which should now be issued to the EETPU. They wearily adjourned again. It was just after seven.

When they re-convened at 9 p.m., it soon became clear that there was more at stake than the exact charges upheld against the electricians. If they directed the EETPU, on threat of suspension, to order its members working in Wapping to stop, they would be asking the union to act unlawfully under secondary-picketing legislation. But if the electricians were not given such a directive, there was very little they could do to bring the union into line.

For the next two hours they debated what could be done. Again, Dubbins was adamant. The General Council should do nothing less than tell electricians in Wapping to stop performing work previously undertaken by print workers. Unless the directive had teeth, 'we are going to look so bloody silly I just don't think it will be treated with any credibility whatsoever,' he said.

Again Dean followed him. She said that there were nearly 6,000 union members out on the streets with no redundancy payments and the papers were being produced by members of another TUC affiliate. 'You have accepted that, this afternoon, in five points out of seven of complaint.' The General Council could not, as suggested, simply ask the EETPU to inform their members that they were doing the jobs of workers who had been sacked. 'They know they are doing those jobs,' she said. If the Council did not admit responsibility, 'I would suggest very respectfully and very humbly that the whole of this investigation has been a complete waste of time.'

Graham told Dean she had done a 'brilliant job' in defending her situation to the public and looking after her members. But, he added: 'We are now talking about the trade-union movement as a whole.' The TUC, he reminded her, could not issue an unlawful directive.

There was a short adjournment at 10 p.m. for Graham to get legal advice. When he returned, he told them that if the directive was strengthened, it would almost certainly lead to an application for an injunction by either the EETPU or News International. That, he said, would 'nullify at a stroke all proceedings to date'.

During the last hour of the long, arduous meeting, they discussed the wording of the draft directive to the EETPU which would be relayed to their members in Glasgow and Wapping. Graham was insistent that it should read: 'Inform their members they were engaged in printers' work.' Some General Secretaries wanted the EETPU to be instructed that their members in Wapping stop work.

Fred Jarvis of the National Teachers Union told them: 'I tend to think it is better not to say it, than say something as pathetic as this.' The words would be a laughing stock, he said, but he was inclined to accept the lawyers' advice.

Ray Buckton of ASLEF told them that if the lawyers' advice was accepted, it meant that the 'whole basic principle of trade unions have gone to the dogs'. He continued: 'Anybody can do anybody else's job of work at any time because the lawyers say so. It is time we stood up to be counted. I am prepared to move that instead of the word "inform",' we ask them to "instruct" the members.'

Buckton was insistent that the EETPU should stop its members in Wapping and Glasgow from crossing the picket lines. 'It is getting to be a bit of a farce as a trade-union movement, quite honestly. You instructed me to tell my members not to cross picket lines.' If they could not ask a trade union to advise members, he said, not to do something done by other trade unionists, they might as well all go home.

There had been forty-three Council members round the table when the meeting started: there were now about thirty. It was late. The General Council was faced with possibly the most important decision it had had to make for thirty or forty years.

Jimmy Knapp of the NUR was getting fed up. 'I have got a wife and a dog back home the same as everybody else,' he said. But he did not agree that they should say nothing at all in the directive. 'We have got to stand up and be counted,' he said.

Ron Todd of the TGWU told them that if the directive was passed merely asking the EETPU to inform their members that they were engaging in work normally done by other trade unionists, it would not only question their competence but their sanity.

The vote was taken, Ray Buckton and Jimmy Knapp lost their amendment to strengthen the directive by just one vote. The General Secretaries wearily left the Council Chamber at 11.35 p.m. The meeting had lasted over thirteen hours.

The directive which had been the cause of so much debate ruled that the EETPU tell its members in Wapping they were engaged on work normally done by members of other unions. The union was told not to conclude any agreement with News International or enter into unilateral talks with them. They

were also directed not to 'facilitate or assist further in recruitment of staff whether directly or indirectly' and that they
should not take into membership workers already in Wapping
or Glasgow. They were given a week to comply. If they did
not, they would be suspended from TUC membership.

Under the headline 'Electricians fail to sway TUC right',
John Lloyd, then Labour Editor of the *Financial Times*, wrote:
'They did not believe him.' He continued: 'What the Council
has done is to produce a formula which both sides can accept
because neither side has won. Its weakness is that it may have
had to tacitly concede that Mr Murdoch has won.' Hammond
had failed to convince his fellow trade unionists, Lloyd
believed, that he had behaved towards News International as
he would have done to any company.[32]

For nine days in May 1985, Brenda Dean had toured North
America with a delegation from Sogat to study technological
changes in newspaper production. They visited four printing
plants and three union offices in Florida, Iowa, Washington
DC and Toronto. 'The impact turned out to be so vast, so
devastating that all of us returned somewhat shaken by what
we had seen,' Dean later wrote.

In her introduction to a 42-page study about the visit sent
to every Sogat member, Dean warned that they were facing
'the eye of the storm'. The ten-person Sogat delegation concluded that opposing technological change was not an option
for trade unions in printing, it was simply a rapid road to de-
unionisation. In America there had been a 50 per cent job loss
in the industry because of new technology. The delegation
realised that some 'unscrupulous employers would use the
opportunity to make staff cuts, possibly with the help of American-
style union bashers'.

'One of the consequences of not concluding successful
negotiations on these difficult changes could be an element of
de-unionisation in the newspaper industry – just as has already
happened in vast areas in America. That, we believe, is one of
the major experiences for us to learn from and make sure a
similar situation does not develop in our industry here,' Dean
advised.

It was already too late. What the Sogat delegation did not

learn in America was that little over a month earlier there
had been a visit of a very different kind to see American newspaper production techniques. Christopher Pole-Carew, the
pioneer of non-union newspapers in Britain, had arrived in
Washington DC on Tuesday, 9 April. He was with Tom Rice,
National Secretary of the EETPU.[33]

They had met up with John Keating, Technical Director of
Murdoch's News America Inc., who had a thorough knowledge of the latest American production systems and who had
contacts in many American papers using the latest technology.
The first papers they toured were the *Washington Post* and *USA
Today*, a national daily first published in 1982. *USA Today* was
produced in Rosslyn, across the Potomac river from Washington, and sent via satellite for printing in twenty-six sites
across the country. It was one of the most electronically
advanced newspapers in America.

Of interest to both Pole-Carew and Rice were the staffing
levels in the press and publishing rooms where *USA Today* was
printed. Normal staffing was eight to a press, with only three
to four people in each publishing room. In Rosslyn, the editorial staff was responsible for typesetting and composition.
Reporting staff also acted as copy-takers.

Dean had written of *USA Today* that, given its success, there
was 'no apparent reason why a new determined proprietor
. . . cannot successfully launch and distribute a national newspaper in Britain'.

From Washington, Pole-Carew, Rice and Keating went on
to Miami, where they visited the offices of the *Herald*, a paper
which had not had a strike in twenty-seven years. John
Hoover, Production Supervisor for the paper, remembers
showing Keating and Rice round the printing operation. It
had been a longer tour than Hoover normally gave. 'We
covered the whole building,' he said. 'They had been particularly interested in plastic plate technology.'[34] A further
trip planned to see the *News and Sentinel* at Fort Lauderdale
that afternoon was cancelled, as they did not think they had
enough time.

The next day, Thursday 11 April, Pole-Carew, Rice and
Keating had arrived in San Antonio, Texas, where they stayed
overnight in the St Anthony Hotel.[35] Murdoch owned the

Express-News in San Antonio, which had a circulation of 269,000. The paper had been using cold-type technology since 1973, two years before his purchase.

From San Antonio they left for New York, where on Monday morning, 15 April, Pole-Carew and Rice were shown round the offices of the *New York Post*, Keating's base. They flew back to London the next day.

Although Rice, Pole-Carew and Keating led such different lives, all got on well during the American trip. Keating had first met Rice in London the week before the American tour had started. An American in all but name, Keating would joke about Rice being a typical Irishman. Their friendship would develop throughout 1985 and on Keating's subsequent trips to London he would visit Rice's home. Keating also toured the EETPU headquarters and went to see their training school, Cudham Hall in Kent.[36]

Pole-Carew, who claimed that his 6 March contract with Murdoch put him in charge of the 'Post Project', would sometimes pull rank with the EETPU official. But there was to be only one moment of tension during the trip. Rice told Pole-Carew he wanted £40,000 per year per man for members who would eventually be working in Wapping. Pole-Carew had assured him in no uncertain terms that if such salaries were ever paid, he would make sure those employees earned every penny.

This American tour, one executive explained later, was crucial in the planning of Wapping. It had been organised to give Rice a 'general understanding of the modern printing industry'.[37] Another said it was to give Rice an 'overview of the equipment'.[38] From the time of the American visit, Rice and Pole-Carew had regular meetings, generally in anonymous London hotels, to discuss manning and shift patterns needed for Wapping.

Rice would later deny that he had any connection with Pole-Carew. At the 5 February meeting at the TUC, when asked about him by Jimmy Knapp of the NUR, Rice had told the General Council: 'There is no connection with Pole-Carew. All of the unions who associate in the industry were concerned to learn from the press some time in the middle of the year that this person had emerged within the Murdoch empire. All of the unions were asked questions about him and sought to find out information. He did attend one meeting at the request of the unions and explained his role. We, the EETPU, had no contact with Pole-Carew.'[39]

Rice was born in Dublin, where he had been a close friend of Sean Geraghty, the Secretary of the EETPU London Press Branch. When he had first come to London to live in Paddington, like many young men in his union in the 1950s he had joined the Communist party. His first job for the EETPU had been as a recruitment officer. He had moved to Kent, working for a time as an electrician for the paper-making company Bowaters, and he had become a national officer in the mid-1970s.

In 1982, Rice, now holding more moderate views, was a contender in the battle for the EETPU leadership after Frank Chapple retired. He had stood down in favour of Hammond: there had been too many candidates for the right. Rice had explained that his candidature 'could only give succour to the Communist-supported candidate'. He had called for his followers to support Hammond and clearly hinted that his two fellow moderates should throw in the towel.[40]

Rice had been closely involved with the single-union agreement with Eddie Shah for *Today*. It was John Grant, a former Labour MP and journalist, the union's press officer, who is said to have first had the idea of doing a deal with the entrepreneur. He had discussed it with Tom Rice, who apparently was immediately enthusiastic. At the first meeting between Shah and the EETPU, in May 1985, the union had been represented by Eric Hammond, General Secretary, Grant and Rice. After this meeting, the deal was as good as signed.[41]

News International executives knew it was not the Shah venture which had convinced Murdoch to use the EETPU for his new plant. Bruce Matthews, for one, believed that Murdoch had been prompted by a single-union deal which the EETPU had done in 1984 with a Finnish-owned paper mill which had taken over an old steel works in Shotton, North Wales.

The company had first offered a deal to Sogat, but had insisted that the union's Merseyside branch, with a history of disputes, should not be responsible for members. When Sogat had insisted Shotton be placed under the branch's aegis, the company began to look elsewhere and settled on the EETPU. Murdoch was said to have been impressed with the way the EETPU had eventually turned the mill into a 'highly efficient plant with healthy labour relations'. It was Shotton, not Shah, which was said to have been his model for Wapping.[42]

Few senior executives involved in the Post Project had ever believed Eddie Shah stood a chance of success. When Shah sold a 35 per cent shareholding to Lonrho in June 1986, one of those closely involved in the planning of Wapping said that part of Shah's problem was his failure to find skilled instructors who could teach recruits how to use new technology, unlike Murdoch, who had called on skilled newspaper employees from both his American and Australian newspapers.

The manning of Wapping and the training of staff had been one of the first problems tackled by those involved with the Post Project. The minutes of the secret planning meetings held throughout 1985 reveal Pole-Carew's role in both these areas. On Tuesday, 21 May, he told Matthews and other senior executives that he would be discussing the number of 'overseas personnel' when he met with Murdoch in two days' time.[43]

The minutes also reveal the role of the EETPU in the project. At the May meeting, Geoffrey Richards, the lawyer, had told executives that any ideas would be 'welcomed on the draft agreement between the LP and the EEPTU [*sic*]'.[44] This was also mentioned in the agenda of the next meeting: 'London Post/EEPTU draft agreement'.

At another planning meeting on Thursday, 8 August, Pole-Carew reported: '. . . Charles Paterson has interviewed twenty-one people, two of whom have already been taken on. Mechanical technicians are now needed, plus electronics people to train on the Atex system.' The minutes reveal: 'CPC feels that the Union will provide the necessary people by the end of this month.' It was decided that 'Charles Paterson should sign the appointment letters to potential employees, against a letter of indemnity from NI'.

Matthews and Pole-Carew had just returned from Los Angeles, where they had been for a meeting with Murdoch to discuss the progress of Wapping. One planning meeting had taken place in Murdoch's cramped office on the run-down lot of the once magnificent 20th Century Fox film studios.[46]

Murdoch had been unable to leave the city. He was within days of agreeing to spend $1.5 billion on six Metromedia television stations, the start of his dream to create a fourth national television network. Servicing the debt on such a sum would cost News Corporation $150 million a year, and no one doubted it was to be the biggest gamble of Murdoch's corporate career. But he had still found time for Wapping. He did not intend losing touch with what was happening in his new British printing plant: he needed the cash-flow from his British newspapers.

Recruitment for Wapping was discussed by his executives again in August. At another planning meeting on Thursday the 15th, Pole-Carew, Bill Gillespie, Managing Director of Times Newspapers, and John Cowley, one of Murdoch's Australian managers, were to draw up 'lists of questions for potential employees to be asked during interviews'. The minutes record: 'It was stressed that the EEPTU is not necessarily the only source of recruitment.'[47]

September found Murdoch in Switzerland. He needed to talk to bankers. Again, he instructed his executives to fly out to him for meetings on Wapping. Two days of discussions took place at the Nova Park Hotel, Zurich, on Wednesday, 11 September, and Thursday, 12 September. Gillespie, Pole-Carew, Keating and Matthews reported progress at the plant and discussed the next stages of the Post Project.[48] One of their main concerns at that time was that the NGA and Sogat officials gathering evidence on Wapping were becoming suspicious. They were pressing for meetings with management.

A week later, on Thursday, 19 September, the executive group planning the plant was beginning to have problems with the EETPU. There was concern about the union's demands. Matthews told them that the electricians had raised the question of a 'one year's notice period'. The 'general understanding now is that the EETPU now want one year's guaranteed work, not a year's pay on termination'. They were told: 'The EETPU also want this to apply to everyone on the staff.'

Matthews was 'seeing Tom Rice on Friday and will discuss the point with him'.

On Thursday, 26 September, the secrecy of the Post Project, so important to all of them, seemed to be breaking down. Matthews had 'received a call from the EETPU to the effect that all recruitment from Southampton must cease forthwith, as there were unfavourable Press reports locally. C. Paterson to tell all potential recruits from Southampton that we will revert to them at a later date.'[49]

The week before this meeting, a local newspaper reporter, Dermot Martin, had rung Vivian Seaman, from the newsroom of the Hythe office of the *Southern Evening Echo*. He had asked her if she could throw any light on a story he had been told by a Labour party contact that electricians and plumbers at Fawley's oil refinery were being offered contracts worth £29,000 to work as printers at Wapping.

Seaman had told him that all enquiries had to go through the EETPU headquarters. Martin said he had telephoned Bromley but had been unable to speak to anyone. He wrote a story for his paper, but it was held back because the Editor felt it needed confirmation. The story was eventually spiked.[50]

NINE

'Anyone could have worked it out'

When the ring of security came down round the Wapping plant early in 1985, a high-level informer in the company began to leak some of News International's most closely held secrets. The leaks went to two print workers who were unique in the ranks of Fleet Street trade unionists. They had already spent almost a year studying the inside of the plant and had produced the only serious assessment the print unions ever undertook of the purpose-built newspaper factory.

They began their own investigation. They started to compile a dossier and eventually built up a network of spies who leaked them dozens of documents. By mid-March, lists smuggled from the security gate had revealed the names of all the Atex personnel. They were told to pay particular attention to a company typed on a list as 'Cadriload'. An informer told them it was a cover for Atex. 'We looked for the company but could not find it,' one of them said. 'We had been told a computer was being tested off-site somewhere in South-East London.' [1]

In July one of them received a telephone call at home. 'Be careful of the EETPU,' a contact warned. Southampton kept cropping up in conversations with informers but it was not until September, when they had taken to spying on the plant and seen the coachloads of new recruits, that they realised the significance of the information. By that time they had a complete list of names and pass numbers of everyone working in Wapping. There were over 500 people.

At first they had met their contacts in pubs in the docklands. 'We had about five regular moles,' one of them said. 'Some were high up in the company.' Others were contractors working on the site. Eventually they became nervous about meeting so near the plant. 'We came back to Fleet Street.' [2]

Neither was politically active. They were from different unions and only held minor Chapel office. Tony Cappi was from the Bouverie Street Engineers' Assistants' Chapel, which belonged to the RIRMA branch of Sogat. It was the lowest in the Street's trade union ranks. These unskilled members were treated with disdain; their only chance of advancement from cleaning the building was to become tool-carriers for the engineers.

His co-investigator, Terry Ellis, a skilled rotary press engineer who repaired the Bouverie Street presses, was one of 110 men providing a twenty-four-hour cover on the machines printing both the *News of the World* and the *Sun*. The AUEW's engineering Chapel in Bouverie Street, of which he was Deputy Father, was far from militant. Members had only been on strike twice in thirty-four years; in 1953 for six weeks for recognition, and during a day of action for their fellow trade unionists in GCHQ, the Government Communications Headquarters in Cheltenham where trade-union membership had been banned.

Ellis, a cautious and unassuming man, took both his engineering job and his job in his union seriously. He had spent most of his career installing press equipment and was not like some of the officials with Fleet Street backgrounds who made sure of a high profile. The only reason he had stood for Chapel office in 1982 was because of his strongly held beliefs about the new building. He thought the engineers would have to accept the rapidly approaching changes in their industry; Tower Hamlets was the future. He had wanted to get involved from the outset.

AUEW Chapel officials assumed they would be offered more jobs when the plant opened. Ellis thought differently. He knew Fleet Street Chapel politics. When he had worked for a short time at the *Observer*, he had got to know a few of the newspaper industry's labour relations customs. When a proprietor asked for staffing cuts, it was generally from all Chapels on the paper. Sogat–NGA infighting meant that one Chapel would not accept a cut unless the others did.

In May 1983, when Bill O'Neill put suggested staffing levels for the new building to the Bouverie Street Chapels, the engineers were told they were to lose two-thirds of their men, like all the other Chapels. Ellis had always believed that when the new building was operational, the company would need more engineers, not fewer. The only way his Chapel would be able to negotiate entry to Wapping was to prove this to management.

Before Ellis had arrived in Fleet Street, he had a job for nine years as an installation engineer for a company manufacturing rotary paper cutters, which had involved assessing the number of staff a client would need to man the equipment. He wanted to undertake the same exercise in Wapping.

In July 1983, when O'Neill agreed that the AUEW Engineers Chapel should be allowed to carry out an assessment of equipment in the building to evaluate staff levels, Ellis was chosen by his Chapel Father to go into Wapping. For the next year, he inspected every piece of machinery which had been installed in the plant.

Early on, he found out that a Chapel official from the RIRMA branch was undertaking his own assessment on how many members from his Chapel would be needed. The Engineers' Assistants' Chapel, whose members worked one-to-one with the skilled engineers, did not usually negotiate its own agreements; they had always been given 86 per cent of any increase given to AUEW members. But when it came to the new building, the RIRMA Chapel, fearing that the one-to-one staffing was threatened, decided for the first time that they would have to negotiate themselves, and they wanted to be well prepared.

Tony Cappi and Terry Ellis decided to join forces. It was not a popular move. When their Chapel members found out that they were working together, there was what Ellis later described as an 'undercurrent'. 'I was a skilled technician,' said Ellis. 'Cappi was an unskilled worker from RIRMA, who would normally be carrying my tools.' They had breached Chapel protocol and they both came under a lot of pressure. It was particularly difficult for Cappi.

'It was hard for us to stick together,' he said. 'It was all so political.'

Cappi, a sensitive man, guarded and suspicious, had the reputation among his fellow members of being difficult to get along with. He had a minor Chapel office – health and safety representative. While he was spending a lot of his time in Tower Hamlets, his work in Bouverie Street was being covered by his colleagues. Some members were making a fuss, particularly

about his night shifts. But he was protected by his Chapel
Father, Harry Spanswick, who told them at one of their regular quarterly Chapel meetings of the importance of Cappi's
work. 'We keep a log of the time he spends working on the
project, quite often five days a week ... Cappi is part of a
team trying to save jobs,' he said.[3]

Cappi's Chapel and Branch officials had been impressed
when they had toured the plant in September 1982 to see the
building. The first phase was almost complete. The Father of
the Engineers' Assistants, Harry Spanswick, had reported to
the Chapel that the press room was 'gigantic'. The Chapel's
neatly typed minutes record: 'Hanging from the ceiling between the presses are long corridors with windows looking left
and right down into the machines. These are called quiet ways
where the button box or control panel for each press will be
installed.'

Spanswick reported: 'It is expected whilst the presses are
running that there will be no person in the press room.' He
described the roadway in the split-level warehouse for loading
papers as 'wider than Fleet Street'.[4] After another visit, he
had told them: 'The overall picture is massive, confused but
looking more like a press house than a building site.'[5]

In May 1983, when O'Neill had given the company's suggested staffing levels to the Bouverie Street Chapels he had
told them that if agreement was reached, they could be
working in the new building towards the end of the year. He
told Spanswick's Chapel that no one would be made redundant, that there would be natural wastage through early
retirement. Spanswick reported to his men: 'We told him
thank you and reminded him that we had worked in Fleet
Street with a reasonable living before Murdoch came ... and
we didn't doubt that a fair number would still be working
with a fair living when he leaves.'[6]

The talks did not go well. Although the staffing cut for the
move in their Chapel was not as 'massive' as that required in
the warehouse or machine room, it was totally unacceptable,
Spanswick said. He said he had told O'Neill to go back to
Murdoch and tell him how lucky he was to have 'a staff that
could earn him enough money to buy *The Times* and a
new £70 million building'. Spanswick had told O'Neill that

although Ken Taylor was a 'mechanical genius' and an expert machine designer, he, Spanswick, was the expert on machinery cleaning, 'with thirty years' experience'. The staffing levels, he said, had been arrived at by 'guesswork' and he refused to even show them to his Chapel. His members would want to hold lengthy meetings. 'It could possibly affect tonight's production,' he had told O'Neill.[7]

Spanswick decided that in order to prepare his Chapel's case on staffing levels, he would need to know about the new machinery installed in Wapping. In October 1983, O'Neill agreed to allow Tony Cappi into the building to make an assessment.

There was no official Chapel acknowledgment that Cappi and Ellis were working together until months later, when labour relations executives in Bouverie Street began to object that two union officials had been allowed to go to Wapping. 'It caused bitter political battles in the company,' said Cappi, who believed that only Ken Taylor, Technical Director of the plant, and O'Neill were keen for them to continue. The problem was that other Chapels were demanding the same rights.

In a complete break with Fleet Street tradition, the Engineers' Assistants' and the AUEW Chapels got together to try to find a meeting point. Spanswick told them they must support each other 'one-for-one'. The officials wanted to keep Cappi and Ellis in the building for as long as possible. They suspected the management of wanting to get them out to stop them being 'too well armed' when it came to negotiating staffing levels.[8]

Ellis and Cappi's 102-page technical report, the only serious study the unions ever undertook into the new plant, was finished in June 1984.

The introduction stated that the technical information and maintenance schedules the report contained were of sufficient depth 'to allow the Chapels to negotiate meaningfully on the project'. It included the specifications of every single piece of machinery in the plant. Production techniques had been assessed and there were sections on the needs of repair and maintenance. 'The sheer volume of plant and machinery coupled with production requirements will necessitate a planned maintenance policy, a feature which has not been present at Bouverie Street,' they recommended. They were critical that there was nothing in production terms which was 'radically different or astonishingly innovative', and although they described the built-in safety features as 'impressive', advised that there would have to be improvements.

The short conclusion on the last page described Tower Hamlets as 'a bold but well-planned step into the future and a fine technical achievement'. The amenities were first class. 'The main building is a spacious, well-ventilated construction which will make a desirable work place. . . . The company have said that Tower Hamlets will be possibly the cleanest and safest working environment yet known in Fleet Street, which is heartening news.'[9]

Ellis was sure he had proved his point on how many engineers would be needed once the plant opened. Based on providing twenty-four-hour cover for Bouverie Street and the new building – the company's plan in 1984 – he thought there would have to be thirty-three more men than the company had proposed. He thought it an accurate and fair figure, and so did some members of the News Group Newspapers management.

But the report was not widely welcomed in the other Chapels. 'Trade unionists in the building said it was wrong,' said Ellis. 'They said we had sold ourselves short. I knew it would upset a lot of people.' Part of the problem, he believed, was that the Fathers in the building did not understand his technical work. 'To them,' he said, 'it was just a big new building.' All he had tried to do, he explained, was to 'equate the machinery so we could sell ourselves into the future'.

In September 1984 the company re-opened the negotiations on Tower Hamlets suspended by O'Neill six months before. Tony Britton, then Assistant General Manager of News Group Newspapers, in negotiations with Chapels gave every indication to the officials that it was now full steam ahead. They were entering the 'transitional period' ready for the move.[10]

Ellis and the Father of the AUEW Chapel, Charles Tucker, had two meetings with Ken Taylor in November, and showed him the report. He was impressed, and called it a 'professional step forward' but when he requested a copy he was told by Tucker that it was Chapel property.[11]

The Ellis–Cappi report had specified one urgent require-
ment; they had asked for a 'thorough training and familiar-
ization programme for all members of the department . . . as
soon as possible.' Ellis said he thought the best approach was
to get the engineers on site to see the machinery. 'We could
have run up a couple of folders,' he said. 'But Taylor said he
did not want us in the building.' Pressed by Tucker, Taylor
eventually agreed that Ellis could bring two AUEW members
on site per day, and show them round.

Over the next three weeks, Ellis took ninety-two Chapel
members round Wapping. Then suddenly, on 5 December
1984, Bill Sooby, Personnel Manager at Bouverie Street,
telephoned one of Ellis's committee men at home and told
him to get his men off the site. 'We withdrew,' said Ellis. 'And
we never went back.' He tried to get in after the New Year
but there was a new security system and he did not have a
pass. 'From then on,' he said, 'our only contact was through
spies.'

It was to the Father of his Chapel, Harry Spanswick, that
Cappi turned when he first had doubts about what was
happening in the plant in mid-January 1985. A twelve-foot
high spiked metal fence now surrounded the perimeter. But it
was in early March that his suspicions were seriously aroused
when he heard that two levels in the new building had been
sealed off.

Cappi's Chapel was given the information about the sealed
floors and told that Murdoch had had 'meetings and confer-
ences with many heads of printing machine manufacturers' at
a quarterly meeting in early March. Spanswick said his personal conclusion was that Murdoch was 'bluffing' and that
'things are going to be tough for the next few months, to say
the very least'.[12]

Spanswick reported his own fears to the Chapel. 'Gradually,
we were made aware by the management that Murdoch had
had enough and had grown tired of Fleet Street,' he told
them.[13] The *Post* had been announced and all negotiations for
the new building had stopped. Murdoch, Spanswick told his
members, 'made claim of his total war on the NGA for
stopping him from printing in Glasgow'.

Shortly after the Chapel meeting, Cappi met one of his contacts and was told that someone had been employed on the site who was 'authorised by Rupert Murdoch to be allowed access day or night'. Cappi vaguely knew the name of the person but it was not until Christopher Pole-Carew's role was revealed on 13 May by *UK Press Gazette* as 'a consultant on new technology for the "Post"', that he began to look seriously into his background.[14] 'Alarm bells started ringing,' he said.

Throughout the spring, Cappi and Ellis were getting more and more information. They knew about Atex. 'When we had done the assessment we had tried to keep up with new technology and we knew what the company did,' said Cappi.

In May, Cappi and Ellis were told by an engineer working on the presses in Wapping that there were plans to convert them from tabloid- to broadsheet-sized paper. Both the *Sun* and the *News of the World* were tabloids. Cappi had been so worried that he had telephoned Brenda Dean's office at Sogat's headquarters in Hadleigh. But there had been no response to his message.

The lists of people going into the site, smuggled from the security gate, were getting longer. Cappi was told by informers to which areas they were allocated. They started breaking down the lists, trying to work out who the people were and for which company they worked. Geoffrey Richards of Farrer and Co. was on the first list, as was John Keating from Murdoch's office in New York, Charles Wilson (Editorial Director of *The Post*) and every one of Smylie's people with their pass numbers.

It was not easy finding out everyone's role in the operation. Each person was described as a 'consultant'. Then someone gave them a 19-page list of companies contracted to work on site with over 500 employees' names, including carpenters, plumbers, engineers, caterers and even gardeners.

It was the equipment being installed in the plant which interested them most. On Monday, 13 May, Cappi and Ellis, posing as prospective customers, went to High Wycombe to meet a sales manager for NAPP Systems (Europe) Ltd, suppliers of photopolymer letterpress printing plates. They had heard from one of their sources that News International was testing NAPP equipment.

The photopolymer technique was not new. Engineers at *The*

Times in Gray's Inn Road had agreed to use plastic plates in 1984 but the NGA members in the foundry had not. So a partial system was used: plastic plates were converted back to hot metal and clamped on the presses. Cappi and Ellis had been told that the NAPP equipment to be used in Wapping was the complete photopolymer technology, never before used in Fleet Street. The presses in the plant would be taking plastic plates.

'We gave them a lot of flannel,' Ellis said of the meeting in High Wycombe. 'We told them we were interested in a complete system and could we see it tested anywhere. They told us that Murdoch was testing it in Wapping but it was a secret.'

By this time, Ellis said later, 'We wanted the world to know.' But there had been little reaction from anyone. Spanswick had contacted the RIRMA Branch officials but no one seemed interested. 'Everyone was playing the political game,' said Cappi. 'No one paid any attention to us.' In a desperate move to warn people, they decided to mount an exhibition of their evidence.

On Monday, 17 June, Harry Spanswick and his deputy Pat Honeywell sat with Tony Cappi in the Spencer Suite on the first floor of the Strand Palace Hotel. On display panels round the room were photographs of Wapping, showing the equipment which News International had installed. There was a complete set of building plans pinned up. There were typed lists of people who were employed on installation work. They had prepared a carefully researched profile on Pole-Carew, whom they described as Murdoch's 'new technology adviser'.

They wrote to Brenda Dean and Bill Miles from Sogat, inviting them to the exhibition. Invitations were also sent to all the union's national officers. Dean replied quickly saying she was unable to attend as she had a meeting in Manchester. Miles declined because he had a meeting organised that day in Bouverie Street with Brian Dibb, Labour Relations Executive.[15]

Only one full-time official turned up at the exhibition – Paul Frizzell, Assistant to David Hutchinson, RIRMA Branch Secretary. Hutchinson had replied to the invitation with a letter: 'I would certainly be of the opinion that your review of the situation is not far off the given truth of the matter.'[16] By late afternoon, when no one else had arrived, they were disheartened. They packed up the exhibition and left. 'It appeared we were taken lightly,' Ellis was to say later.

Then suddenly things started to happen. Frizzell had been so surprised at what he had seen that he contacted Dean. Within a week of the abortive exhibition, a meeting was arranged. Cappi was told to go to the Waldorf Hotel with Spanswick and wait in the bar. They took along two other Chapel officials and were met there by John Mitchell, then Branch Secretary of the London Machine Branch and Secretary of the London District Council, who took them in a hired car to the TUC. They were shown to the top floor of the building, to a private apartment, where Dean and Miles were waiting for them.

Complying with tradition, the Father of the Chapel opened the conversation. Spanswick told Dean of the network of moles in the building and about the evidence they had been given. He said that if she did not listen to what they had to say she would find herself 'General Secretary of nothing'.[17]

Dean put them through what Cappi later described as an interrogation. Taking notes throughout, she said she wanted to be sure of the facts. She had been 'put through this hoop before'. Miles said nothing. There was a feeling among Chapel Fathers in Fleet Street that the General Officer always needed pushing into action. 'Unless he was steam-rollered, we never got anything out of him,' Cappi said. It was Dean they had come to see. 'There was no one else left who could help us,' he said.

'She was a breath of fresh air, I suppose,' said Cappi. 'We had finally broken down one barrier. It was unheard-of for any lay member of a Chapel to meet the General Secretary. That someone like me could have access was unheard-of in the union.'

Dean later wrote to Spanswick to thank him for the meeting. 'It is helpful,' she wrote, 'to have members who are concerned about the future and are willing to work with us to a common goal.'[18] Cappi was given what he described as 'twenty-four hour access' to Dean, and from then on he kept her supplied with a continual flow of information.

To John Mitchell, the Secretary of the union's London District Council, Dean wrote: 'I believe we should be preparing ourselves for what may well be a very difficult problem' and she had asked him to make a few discreet inquiries. She wanted to know who supplied and delivered the ink and newsprint to the Bouverie Street papers and how much was stored in the building. She also wanted to know 'to what degree the journalists are organised into the NUJ in each of the titles of both News Group Newspapers and Times Newspapers Ltd' and how many had received new-technology training. Dean told him she had requested a meeting with Murdoch as he was due in London for the celebrations for the 200th anniversary of *The Times*.[19]

In early July, Dean met Murdoch in the Waldorf Hotel where he told her he had had enough of 'obstruction and delay'. He said that the NGA was 'impossible to deal with' and was surprised that Sogat was prepared to tolerate another union having a severe influence on the best interests of its members. He said he would be returning to London in September and would meet with her then.[20] Miles remembers it as a friendly meeting which lasted about an hour. 'Murdoch reassured us,' he said later. 'He said there was nothing going on in Wapping.'[21]

It was not until Tuesday, 30 July, when Dean called together all News International Fathers and full-time officials at the assembly hall in Congress House, that some of the information from Cappi and Ellis was made public. She told them about the construction going on and said there were reports about recruitment. 'She did not give them as many details as I thought she would,' Cappi said later.

The next day, after a National Executive meeting, Sogat issued a press release. The union was to seek immediate talks with News Group Newspapers on the move of the production of the two Bouverie Street titles. Chapel members were no longer prepared to accept a delay in concluding negotiations.

At the end of the press release was a personal statement from Dean. 'The move has been delayed too long and working conditions for the employees in Bouverie Street . . . are appalling.' They were prepared to have constructive discussion on the *Post*, the move to Wapping and also, 'subject to dis-

cussion with our Branches', production of copies of the *Sun*
into Scotland, 'not at any price but based on sensible
agreements'.[22]

Throughout August, Dean and full-time Sogat and NGA
officials pressed management for a meeting. One was finally
arranged over the telephone by Bill Miles. He told Dean that
Matthews had said the presses at Wapping were going to be
tested by engineers. Miles wrote to Dean in an internal
memorandum dated 29 August that 'Mr Paul Crew has apparently recruited [those] who have considerable experience apparently with this type of work'. The memo informed Dean that
'Mr Paul Crew' would not be at the meeting as he was not on
Matthews's 'pay roll' and was directly accountable to Murdoch.[23]

The meeting took place at 9 a.m. in Bouverie Street on
Friday, 30 August. The General Secretaries and their national
and branch officials were told by Matthews that he was not
responsible for Wapping and that they should talk to Pole-
Carew. When Pole-Carew arrived, Miles remembers him
telling them that he was conducting a feasibility study into
the plant and he was not responsible for 'industrial relations
matters'. He said that no production was being carried out
and that the rumour of people being bussed in from Southampton was incorrect. The officials asked to go to Wapping.
Matthews and Pole-Carew said they could not.[24]

Miles would later describe it as a 'silly meeting'. No one
wanted to admit to responsibility for the plant. At one stage,
Matthews had got up from his chair and said he did not want
'any more of this shit'.[25]

Dean issued another statement informing her members that
the meeting with management had been helpful in 'clearing
the air of speculation concerning developments at Wapping'.

The statement went on: 'This morning we met with Mr
Bruce Matthews and Mr Pole-Carew and raised with them
the concern of our membership. I am pleased to say that they
both totally denied that any personnel were being recruited or
were currently working in the premises being trained in jobs
traditionally done by Sogat members. The electricians and
engineers working in the plant are engaged on the installation
of electrical wiring and equipment.'

Dean reported that Matthews had spoken to Murdoch in the last two days and he had confirmed that 'no agreements would be reached with any union until his visit to the UK during September'. Matthews had told Dean that Murdoch would meet her during that visit.

'Sogat also contacted the EETPU, who confirmed that their members working in Wapping were engaged on traditional electricians' work only and certainly were not doing any work which would normally be that of the members of Sogat,' the statement concluded.[26]

'I could not believe it,' said Cappi. 'She swallowed everything Pole-Carew said. If I had been there when she met him, I could have shot him to pieces.'

Ten days later, Matthews wrote a reassuring letter to Dean, reiterating the points he had made at the meeting. 'We are currently investigating the possibility of a product known as the *Post*,' he wrote, adding that Pole-Carew was undertaking a study into the type of technology that would be required for the paper's production. Murdoch would be in London towards the end of September, he told her, when he would be prepared to outline his policy on Tower Hamlets. The penultimate paragraph contained a warning: 'I must once again point out, and Mr Murdoch made this clear to me at the weekend, that his promise to meet with you and whichever other unions are involved in the traditional publication of our products at News Group Newspapers, is conditional on normal production being maintained until these discussions take place.'[27]

By now, Cappi and Ellis were not the only members warning Dean. In September she received a letter from Ted Chard, Secretary of the London Central Branch. He had been told by a contact of 'two bus-loads of people' who had gone into Wapping. 'I very seldom respond to rumours, Brenda,' he wrote, 'but I do believe this is a case of facts and it does really confirm our suspicions that on every occasion we have had an exchange with News Group, we are being told far from the truth.'[28]

The National Union of Journalists was alerted by Dean in early September about the large numbers of computer terminals which were to be installed in Wapping. Harry Conroy, General Secretary, wrote to her to say how concerned he was about the plant. 'If the company is installing anywhere near the number of terminals indicated in your letter, then the employment of journalists at Wapping would seem to be more than just a possibility,' he had replied.[29]

In the first week of September, Cappi noticed that heavy eye-bolts had been fitted to all ground-floor doors at Bouverie Street. He suspected that management was preparing for a lock-out. When he was told that a 16-page paper had been produced at Wapping, he concluded immediately that the plant was gearing up for production.

It was the last day of the TUC conference in Blackpool, on Friday, 6 September, that a dummy newspaper, printed in Wapping and smuggled out of the plant, was given to the General Secretaries of the print unions. Dean and Tony Dubbins of the NGA were sure their members would react. 'If they don't go out now,' Dean remembers saying to an official, 'they never will.' Dubbins was certain too. There was now so much evidence. He approached one of the labour correspondents covering the conference and told him not to bother to write his story. There would be no papers the next day.[30] Dubbins was wrong.

When Dean arrived back in London on the Saturday, she was sure that Murdoch's Sunday papers would be stopped. That afternoon, Bill Miles, who had been speaking with the union's Fleet Street officials, rang her at home in Islington. There would be no action. Miles told her that the Fathers had decided to wait until she had seen Murdoch at the end of the month. 'I don't believe what you are telling me,' she remembers saying.[31]

The next week, the London Machine Branch held a packed meeting at Central Hall, Westminster, calling for a twenty-four-hour strike on all News International titles. The motion, submitted by the branch committee, mentioned the 'outrageous actions of the company in introducing non-print-union scab labour into its Wapping factory despite assurances and guarantees to the contrary.'[32]

There was an impassioned debate. Roy 'Ginger' Wilson, the Father of the *Sunday Times* Machine Chapel, urged them to strike. 'If you don't come out now,' he said, 'you will lose everything we have ever fought for.'[33] There was more than enough evidence to prove that the machines were running, staffed by 'scab labour'. 'We must show Murdoch we mean business.'

Ray James, Father of the *Sun* Machine Chapel, spoke against the motion. If there was to be any action, he told them, all the branches had to strike. 'Why should we be the first to fight?' he asked. 'We are always in the firing line.' The motion was lost: 520 machine men were against strike action, 306 were for it.

Again, Cappi and Ellis thought there was now no hope of anyone heeding their warning. There had been so many lost chances. They had no faith left in their national officials. 'We just got bogged down in the politics of it,' said Cappi. But, undeterred, they set up the exhibition of evidence in Bouverie Street, in a storeroom above the Chapel office, and notified every Father in the building.

There was not a great deal of interest. Tony Isaacs, Imperial Father of the *News of the World* Machine Chapel, told Spanswick that he knew best. 'The balls are in the air . . . I'm the juggler,' he had said. Some Fathers told Cappi he was interfering with the 'due process', while others thought it beneath them to go. After all, Cappi was only a health and safety representative for a RIRMA Chapel. Members still could not understand why Cappi and Ellis, not only from different Chapels, but from different unions, were working together.

'We always thought that someone somewhere would be bright enough or intelligent enough to see what was happening,' said Cappi. 'People have always wanted what's best only for themselves in Fleet Street. There was always Chapel and inter-union rivalry. No one cared about the overall situation.'

'I said to Brenda once,' Cappi was to say months later, 'that we really needed to change how we operated. We should have got rid of all that structure and got up to date.' He was not quite sure she had understood him. 'We should get out of the cloth-cap image,' he had continued. 'The EETPU had done it.' Perhaps, he had said, that might have been too radical a change for everyone. 'But it could all have been so different.'[34]

*

Bill Miles, General Officer of Sogat, looked across the table at Bill O'Neill, Vice President, Personnel and Labor Relations, of Murdoch's News American Publishing Inc. Both men were tired. 'You need to understand,' Miles told him, 'you are talking of things which cut across the principles of our trade union which we have taken 200 years to achieve.' Like most of the meetings to negotiate the manning of the *London Post* in the last three months of 1985, it had reached stalemate very early on.

Tony Isaacs, Imperial Father, Sogat Machine Room Chapel, *News of the World*, was at Miles's side. His tirade that day was familiar. Murdoch's employees at Bouverie Street earned the company millions. 'No one you employ off the street can achieve this, nor will they.' At issue were legally binding agreements. 'Would you do us the kindness not to treat us as idiots because you will find out that is a major mistake,' Isaacs told O'Neill.

Miles, with his years of experience of Fleet Street industrial relations, could not understand why the company suddenly seemed to be digging in its heels. 'You don't seem to want to negotiate,' he said to O'Neill. They were going round in circles. Miles, in desperation, said at one stage: 'I have run out of ideas. I don't know what to do.'[35]

The new beginning which was promised at the much-awaited 30 September meeting with News International had been short-lived. The very next day, the print-union General Secretaries had been amazed to see that the verbal assault levelled against them by Murdoch as the talks had opened was published in full, covering almost half of the front page of *The Times*.

The 'splash' – the lead story – was headlined: 'Fleet Street unions agree to talks on printing plant for News International'. Two short paragraphs underneath pointed out that in a 'fresh spirit of unity' both sides were now committed to conclude an industrial-relations deal for the new *London Post* which was to be printed in Wapping.

Below was printed the text of the statement Murdoch had read to them at the Inn on the Park, in which he had lambasted them for constant disruptions, breaches of discipline, closed shops, high wages and short hours. Fleet Street industrial relations, he had said, were a national disgrace. He had told them he had been met with nothing but 'cynicism, broken promises and total opposition'. Three short crossheads – smaller headlines – broke up the text: 'A continuing disgrace', 'Little sign of progress' and 'Need for new titles'.[36]

The General Secretaries were furious. They had assumed that the only statement to be issued after the meeting was the joint press release announcing the start of negotiations for the *London Post*.

Dean wrote a letter to *The Times*, pointing out that the 30 September meeting had been the first positive step in the right direction after nearly a year of no talks at all. 'We have the commitment and good will to reach a successful conclusion. Mr Murdoch indicated that he had too, and if that joint goodwill continues then an agreement with the unions on Wapping will emerge.'[37]

When the *London Post* talks started in the middle of October, Bill O'Neill, leading the negotiations, made it clear to Sogat that there would be a 50 per cent cut in manning levels in the distribution and machine room areas in Wapping. An internal Sogat report about those first weeks of talks, prepared for head office, concluded that the major issues which had developed meant that meeting the Christmas deadline was a 'near impossibility'.

Compounding the problems was the fact that the NGA appeared to have reversed an earlier decision not to lay claim to 100 per cent membership in the machine room – at Sogat's expense. The Sogat London Machine Branch said that O'Neill had hinted that the NGA would consider a one-union agreement with the company: '. . . no details as to what was stated by the NGA were given to us', the interim report on negotiations noted.[38] The NGA was later to deny this.

Sogat officials told head office that as the plant was now going to use cold-type technology, the negotiations of manning agreements would be more difficult. They reported: 'Although persistent requests have been made for a visit to Tower Hamlets, this has been resisted by the company. They have stated that they consider when the negotiations have made constructive progress, the visit would then be appropriate.'[39]

When O'Neill met the NGA, he dropped a bombshell. He told them that the company intended to use full direct-input technology in both editorial and advertising on the *London Post*. It was the first time any national newspaper proprietor had tried to eradicate jobs traditionally organised by the powerful craft union. It would make not only the job of the compositors redundant but also those of the readers and readers' assistants. The news sent a chill round the Street's composing rooms.

At the end of October, O'Neill met the officials of the National Union of Journalists. He was with Charles Wilson, then Editorial Director of the *London Post*. Harry Conroy, General Secretary, was told that the paper's launch date was set for 17 March 1986. It would have three main editions, with a print run in the region of 600,000. They told him that 130 journalists would be needed.

O'Neill told Conroy that the company had not yet worked out proposals for his union for the *London Post*. But draft agreements had been prepared for the other print unions and were to be given to Sogat the following day.

The proposals stunned Sogat and the NGA: legally binding agreements, no strikes, management's right to manage and no closed shops. Each branch was given a document, marked 'In Confidence' and called 'London Post (Printers) Limited's Initial Proposal'. There would be no more Chapels, the company would decide manning levels and anyone who went on strike would be sacked. The document, they were told, was negotiable.

Dean reported to her National Executive Council on 6 November that the proposals were 'repugnant'. They could be interpreted, she told them, as an invitation to walk out of the talks. 'This would be fatal in my view,' she added.[40]

It was the NGA who took the next step. On Friday, 22 November, they conceded direct inputting to News International for the *London Post*. The historic move which could lead the whole of Fleet Street to change to computerised production was made in a letter to O'Neill. 'We wanted to find out if there was serious intent,' said Alf Parish, the NGA's National Secretary. O'Neill, said Parish, pushed the offer aside: 'We intend to have that anyway.'[41]

The NGA's concession had come with a condition. Tony Dubbins, the General Secretary of the NGA, explained his position four days later at a meeting of the Printing Industries Committee of the TUC.

Dubbins had told the company he would concede direct input only if there was a common approach to all unions. He told the other print-union officials that News International's management did not appear to have taken a consistent line with all of them. The NGA had been asked if it was prepared to sign a single-union agreement. It had not been. At the same time, management was promising the EETPU members, 'recruited in Southampton to install printing machinery, permanent jobs once the production was underway'. It was in everyone's interest that there be a common approach.[42] They agreed to hold a special meeting in early December.

By the time that meeting took place on 9 December, every General Secretary had received a letter from Norman Willis, TUC General Secretary, urging them to adopt a 'common approach'. The leaders of the five unions, Sogat, NGA, AUEW, EETPU and the NUJ, decided that they would jointly reject Murdoch's proposals and tell him they were ready to negotiate 'the introduction of agreements which will provide for flexibility and avoid disruption . . . and promote close inter-union working'. They decided to ask for an urgent meeting with Murdoch.

They met Murdoch on Tuesday, 10 December. He was firm. He told them they had no 'God-given right' to be in Wapping.[43] 'I've had seventeen years of hell,' he said. No one would go to Tower Hamlets without a legally binding agreement. Those currently employed by the company would not automatically transfer to the new plant and management would have total right to select the staff. He told them that as long as there was no agreement for the *London Post*, it was 'nothing to do with them' if he decided to print an extra million copies in Wapping. He ended the meeting by telling them that the next move was theirs.[44]

Tom Rice, National Secretary of the EETPU, had arrived fifteen minutes late. During the first adjournment, he told the print-union officials that they ought to know that his Executive was not opposed to legally binding agreements and that they recognised the management's right to manage and supported binding arbitration to avoid strikes. In Rice's hand was a press release detailing the EETPU's response to the four clauses. It had been given to the press at midday before the meeting started. 'It was clear to us that Murdoch was probably aware of that press statement even before meeting with us,' Dean said.

She asked Rice if it was likely that the EETPU would seek a single-union agreement with the company. She later reported: 'Tom Rice said that he could not answer . . . it was a matter for his Executive Council.' Dean pressed him further, asking him if he realised that the unions were now divided. 'Don't you realise how serious that is?' she had said.

After the adjournment, Dean asked Murdoch to reconsider and amend the four clauses. She suggested that all unions negotiate with him jointly. His reply made it clear that he was not going to budge. 'Don't go away believing there's any likelihood I'll change my mind,' he had said.[45]

The next day, Wednesday, 11 December, the four unions met Ken Graham, Deputy General Secretary of the TUC, and registered a complaint against the EETPU.

When Dean discussed strike action with the Secretaries of her nine London Branches the following week, the situation looked grim. They believed that Wapping was ready to run and could produce the *Sun*. But they decided that no ballot should take place before Christmas.

On Thursday, 19 December, as the Christmas deadline for the *London Post* approached, the company decided to extend it –but only for the EETPU. The gap between the electricians and the other unions was widening. Willis summoned all the unions involved to the TUC under Rule 11, thus raising the possibility of disciplinary action against any member not accepting TUC advice.[46]

A day later, talks for manning the *London Post* broke down. The General Secretaries and officials of the four unions, Sogat, NGA, AUEW and NUJ, tried, each in turn, to persuade O'Neill to withdraw the legally binding no-strike clauses. It was a gruelling four and a half hours for them all. O'Neill told them he could not substitute the legally binding clause: if they were not prepared to accept that, there was no point in meeting again.

'O'Neill and I looked at each other,' Miles recalled. 'We were exhausted.' He said they had talked for hours and hours and had got nowhere. 'We could sit here till dawn. Let's leave it there,' said Miles. He remembered them standing up together and shaking each other by the hand. 'In the end,' he said, 'there was nothing more to say.'

Parish said later that he knew there had been no prospect of agreement as O'Neill seemed determined to stand his ground. 'It was like seeing a film for the second time round that had not been any good the first time.'

That weekend, on Sunday, 22 December, Dean spoke to O'Neill on the telephone. He had called her at home in the early evening. 'What are you doing?' she had asked him. 'I thought you had gone home for Christmas.' He had replied that he had been waiting for her to call him. Dean remembers being surprised. 'If you are ready to talk, we can meet tomorrow,' she had told him.

She later recalled: 'O'Neill told me that was not possible as Murdoch was skiing in Colorado. He said if he negotiated the legally binding agreement, he would be fired. I told him in that case I could not get involved and he ended the conversation by telling me I had arrived on the scene too late.'[47]

On Monday morning, Sogat and the NGA took the offensive. Miles wrote to Bruce Matthews to tell him that the union was amending its claim in the forthcoming revision of their agreements with both News Group Newspapers and Times Newspapers Ltd. 'The unions are concerned about the security of their members' employment at Bouverie Street and Gray's Inn Road,' he wrote. Sogat now wanted a guarantee of employment for their News International members and index-linked wage increases. If there was any transfer of work to Wapping, the company had to guarantee that their members would be offered jobs.

The last paragraph of Miles's letter contained a threat. The union wanted to avoid industrial action but if the company was not prepared to discuss the claims, there would be no alternative.[48]

On Christmas Eve, O'Neill wrote to Dean from America. 'I was disappointed last Sunday when you confirmed to me that the unions did not intend meeting with me again over the

Tower Hamlets plant.' He told her he had had difficulty understanding the unions' opposition to a sound agreement backed by law with 'provisions and a built-in mechanism to eliminate disputes'. The proposal had many clauses he had been prepared to negotiate, delete or amend, but whatever they agreed had to be legally enforceable.

'The statements expressed by union leaders to Mr Murdoch at our hotel meeting on September 30 led us to believe there could be a change of attitude,' he wrote, 'but if the unions were not prepared to join us in entering into an agreement that was designed to ensure both sides honoured it . . . it is regrettable to say the least.'[49]

After Christmas, Murdoch issued another statement, which was printed in *The Times*. The deadline had passed and as the talks with the print unions had broken down, he was bringing Tower Hamlets and Kinning Park into a 'state of operational readiness' both for the launch of the *Post* and to enable the company to 'meet the urgent requirements of other group newspapers'. The unions, he said, had failed to address the four points put forward in the proposal in any 'realistic fashion'. The main stumbling block appeared to have been the failure of the unions to accept the principle of legally binding collective agreements.[50]

On New Year's Eve, Bill Gillespie wrote to Miles, turning down his union's claim for index-linked pay increases and jobs for life. The Managing Director of Times Newspapers Ltd told Miles there was something 'highly artificial' about the claims. It was not without 'significance' that they should come within days of the breakdown of talks over the *London Post*. Gillespie had found the last paragraph of Miles's letter 'most unfortunate'. He wrote: '. . . your letter suggests very strongly that if your points are not met, and quickly at that, your members will not hesitate to break their contracts by taking industrial action.'

Gillespie told Miles that all that had been established was that Sogat, NGA and the AUEW would not be recognised by London Post (Printers) Ltd. Significantly, he did not mention the electricians' and the journalists' unions.

The letter, which Gillespie's secretary also sent to the General Secretaries of the other unions and to Norman

Willis, ended: 'On a personal note, my best wishes to you for 1986'.[51]

Murdoch flew back to London from his skiing holiday early in the New Year. News International announced that he was to take charge of the talks for the *London Post*, which was still on course for 17 March. The company was prepared to hold meetings with the NUJ and the EETPU. Negotiations with the other three unions were at an end.

On 8 January, Harry Conroy, General Secretary of the NUJ, met journalists from *The Times* and *Sunday Times* and told them that the union would consider any deal offered 'in consultation with the other unions and the TUC'. And he added that he thought the *London Post* was 'a sham'. The company's plan, he believed, was to switch some or all of the titles to Wapping.[52]

The next day it was the company which assumed the offensive. Both Times Newspapers Ltd and News Group Newspapers gave six months' notice of termination of all union agreements with 5,500 News International members of Sogat, NGA, AUEW and the EETPU. Only the journalists were exempt. This did not mean that the contracts of employment had been altered, Gillespie wrote to Sogat. 'These contracts remain terminable with appropriate notice, or without notice, depending on the circumstances.'[53] They all knew a crisis could not be far away.

On Sunday, 12 January, the *Sunday Times* carried a front-page announcement that a section of the paper would be printed in Wapping the next week. 'For years the *Sunday Times* has been under production restraints which have limited it to a maximum of 80 pages. But next week it will be even greater value for money – with four sections totalling at least 96 pages. This additional section has been made possible by the commissioning of News International's spectacular new printing plant at Tower Hamlets in London's docklands.'

On the Monday, Dean told news reporters that the 'consequences would be serious'. She was not prepared to see her members treated like 'eighteenth-century mill workers or Australian convicts'.[54] She said: 'Mr Murdoch and his lieutenants have assessed this and prefer some kind of macho showdown rather than sensible, rational negotiations.'

Murdoch issued his own statement: the unions had failed to accept 'our sensible and reasonable demand that any agreement would be legally binding on both sides. Printing extra sections or copies of existing publications in no way breached any industrial agreements.'[55]

Dean asked Norman Willis to step in. On the Wednesday, the TUC General Secretary met Eric Hammond of the EETPU at Congress House. Hammond argued that the mere pursuit of separate negotiations by the EETPU did not conflict with Willis's formal advice on joint negotiations. The meeting ended with Willis writing a formal request to Hammond to take steps to stop his members producing the *Sunday Times* section in Wapping that weekend.

The print run went ahead. The special section, printed in Wapping and inserted into the 19 January edition of the paper, carried the most revealing interview Rupert Murdoch had ever given about Wapping. Headlined 'The Future of Fleet Street', it led the 12-page 'Innovation Special'. His answers about the plant were fitted between an editorial on the 'national disgrace' of Fleet Street and a quarter-page advertisement from the London Docklands Development Corporation.

In the unsigned interview conducted by Mike Hoy, who was then Acting Editor of the *London Post*,[56] Murdoch was asked why a legally binding, no-strike agreement was so important to him. He replied: 'Newspapers are under threat all over the world from electronic competition, and in many countries there is a decline of readership. The greatest asset newspapers have is the habit factor. We cannot afford to go on interrupting that.'

His response to a question on whether he had the capacity to print all four titles at Wapping was: 'We don't want to do that because of course we don't have sufficient presses to do that satisfactorily. We want to start the *Post* there and we want to put work there as we grow out of our existing two plants. But if we are struck in the manner in which the unions are now threatening, then we will have no choice but to try and keep producing as best we can. It is both our duty to do that as publishers and our obligation as business people.'

There were twenty-two advertisements in the section from

companies that had helped to create the plant. Atex, in a full-page ad, proclaimed itself 'The only choice for today's publishing environment.' Opposite was a picture of forest scenery with congratulations from the Finnish newsprint supplier, Finnpap, and its London distributor, Lamco Ltd. Pipe- and duct-fitters, surveyors, caterers, accountants, fabricators and floor finishers all added their best wishes.

A full-page ad for Ferag AG, the Swiss company that provided paper-handling equipment, pictured a newspaper with the words 'Partner to the world's printers' bannered across the top. 'Where the future happens first', was the message of the computer engineering firm, Siemens Ltd. Marine Bank invited loan queries from business people who 'can demonstrate a highly motivated and imaginative approach to management'.

'Wimpey meets newspaper deadlines', the building contractor announced in bold three-inch letters. Rockwell International, owner of press manufacturers Goss Products, displayed a picture of the space shuttle *Columbia* with the line that Rockwell both prints and makes news. NAPP Systems featured its slick, state of the art presses that turn out plastic printing plates.

In between the commercial messages were articles about the plant and its dockland surroundings. Photographs contrasted an aerial shot of the congestion of Fleet Street with a view of the new plant from 'St Katherine's Dock, transformed to a setting for luxury homes'. A map for the docklands area accompanied stories about the area's booming development. 'Wapping . . . has seen a spectacular change in its fortunes, and now rivals more traditional riverside locations such as Chelsea in terms of property prices.'

Another article titled 'Drama of Project X' told how the computers 'were installed in a secret operation that sounds more like an old thriller than a story about high technology'. It described the undercover company set up to buy equipment, the company's packing crates spray-painted to obscure its name, and orders it placed for unrelated equipment in order to cover its tracks.

Along with Murdoch's interview – and the section itself – the Project X story confirmed that the plant could print more than one newspaper. 'Although Atex is coy about some of the figures involved at Wapping, it becomes clear that the system would be capable of handling more than the *London Post*.'

The story as originally filed from America by journalist Will Ellsworth-Jones was more explicit. It read: '. . . it becomes clear that they were being asked for a system that would serve all four of Murdoch's existing titles – the *Sun*, the *News of the World*, *The Times* and the *Sunday Times*. Indeed, in an afternoon's conversation with Atex officials, the new Murdoch evening newspaper supposed to be launched at Wapping, the *Post*, was not mentioned once.'[57]

The main message of the section came in the editorial, and it was loud and clear:

'Wapping represents the Fleet Street of the future, in which the latest technology goes hand-in-hand with progressive labour practices. While newspapers have continually lectured the rest of British industry on its inadequacies, Fleet Street itself has remained a microcosm of Britain's industrial malaise at its worse: ridiculous overmanning; absurd restrictive practices; pusillanimous management; top-of-the-league pay levels which bear little relation to the work done or the skills involved; and the technology of the nineteenth century. Both government and private inquiries had recommended that Fleet Street should 'put its shameful house in order. But the arrogance of print-union power and the abdication of managerial control have always conspired to keep things as they are.'

'Fleet Street is, in effect, a cartel – a conspiracy against the consumer,' the editorial went on, because the costs of out-of-date technology and 'crazy labour practices' were passed along to readers and advertisers.

But, it declared: 'Change is coming to Fleet Street and faster than most people think: direct input of copy by journalists, progressive labour agreements and the latest techniques are all on their way . . . the question is no longer if this will happen, but only how, and the answer to that lies very much in the hands of the print unions.'

The piece had a grim conclusion. 'It will be a painful process of adaptation for some of the country's most conservative unions, but it is inevitable if the print unions are to survive the coming revolution. Their alternative, of course, is to use their industrial muscle to try to keep things as they are. But that way they risk losing everything.'

When it came to the question about conflict with print unions over Wapping, the Murdoch interview revealed: 'There is no dispute. They have refused to work at Wapping and agreements are in place at our existing plants.'

Asked what would happen if, in fact, the unions decided not to strike, Murdoch replied: 'Well, my fingers are crossed. Of course, we would then have to negotiate house agreements that are coming up and try to get improved efficiencies in the existing two plants. We are looking for security of production, greater capacity, modern competitive costs, and flexible working practices.'

On Wednesday, 22 January, the unions announced the results of their strike ballots. In an eleven-page document, explaining the background to the dispute, Sogat's National Executive Council recommended a 'yes' vote. 'If a strike does take place,' Dean wrote, 'it could possibly develop into the most important industrial dispute this union has had since the war.' There had clearly been a deliberate attempt to 'provoke conflict'. She warned her members that if they did strike, they would be in breach of their contracts.

A majority of 82 per cent of Sogat members balloted voted for strike action: 3,534 to 752. The NGA vote was 843 to 117. 'We are not looking for a dispute,' said Dubbins after the announcement, 'but we will not shrink away from a dispute if what we have to do is to defend our members' employment.' Dean still pushed for negotiation. She said she wanted to give the company one last opportunity to resolve the crisis.

Murdoch, in what he described as a 'final appeal', wrote a two-page letter to all his News International employees telling them that for five years, through 'consultation and scores of meetings', he had tried to agree a way of bringing Tower Hamlets into production. '. . . I have told the unions concerned this morning through ACAS, that our door is open for talks on Gray's Inn Road and Bouverie Street. I still hope that we can avoid the strike action that has been threatened. I want us to continue to produce our titles at both the existing plants, at the same time as we see our needed expansion going ahead at Tower Hamlets.'[58]

A meeting was hurriedly arranged. Murdoch was offered an unprecedented package – the best ever offered to a national newspaper proprietor. The print union General Secretaries gave away Chapel power. They would agree to binding arbitration triggered by either side.

This last meeting failed to avert the dispute. The next day, 5,500 print workers went on strike. It was Friday, 24 January 1986, and it was the end of the Street.

Epilogue

The following week, the *Guardian* announced that it would change over to computer typesetting. It involved moving production from Fleet Street to docklands and cutting 200 employees from the staff of 1,000. 'There is precious little time,' Managing Director Harry Roche warned in a letter to all staff. 'We must go to direct input and the all-electronic newsroom to be competitive.' Its £23 million plant in the docklands area was due to become operational in autumn 1987.

The week after that Associated Newspapers announced that it would move the *Daily Mail, Mail on Sunday* and *London Standard* to South London by 1988. The company was spending £100 million on the move, 600 people would be cut from its staff of 4,200 but the eventual goal was to halve the staff.

In May, United Newspapers said it was considering a move out of Fleet Street for the *Sunday* and *Daily Express* and the *Daily Star.* The company was to decide about the move by the end of the year.

In July, the *Financial Times* announced that it would move its printworks and it was looking for a site in the East India Docks. The target date for a complete switch to direct-input typesetting was 1988. Cuts of 400 were expected from its staff of 1,500.

In September 1986 the *Daily* and *Sunday Telegraphs* announced that they would print in docklands and the company was looking for a South London site for their editorial offices. It aimed to cut 2,000 from its staff of 3,300.

The *Observer* planned to move its editorial offices to Battersea in March 1987. The paper would be printed in regional centres at Portsmouth, Bradford, Peterborough and Worcester. Its goal was a 500 cut in a staff of 1,200.

The Mirror Group Newspapers planned to move the *Daily Mirror, Sunday Mirror* and *Sunday People* to a docklands plant in spring 1987. The company already had an agreement to cut its staff of 6,000 to 3,900.

The Cast

(Titles as at January 1986)

Sir Peter Abeles, founder and world chairman of Thomas Nationwide Transport, Inc. (TNT)

Ken Ashton, former General Secretary of the National Union of Journalists (NUJ)

David Banks, Executive Editor of the *Sun*, in charge of direct-input equipment and training at Wapping

Tom Bell, Manager of the Newsfact Division of TNT Inc.

Don Berry, Executive Features Editor of the *Sunday Times*

John Breen, Deputy Imperial Father of the NGA *News of the World* Composing Room Chapel

Bert Brown, member of the EETPU Southampton branch committee and former shop steward at Vospers Thorneycroft Shipbuilders

Tony Britton, former Assistant General Manager of News Group Newspapers Ltd

John Brown, Imperial Father of the NGA *Sun* Composing Room Chapel

Ronald A. Brumback, President of Atex Inc. USA

Tony Cappi, Health and Safety representative for the Sogat Revisers, Ink and Roller Makers and Auxiliaries (RIRMA) Engineers' Assistants' Chapel in Bouverie Street

Harry Conroy, General Secretary of the National Union of Journalists (NUJ)

John Cowley, Joint General Manager of News International

Brenda Dean, General Secretary of the Society of Graphical and Allied Trades (Sogat '82)

Tony Dubbins, General Secretary of the National Graphical Association (NGA)

Vic Dunn, Father of the NGA *Sunday Times* Machine Managers Chapel

Les Elliott, London divisional organiser for the Amalgamated Union of Engineering Workers (AUEW)

Terry Ellis, deputy Father of the AUEW Chapel in Bouverie Street

Sean Geraghty, Secretary of the EETPU London Press Branch

Ken Gill, General Secretary of TASS, and Chairman of TUC General Council (5 February 1986)

Bill Gillespie, Managing Director of Times Newspapers Ltd

Eric Hammond, General Secretary of the Electrical, Electronic Telecommunications and Plumbing Union (EETPU)

Ernie Hardcastle, Deputy Father of the Sogat *Sun* Machine Room Chapel

Joan Herring, Atex Manager for 'Project X'

Tony Isaacs, Imperial Father of the Sogat *News of the World* Machine Chapel

Ray James, Father of the Sogat *Sun* Machine Room Chapel

John Keating, Technical Director for News America Inc.

Kelvin MacKenzie, Editor of the *Sun*

John Manaras, Vice President and General Counsul of Atex Inc. USA

Bruce Matthews, Managing Director of News International

Robert Maxwell, Chairman of Mirror Group Newspapers

Bill Miles, General Officer of Sogat

John Mitchell, former Secretary of Sogat London Machine

Branch and former Secretary of Sogat London District
Council

Rupert Murdoch, proprietor and Chairman of News International

Greg Neale, Father of *The Times* NUJ Chapel

Andrew Neil, Editor of the *Sunday Times*

Bill O'Neill, Vice President for Personnel and Labor Relations for News America Publishing Inc.

Tony Norbury, Production Editor of the *London Post*

Patrick O'Hanlon, Area official EETPU, Motherwell

Bob O'Hagan, security consultant for News International

Alf Parish, National Secretary of the NGA

Sir Edward Pickering, Executive Vice President of Times Newspapers Ltd

Christopher Pole-Carew, consultant to News International

Tom Rice, National Secretary of the EETPU

Geoffrey Richards, lawyer, partner of Farrer and Co

Peter Roberts, Managing Editor of the *Sunday Times*

Mick Scanlon, Area Secretary EETPU, Southampton

Eddie Shah, founder of *Today* newspaper

Mike Smith, National Organiser of the NUJ

Ben Smylie, Atex Manager of News International account

Harry Spanswick, Father of Sogat RIRMA Engineers' Assistants Chapel in Bouverie Street

Ken Taylor, Technical Director, News Group Newspapers

Charles Tucker, Father of the AUEW Chapel in Bouverie Street

Norman Willis, General Secretary of the Trades Union Congress (TUC)

Charles Wilson, Editor of *The Times*

Roy 'Ginger' Wilson, Father of Sogat *Sunday Times* Machine Room Chapel

Sources

CHAPTER ONE

1. Minutes of a meeting between News International and representatives of Sogat '82, NGA, AUEW and NUJ, held at the Park Lane Hotel, London, on 23 January 1986. Minutes prepared by Geoffrey Richards, Farrer & Co.

2. Interview with Brenda Dean, General Secretary, Sogat '82, 8 May 1986, London.

3. Barrie Clement, 'Fleet Street unions agree to talks on printing plant for News International', *The Times*, 1 October 1985.

4. Interview with Harry Conroy, General Secretary, NUJ, 6 May 1986, London, and minutes of a meeting between News International and representatives of Sogat '82, NGA, AUEW and NUJ, held at the Park Lane Hotel, London, on 23 January 1986. Minutes prepared by Geoffrey Richards, Farrer & Co.

5. 'Statement on Post talks failure', *The Times*, 30 December 1985.

6. Interview with Tony Dubbins, General Secretary, NGA, 5 June 1986, London.

7. The News Corporation Limited Annual Report 1985.

8. Interviews with Tony Dubbins, General Secretary, NGA, 5 June 1986, London; Alf Parish, National Secretary, NGA, 1 May 1986, London; Harry Conroy, General Secretary, NUJ, 6 May 1986, London; Mike Smith, National Organiser, NUJ, 30 May 1986, London; Brenda Dean, General Secretary, Sogat '82, 8 May 1986, London; Bill Miles, General Officer, Sogat '82, 14 May 1986, Southend.

9. 'Print union's new woman chief wants jaw, not war', *Daily Telegraph*, 11 March 1985.

10. David Goodhart and Patrick Wintour, *Eddie Shah and the Newspaper Revolution* (London: Coronet, 1986).

11. Interview with Harry Conroy, General Secretary, NUJ, 6 May 1986, London.

12. Interview with Alf Parish, National Secretary, NGA, 1 May 1986, London.

13. Interview with Bill Miles, General Officer, Sogat '82, 14 May 1986, Southend.

14. Transcript of press conference given by Rupert Murdoch on 23 January 1986, taken from recording by Nick Jones, Labour Correspondent, BBC Radio.

CHAPTER TWO

1. The News Corporation Limited Annual Report 1985.

2. Letter dated 14 April 1982 from R. James, Father, Sun Machine Chapel, Sogat '82, to B. Matthews, Managing Director, News Group Newspapers Ltd.

3. Minutes of meeting held on 6 September 1984 at 3 p.m. at the Tower Hamlets Conference Centre between A. Britton, Labour Relations Manager, News Group Newspapers Ltd, and A. Isaacs, Imperial Father, Sun Machine Chapel, Sogat '82.

4. David Goodhart and Patrick Wintour, *Eddie Shah and the Newspaper Revolution* (London: Coronet, 1986).

5. 'Summary of Noise Surveys for Members of the Newspaper Publishers Association Ltd', by W. I. Acton, Senior Consultant, Institute of Sound and Vibration Control, University of Southampton. Project Number 1551/C9/F5, Report Number 1970 (July 1977).

6. Letter dated 28 January 1986, ref. PBM. 5/86, from B. Dean, General Secretary, Sogat '82, to all Branch Secretaries, Sogat '82.

7. Minutes of meeting held on 31 August 1983 between W. O'Neill, Tower Hamlets Project Director, News Group Newspapers Ltd, and the NGA/Sogat '82 Sun Machine Joint Chapel.

8. Minutes of meeting held on 14 September 1983 between W. O'Neill, Tower Hamlets Project Director, News Group Newspapers Ltd, and the NGA/Sogat '82 Sun Machine Joint Chapel.

9. News Group Limited computer print out, 'Plate Breaks, 1984/1985'.

10. *Ibid.*

11. Minutes of meeting held on 6 September 1983 between W. O'Neill, Tower Hamlets Project Director, News Group Newspapers Ltd, and the NGA/Sogat '82 Sun Machine Joint Chapel.

12. 'Injunction against Sun unions', *The Times*, 25 March 1985.

13. Mark Hollingsworth, 'Sun lock-out linked to Murdoch plans for Post?', *New Statesman*, 29 March 1985.

14. Letter dated 17 April 1985 (dictated 10 April 1985), ref. EH/GP/568, from Eve Horwood, Health and Safety Adviser, Sogat '82, to B. Dean, General Secretary, Sogat '82.

15. Letter dated 25 April 1985, ref. JM:JN, from J. Mitchell, Secretary London Machine Branch, Sogat '82, to A. Fisher, Production Director, News Group Newspapers Ltd.

16. Letter dated 7 May 1985, ref. NR/EL, from N. Ratty, H.M. Inspector of Factories, to W. Sooby, Company Safety Officer, News Group Newspapers Ltd.

17. Interview with Richard Davies, Imperial Father, NGA Composing Room, *Daily Express*, 29 May 1986.

18. *The London Compositor*, edited by Ellic Howe (London: The Bibliographic Society, 1947).

19. London Society of Compositors, Newspaper Scales of Charges, for Daily, Evening and Sunday Newspapers, 29 December 1947.

20. Interview with John Tebb, Father, Lino Operators, the *Sun*, 30 May 1986.

21. Eric Jacobs, *Stop Press – The Inside Story of the Times Dispute* (London: Andre Deutsch, 1980).

22. Letter dated 11 October 1984 from B. Matthews, Managing Director, News Group Newspapers Ltd, to R. James, Father, Sun Machine Chapel, Sogat '82.

23. Letter dated 21 January 1986 from A. Fisher, Production Director, News Group Newspapers Ltd, to R. James, Father, *Sun* Machine Chapel, Sogat '82.

24. Letter dated 5 March 1981 from Rupert Murdoch to R. James, Father, *Sun* Machine Chapel, Natsopa.

25. Letter dated 10 April 1985 from R. James, Father, *Sun* Machine Chapel, Sogat '82, to Rupert Murdoch.

26. Letter dated 11 June, 1981 from Rupert Murdoch to R. James, Father, *Sun* Machine Chapel, Natsopa.

27. Letter dated 31 October 1985 from R. James, Father, *Sun* Machine Chapel, Sogat '82, to Rupert Murdoch.

28. Letter dated 11 June 1983, ref. AJI/NBI, from A. Isaacs, Imperial Father, *Sun* Machine Chapel, Sogat '82, to W. O'Neill, Tower Hamlets Project Director, News Group Newspapers Ltd.

29. Minutes of meeting held on 12 September 1983 between W. O'Neill, Tower Hamlets Project Director, News Group Newspapers Ltd, and A. Isaacs, Imperial Father, *Sun* Machine Chapel, Sogat '82.

30. Minutes of meeting held on 20 October 1983 between W. O'Neill, Tower Hamlets Project Director, News Group Newspapers Ltd, and A. Isaacs, Imperial Father, *Sun* Machine Chapel, Sogat '82.

31. Letter dated 12 January 1985 from A. Isaacs, Imperial Father, *Sun* Machine Chapel, Sogat '82, to A. Britton, Labour Relations Manager, News Group Newspapers Ltd.

32. Minutes of meeting held on 11 April 1985 between A. Britton, Labour Relations Manager, News Group Newspapers Ltd, and A. Isaacs, Imperial Father, *Sun* Machine Chapel, Sogat '82.

33. Letter dated 6 April 1985 from A. Isaacs, Imperial Father, *Sun* Machine Chapel, Sogat '82, to B. Matthews, Managing Director, News Group Newspapers Ltd.

34. Letter dated 6 December 1985 from A. Isaacs, Imperial Father, *Sun* Machine Chapel, Sogat '82, to A. Fisher, Production Director, News Group Newspapers Ltd.

35. Letter dated 18 December 1985 from A. Fisher, Production Director, New Group Newspapers Ltd, to A. Isaacs, Imperial Father, *Sun* Machine Chapel, Sogat '82.

CHAPTER THREE

1. Henry Porter, *Lies, Damned Lies and Some Exclusives* (London: Chatto & Windus, 1984).

2. Alastair Hetherington, *News, Newspapers and Television* (London: Macmillan, 1985).

3. Henry Porter, *op. cit.*

4. Tom Baistow, *Fourth-Rate Estate* (London: Comedia, 1985).

5. 'Independent Sun pledge', *The Times*, 4 September 1969.

6. *Sun*, 15 November 1969.

7. *Sun*, 17 November 1969.

8. *Sun*, 22 November 1969.

9. Anthony Smith, *The British Press Since The War – Sources for Contemporary Issues* (Newton Abbot: David & Charles, 1974).

10. Robert Harris, *Gotcha! – The Media, the Government and the Falklands Crisis* (London: Faber, 1983).

11. *Ibid.*

12. *Ibid.*

13. Simon Jenkins, *Newspapers – The Power and the Money* (London: Faber, 1979).

14. 'Sun peace talks fail after eight hours', Donald Mcintyre, *The Times*, 1 August 1978.

15. Interview with executive members, National Union of Journalists, 5–8 April 1986.

16. Interview with John Hill, sub-editor, *Sun*, 2 May 1986.

17. Transcript of address to staff by Editor of the *Sun*, Kelvin Mac-Kenzie, Friday, 24 January 1986 (tape in possession of author).

18. Letter dated 24 October 1985 from O. Duke, Committee Member, *Sun* National Union of Journalists Chapel, to H. Conroy, General Secretary, National Union of Journalists.

19. Dorothy Byrne, 'Union World', Granada Television.

20. *Ibid.*

CHAPTER FOUR

1. 'The "Times" voices that are educating Charlie', Michael Davie, *Observer*, 13 January 1985.

2. Michael Leapman, *Barefaced Cheek – The apotheosis of Rupert Murdoch* (London: Hodder and Stoughton, 1983).

3. *Ibid.*

4. *Ibid.*

5. *Ibid.*

6. *Ibid.*

7. 'Throwaway lines saved for posterity', Philip Howard, *The Times*, 2 January 1985.

8. Michael Leapman, *op. cit.*

9. Harold Evans, *Good Times, Bad Times* (London: Weidenfeld and Nicolson, 1983).

10. 'There's more than one road to success', *UK Press Gazette*, 4 November 1985.

11. 'The London Times: Thunderer or trained seal?', R. W. Apple Jr, *New York Times* Service, *Herald Tribune*, 11 October 1984.

12. 'Is that a fact?', Ian Jack, *Spectator*, 26 April 1986.

13. Meeting of *Times* journalists addressed by the Editor, Charles Wilson, on Wednesday, 6 November 1985. Notes taken by senior *Times* executive.

14. Interview with News International Executive, 15 July 1986, London.

15. Meeting of *Times* journalists addressed by the Editor, Charles Wilson, 8.20 p.m., Friday, 24 January 1986. Notes taken by Martin Huckerby, former Assistant Foreign News Editor, *The Times*.

16. Interviews with *Times* journalists, 15 July 1986, London.

17. 'Why I could not board the bus to Wapping', Martin Huckerby, former Assistant Foreign News Editor, *The Times*, *UK Press Gazette*, 3 February 1986.

18. Interview with Greg Neale, former Father, NUJ *Times* Chapel, 14 July 1986, London.

19. 'To Wapping, with principles still intact', Clifford Longley, Religious Affairs Correspondent, *The Times*, in *The Times*, 5 February 1986.

20. 'Chapels roofless under the storm', *New Statesman*, 7 February 1986.

21. Michael Leapman, *op. cit.*

CHAPTER FIVE

1. Harold Evans, *Good Times, Bad Times* (London: Weidenfeld and Nicolson, 1983).

2. 'The View from the Goldfish Bowl', profile of Andrew Neil, *Guardian*, 22 October 1983.

3. *Ibid.*

4. 'Nightmare on Fleet Street: Andrew Neil and the Brothers', *Media Week*, 8 February 1985.

5. *Ibid.*

6. 'The Nouveau-Right Sunday Times', *Literary Review*, January 1985.

7. 'The View from the Goldfish Bowl'.

8. *Ibid.*

9. 'The Nouveau-Right Sunday Times'.

10. David Goodhart and Patrick Wintour, *Eddie Shah and the Newspaper Revolution* (London: Hodder and Stoughton, 1986).

11. 'The View from the Goldfish Bowl'.

12. 'Rupert Murdoch and The Sunday Times: A Lamp Goes Out, The first of a series of occasional articles examining the state of the British Press', Hugo Young, *Political Quarterly*, Vol. 35, No. 4, October–December 1984.

13. Interview with Don Berry, former Executive Editor Features, *Sunday Times*, 12 April 1986.

14. Harold Evans, *op. cit.*

15. Interview with Don Berry, 12 April 1986.

16. *Ibid.*

17. *Ibid.*

18. *Ibid.*

19. Transcript of 'This Week Next Week', BBC 1 TV programme, transmitted 2 February 1986. (Transcript in possession of author.)

20. Interview with Roy Wilson, Father, Sogat Machine Chapel, *Sunday Times*, 27 April 1986.

21. *Ibid.*

22. *Ibid.*

23. Letter dated 15 January 1986 from Nigel Harris, Father, NUJ Chapel *Sunday Times*, to W. Gillespie, Managing Director, Times Newspapers Ltd.

24. Letter dated 16 January 1986 from W. Gillespie, Managing Director, Times Newspapers Ltd, to Nigel Harris, Father, NUJ Chapel, *Sunday Times*.

25. Interview with David Blundy, former Middle East Correspondent, *Sunday Times*, 10 February 1986.

26. Interview with Don Berry, 12 April 1986.

27. Interview with David Blundy, 10 February 1986.

CHAPTER SIX

1. Interview with senior executive, News International, 27 July 1986, London.

2. Interview with Vic Dunn, NGA Father, Machine Managers' Chapel, *Sunday Times*, 7 August 1986.

3. Barrie Clement, 'Fleet Street unions agree to talks on printing plant for News International', *The Times*, 1 October 1985.

4. *Ibid.*

5. Interview with Bill Miles, General Officer, Sogat, 6 August 1986, London.

6. Barrie Clement, 'Fleet Street unions agree to talks on printing plant for News International', *The Times*, 1 October 1985.

7. *Akron Beacon Journal*, 3 January 1985, quoting a television interview with Rupert Murdoch.

8. Interview with senior executive, News International, 27 July 1986, London.

9. Hilary Robinson, 'The man defending Murdoch's front line', *Marketing Week*, 25 July 1986.

10. *Ibid.*

11. Interviews with executive, News International, 8 July 1986, London, and senior manager, News Group Newspapers, 18 June 1986, London.

12. Interview with senior executive, News Corporation, 11 May 1986, London.

13. Affidavit of Charles Martin Wilson, sworn July 1986, Queen's Bench Division, High Court of Justice.

14. Stephen Cook, 'War of words in Nottingham press battle', *Guardian*, 8 February 1979.

15. Interview with Christopher Pole-Carew, 13 August 1986, London.

16. Interview with senior executive, News Corporation, 10 June 1986.

17. Interview with Christopher Pole-Carew, 13 August 1986, London.

18. 'A 24-hour Post from Murdoch', *Sunday Telegraph*, 10 March 1985.

19. Affidavit of Charles Martin Wilson, sworn July 1986, Queen's Bench Division, High Court of Justice.

20. Robert G. Kaiser, 'The Strike at the Washington Post', Appendix IV, *New Technology – The American Experience*, Report of Sogat Study Group's Visit to USA and Canada Newspaper Industry 1985.

21. *Ibid.*

22. Chalmers M. Roberts, *The Washington Post; The First 100 Years*, (Boston: Houghton Mifflin, 1977).

23. *Ibid.*

24. Interviews senior executives, News Corporation, 15/16 July and 4 August 1986, London.

25. *Ibid.*

26. Interview with Ronald Brumback, President, Atex Inc., 23 July 1986, Atlanta.

27. Interviews with Atex personnel, 22 July 1986, Atlanta.

28. Interviews with Atex personnel, 6/7 August 1986, London.

29. Interview with Atex employee, 8 August 1986, London.

30. Interview with Jim Lennane, President, Systems Integrators Inc., 22 July 1986, Atlanta.

31. Interviews with senior executives, News International, 27/29 July 1986, London, and Atex personnel, 8 August 1986, London.

32. *Ibid.*

33. Interviews with Atex personnel, 4/8 August 1986, London.

34. Interview with Atex employee, 20 July 1986, Atlanta.

35. Interview with Chris Grad, Chairman, Aerload Ltd, 20 August 1986, Slough.

36. Interview with Atex employee, 4 August 1986, London.

37. *Ibid.*

38. *Ibid.*

39. *Ibid.*

40. *Ibid.*

41. Interview with executive, News International, 15 July 1986.

42. Minutes of a meeting held at Tower Hamlets on 21 May 1985. Item 1 (a).

43. Minutes of a meeting held at Tower Hamlets on 21 May 1985. Item 2 (i).

44. Minutes of a meeting held at Tower Hamlets on 21 May 1985. Item 2 (b).

45. Interview with Chris Grad, Chairman, Concorde Transport Ltd, 20 August 1986, Slough.

46. Minutes of a meeting held at Tower Hamlets on 21 May 1985. Item 2 (e) and Item J (iii).

47. Interview with executive, News Corporation, 8 August 1986, London.

48. News International Security Pass List – Card Numbers and Owners, for Tower Hamlets plant, June 1985.

49. 'Confidential', R. P. O'Hagan, Security Consultant, 28 August 1985.

50. Interview with James Stuckey, Executive Director and General Manager, Southern Productions Program Inc., 15 August 1986, Oklahoma.

51. Minutes of a meeting held at Tower Hamlets on 15 August 1985.

52. Barrie Clement, 'Fleet Street unions agree to talks on printing plant for News International', *The Times*, 1 October 1985.

53. Notes taken by Brenda Dean, General Secretary, Sogat '82, of meeting with News International on Monday, 30 September 1985 at the Inn on the Park Hotel, London.

54. Interviews with Mike Smith, National Organiser, NUJ, 8 August 1986; Alf Parish, National Secretary, NGA, 18 July 1986; and Brenda Dean, General Secretary, Sogat '82, 31 July 1986.

55. Interview with executive, News Corporation, 4 August 1986, London.

56. Interview with executive, News International, 15 July 1986, London.

57. Interview with senior executive, News International, 8 August 1986, London.

58. Affidavit of Bruce Robert Matthews, sworn July 1986, Queen's Bench Division, High Court of Justice.

59. Interview with senior manager, production, Tower Hamlets, 3 June 1986, London.

60. Interview with senior managers, production, Tower Hamlets, 3/8 June 1986, London.

61. Interview with senior executive, News International, 3 August 1986, London.

62. Interview with senior managers, production, Tower Hamlets, 3 June 1986, London.

63. *Ibid.*

64. *Ibid.*

65. John Lloyd and Helen Hague, 'Murdoch wins first round in the battle over Wapping', *Financial Times*, 27 January 1986.

66. Crispin Aubrey, 'Rocked in the Wapping waves', *Guardian*, 12 May 1986.

67. 'Shah thinks twice on distribution', *Sogat Journal* special issue, January 1986.

68. Barrie Clement, 'Fleet Street unions agree to talks on printing plant for News International', *The Times*, 1 October 1985.

69. John Lloyd, 'TNT seeks more Fleet St delivery contracts', *Financial Times*, 21 January 1986.

70. Interview with David Forbes, Group Security Manager, TNT UK Ltd, Atherstone, London, 8 August 1986.

71. News International TNT Operational Proposal, prepared by Tom Bell, TNT Project General Manager, 16 April 1985.

72. *Ibid.*

73. Affidavit of Bruce Robert Matthews, sworn July 1986, Queen's Bench Division, High Court of Justice.

74. *Ibid.*

75. *Ibid.*

76. Deed of Indemnity between News International Plc and TNT Roadfreight (UK) Ltd dated 28 June 1985.

77. Interview with circulation representative, News International, 17 August 1986.

78. Interview with Michael Bowen, Secretary, Provincial Wholesale Newspaper Distributors Association, 12 August 1986, Rochdale.

79. Interview with senior executive, News International, 16 August 1986.

80. Interview with Kevin Cahill, writer specialising in computer technology, 17 August 1986.

81. Interview with Chris Grad, Chairman, Aerload Ltd, 20 August 1986, Slough.

82. Interview with former senior manager, News International, 15 August 1986.

CHAPTER SEVEN

1. Metropolitan Police document, 'Demonstrations in the London Borough of Tower Hamlets. Commissioner's Directions', signed by Sir Kenneth Newman, Commissioner of Police of the Metropolis, dated 22 January 1986, reference TF122/83/113 pt VII.

2. Notes taken at meeting in Free Trade Hall, Manchester, 30 January 1986.

3. Philip Bassett, Helen Hague and Raymond Huges, 'Sogat calls emergency session after court orders sequestration', *Financial Times*, 11 February 1986.

4. ITN 'News at Ten', 10 February 1986.

5. Letter from G. W. Richards, Farrer & Co., to Bruce Matthews, Managing Director, News International, dated 20 December 1985, published in full in the *Morning Star*, 4 February 1986.

6. Thames Television programme 'TV Eye', 13 February 1986.

7. BBC Television programme 'This Week, Next Week', 2 February 1986.

8. *Ibid*.

9. 'Sogat chief pleads for end to violence', *Daily Express*, 17 February 1986.

10. John Hunt, 'Wapping "may lead to tighter union law" ', *Financial Times*, 13 February 1986.

11. Interview with Brenda Dean, General Secretary, Sogat '82, 31 July 1986, London.

12. *Ibid*.

13. Interviews with Brenda Dean, General Secretary, Sogat '82, 28 July 1986, Hadleigh, Essex, and Mike Smith, National Organiser, NUJ, 25 July 1986, London.

14. Interview with News International executive, 27 July 1986.

15. Letter to the Editor, written by D. P. Forbes, published in *The Times*, 27 February 1986.

16. Interview with Brenda Dean, General Secretary, Sogat '82, 31 July 1986, London.

17. Patrick Wintour and Andrew Rawnsley, 'Murdoch offers unions plant as gift', *Guardian*, 5 April 1986.

18. Philip Bassett, 'Murdoch sets print unions a new problem', *Financial Times*, 8 April 1986.

19. Patrick Wintour, 'Police horses charge Murdoch picket as unions study "gift" offer', *Guardian*, 7 April 1986.

20. Patrick Wintour, 'Murdoch's PR diversion on unions' Wapping road', *Guardian*, 8 April 1986.

21. Notes taken by Alf Parish, National Secretary, NGA, during meeting on 16 April 1986.

22. Interview with senior EETPU trade unionist, 14 July 1986.

23. Interview, senior police officers, London, 15–16 May 1986.

24. Patrick Wintour and David Rose, 'Sogat calls for Wapping policing inquiry', *Guardian*, 5 May 1986.

25. Patrick Wintour, 'A Wapping stalemate', *Guardian*, 8 May 1986.

26. *Ibid.*

27. Minutes of a meeting held at Carlisle Avenue between News International executives and Unity Trust representatives on 2 May 1986.

28. Letter from Michael Marsden, Executive Director, Unity Trust Plc, to John Monks, TUC, dated 12 May 1986, reference MM/jk/M34, headed 'News International Plc – Gray's Inn Road'.

29. Interview with Brenda Dean, General Secretary, Sogat '82, 31 July 1986, London.

30. Interview with Brenda Dean, General Secretary, Sogat '82, 8 May 1986, London.

31. Interview with Brenda Dean, General Secretary, Sogat '82, 31 July 1986, London.

32. 'Front-line sister of the print', *Observer* profile of Brenda Dean, 10 November 1985.

33. Interview with Brenda Dean, General Secretary, Sogat '82, 31 July 1986, London.

34. *Ibid.*

35. *Ibid.*

36. Interview with Bill Miles, General Officer, Sogat '82, 6 August 1986, London.

37. Interview with Brenda Dean, General Secretary, Sogat '82, 31 July 1986, London.

38. Notes taken by Sogat member at Sogat '82 London District Council meeting held at Central Hall, Westminster, London, 19 May 1986.

39. Interview with Tony Isaacs, Imperial Father of the Sogat *News of the World* Machine Chapel, 2 August 1986.

40. Interview with Brenda Dean, General Secretary, Sogat '82, 31 July 1986, London.

41. Interviews with Brenda Dean, General Secretary, Sogat '82; Mike Smith, National Organiser, NUJ; Bill Miles, General Officer, Sogat '82; Alf Parish, National Secretary, NGA; Tony Dubbins, General Secretary, NGA, July 1986.

42. 'Murdoch postpones London Post launch', *UK Press Gazette*, 24 February 1986.

43. Affidavit of Bruce Robert Matthews, sworn July 1986, Queen's Bench Division, High Court of Justice.

44. Interview with News International executive, 27 July 1986.

45. 'Final Offer' document drafted by News International.

46. ITN News, 26 May 1986.

47. Patrick Wintour, 'Sogat to ballot members on Murdoch print offer', *Guardian*, 28 May 1986.

48. Interview with Brian Redhead, BBC Radio Four presenter, 10 June 1986.

49. Interview with Brenda Dean, General Secretary, Sogat '82, 31 July 1986, London.

50. BBC Radio 4, 'The World Tonight', 6 May 1986.

51. Peter Wilsher, 'No Deal', *Sunday Times*, 8 June 1986.

52. Brenda Dean, General Secretary, Sogat '82, transcript of speech to biennial delegates conference, Scarborough, 9 June 1986.

53. Helen Hague, 'Sogat activists mend split with leaders on Wapping', *Financial Times*, 13 June 1986.

54. Helen Hague, 'Willis discusses strategy with Sogat leaders', *Financial Times*, 12 June 1986.

55. Interview with Bill Miles, General Officer, Sogat '82, 6 August 1986, London.

56. Interview with Brenda Dean, General Secretary, Sogat '82, 31 July 1986, London.

57. *Ibid.*

CHAPTER EIGHT

1. Letter from Tom Rice, Secretary, Committee of Enquiry London Press Branch, EETPU, to Sean Geraghty, Secretary, London Press Branch, EETPU, reference TJR/AP, dated 20 January 1983.

2. Interview with Sean Geraghty, Secretary, London Press Branch, EETPU, 4 July 1986, London.

3. Patrick Wintour, 'Chapple to sell press branch?', *New Statesman*, 20 August 1982.

4. Letter from Frank Chapple, General Secretary, EETPU, to Len Murray, General Secretary, TUC, reference FJC/LHF, dated 16 March 1983.

5. Paul Routledge, 'Union dispute threatens papers', *The Times*, 21 May 1983.

6. Letter from Tom Rice, National Secretary, EETPU, to John Mitchell, Secretary, Sogat London Machine Branch, reference TJR/JRW, dated 14 June 1983.

7. Interview with Sea Geraghty, Secretary, London Press Branch, EETPU, 4 July 1986, London.

8. Attachment to circular from Eric Hammond, General Secretary, EETPU, to Executive Councillors, Full-time officials, all branches, ref. 4880/EAH/AP, dated 31 January 1986.

9. 'The Tojan horse of the TUC', *Observer*, 2 February 1986.

10. Philip Bassett, *Strike Free* (London: Macmillan, 1986).

11. Eric Hammond, 'We reach the parts other unions can't', *Sun*, 5 July 1985.

12. John Torode, 'Tainted cash won't hurt the TUC's marked man', *Guardian*, 3 December 1985.

13. Barrie Clement, 'Livewire on the union circuit', *The Times*, 4 July 1985.

14. Kim Fletcher, 'Electrician who strikes sparks', *Sunday Times*, 12 January 1986.

15. Barrie Clement, 'Livewire on the union circuit', *The Times*, 4 July 1985.

16. McIntosh and Ireland, 'Report of proceedings of the General Council of the Trades Union Congress held at Congress House, London', 5 February 1986.

17. Interview with Bert Brown, former member of EETPU Southampton branch committee, 30 August 1986, London.

18. *Ibid.* and interview with Arthur Pearse, President, EETPU Southampton branch, 3 September 1986, London.

19. Interview with John Fraser, former employee at Wapping, 21 August 1986, London.

20. Interview with News International executive, 8 July 1986, London.

21. Minutes of TUC Eighth (Special) Meeting (1985–1986) held in Congress House on 30 January 1986.

22. *Ibid.*

23. Interview with Arthur Pearse, President, EETPU Southampton branch, 25 August 1986, London.

24. *Ibid.*

25. Barrie Clement and David Felton, 'Deadline on Post deal extended', *The Times*, 19 December 1985.

26. Maurice Weaver, 'Willis warns electricians on "Post" deal', *Daily Telegraph*, 21 December 1985.

27. Memo to Norman Willis, General Secretary, and Members of the General Council of the TUC, from AUEW, NGA, NUJ and Sogat, headed 'Situation with News International/EETPU', 21 January 1986.

28. Letter to Norman Willis, General Secretary TUC, from Eric Hammond, General Secretary, EETPU, reference EAH/SEH, 29 January 1986.

29. Circular from Eric Hammond, General Secretary, EETPU, to Executive Councillors, Full-time Officials, all branches, ref. 4880/EAH/AP, dated 31 January 1986.

30. Interview with Donald Macintyre, former Labour Editor of *The Times*, 31 July 1986, London.

31. McIntosh and Ireland, 'Report of proceedings of the General Council of the Trades Union Congress held at Congress House, London', 5 February 1986.

32. John Lloyd, 'Electricians fail to sway TUC right', *Financial Times*, 7 February 1986.

33. Interviews with senior executives, News International, 7/8 July 1986.

34. Interview with John Hoover, Production Supervisor, *Miami Herald*, 25 August 1986, Miami.

35. Interview with Robin Guinaugh, Accounts Receivable, St Anthony Hotel, San Antonio (USA), 28 August 1986, San Antonio.

36. Interviews with EETPU official, 7 August 1986; and News International executives, 5, 6, 7 August 1986, London.

37. Interview with News International executive, 6 July 1986, London.

38. Interview with News International executive, 5 August 1986, London.

39. McIntosh and Ireland, 'Report of proceedings of the General Council of the Trades Union Congress held at Congress House, London', 5 February 1986.

40. John Fryer, 'Left leaps for electric chair', *Sunday Times*, 10 October 1986.

41. David Goodhart and Patrick Wintour, *Eddie Shah and the Newspaper Revolution* (London: Coronet, 1986).

42. Derek Jameson, 'Paper pattern', *UK Press Gazette*, 10 February 1986.

43. Minutes of a meeting held at Tower Hamlets, 21 May 1985, Item (h) 'Overseas equipment/personnel'.

44. Minutes of a meeting held at Tower Hamlets, 21 May 1985, 'Any Other Business', point 2.

45. Agenda for a meeting to be held on 29 May 1985, Item 2 (c).

46. Interview with Deborah Light, *Business Review Weekly* (Australia), 29 August 1986, London.

47. Minutes of a meeting held at Tower Hamlets on 15 August 1985, 'Recruitment'.

48. Interviews with News International executives, 5/6 August 1986.

49. Minutes of a meeting held at Tower Hamlets, 26 September 1985, 'BRM Comments'.

50. Interview with Dermot Martin, Reporter, *Southern Evening Echo*, 2 September 1986.

CHAPTER NINE

1. Interview with Terry Ellis, Deputy Father of the AUEW Chapel, Bouverie Street, 25 August 1986, London.

2. Interview with Tony Cappi, Engineers' Assistants' Chapel, Sogat RIRMA, 27 August 1986.

3. FoC's Report, Quarterly Chapel Meeting, Bouverie Street Engineers' Assistants' Chapel, Sogat RIRMA, 14 March 1984.

4. FoC's Report, Quarterly Chapel Meeting, Bouverie Street Engineers' Assistants' Chapel, Sogat RIRMA, 13 October 1982.

5. FoC's Report, Quarterly Chapel Meeting, Bouverie Street Engineers' Assistants' Chapel, Sogat RIRMA, 21 March 1983.

6. FoC's Report, Quarterly Chapel Meeting, Bouverie Street Engineers' Assistants' Chapel, Sogat RIRMA, 13 July 1983.

7. *Ibid.*

8. Interview with Terry Ellis, Deputy Father of the AUEW Chapel, Bouverie Street, 25 August 1986, London.

9. Assessment of News Group Newspapers Ltd Tower Hamlets Development for an Additional Newspaper Printing Facility at Pennington Street, Wapping, London E1, June 1984.

10. Interview with Terry Ellis, Deputy Father of the AUEW Chapel, Bouverie Street, 21 August 1986, London.

11. *Ibid.*

12. FoC's Report, Quarterly Chapel Meeting, Bouverie Street Engineers' Assistants' Chapel, Sogat RIRMA, 13 March 1985.

13. *Ibid.*

14. Jon Slattery, 'Pole-Carew at docklands as Post adviser', *UK Press Gazette*, 13 May 1985.

15. Letter from Brenda Dean, General Secretary, Sogat '82, to Harry Spanswick, FoC, Engineers' Assistants' Chapel, ref. BD/MVT/830, 11 June 1985; and letter from David Hutchinson, London Branch Secretary, RIRMA, to Bill Miles, General Officer, Sogat '82, ref. DEH/RK, 6 June 1985.

16. Letter from David Hutchinson, London Branch Secretary, RIRMA, to Harry Spanswick, FoC, Engineers' Assistants' Chapel, Bouverie Street, Sogat RIRMA, ref. DEH/RK, 6 June 1985.

17. Interview with Tony Cappi, Engineers' Assistants' Chapel, Bouverie Street, Sogat RIRMA, 25 August 1986, London.

18. Letter from Brenda Dean, General Secretary, Sogat '82, to Harry Spanswick, FoC, Engineers' Assistants' Chapel, Bouverie Street, Sogat RIRMA, ref. BD/BD/56, 3 July 1985.

19. Letter from Brenda Dean, General Secretary, Sogat '82, to John Mitchell, Secretary, London District Council, Sogat, ref. BD/MVT/981, 25 June 1985.

20. Report to National Executive Council, Sogat '82, headed 'News Group/TNL – Wapping', from Brenda Dean, ref. BD/MVT/11.9.85.

21. Interview with Bill Miles, General Officer, Sogat '82, 14 May 1986, Southend.

22. Press statement issued by Sogat '82, 31 July 1985.

23. Inter-departmental memo from Bill Miles, General Officer, Sogat '82, to Brenda Dean, General Secretary, Sogat '82, headed 'News Group Newspapers', ref. HWM/CJE/800, 29 August 1985.

24. Interview with Bill Miles, General Officer, Sogat '82, 14 May 1986, Southend.

25. *Ibid.*

26. Press statement issued by Sogat '82, 30 August 1985.

27. Letter from Bruce Matthews, Managing Director, News Group Newspapers Ltd, to Brenda Dean, General Secretary, Sogat '82, 9 September 1985.

28. Letter from Ted Chard, Secretary, London Central Branch, Sogat '82, to Brenda Dean, General Secretary, Sogat '82 ref. ERC/PI/0011, 10 September 1985.

29. Letter from Harry Conroy, General Secretary, NUJ, to Brenda Dean, General Secretary, Sogat '82, ref. SOG/G, 19 September 1985.

30. Interview with Donald Macintyre, former Labour Editor with *The Times*, 31 July 1986, London.

31. Interview with Brenda Dean, General Secretary, Sogat '82, 8 May 1986, London.

32. Point 42 of minutes of sectional meeting – Members Employed by News International – held on 12 September 1985 ('Private and Confidential').

33. Interview with Roy 'Ginger' Wilson, Father of the Sogat Machine Room Chapel, *Sunday Times*, 27 August 1986, London.

34. Interview with Tony Cappi, Engineers' Assistants' Chapel, Sogat RIRMA, 27 August 1986, London.

35. Report of meeting between London Post (Printers) Ltd and representatives of Sogat '82. Notes taken by A. J. Isaacs, 4 December 1985.

36. Barrie Clement, 'Fleet Street unions agree to talks on printing plant for News International', *The Times*, 1 October 1985.

37. Letter to the Editor, *The Times*, from Brenda Dean, General Secretary, Sogat '82, 3 October 1985.

38. Report by London Machine Branch, Sogat '82, of meeting held with News Group Newspapers on 16 October 1985.

39. Interim report by Sogat '82 Branch Officials and Delegates of meetings with News Group Newspapers held 14–17 October 1985.

40. Report by Brenda Dean, General Secretary, Sogat '82, to National Executive Council meeting held on 6/7 November 1985.

41. Interview with Alf Parish, National Secretary, NGA, 28 August 1986, London.

42. Minutes of Printing Industries Committee, Trades Union Congress, ref. PIC4, 25 November 1985.

43. Report by Brenda Dean, General Secretary, Sogat '82, to National Executive Council meeting held on 19 December 1985.

44. *Ibid.*

45. Interview with Brenda Dean, General Secretary, Sogat '82, 31 July 1986, London.

46. Barrie Clement and David Felton, 'Deadline on Post deal extended', *The Times*, 19 December 1985.

47. Interview with Brenda Dean, General Secretary, Sogat '82, 8 May 1986, London.

48. Letter from Bill Miles, General Officer, Sogat '82, to Bruce Matthews, Managing Director, News International, ref. HWM/CJE/0046, 23 December 1986.

49. Letter from Bill O'Neill, Vice President Personnel and Labor Relations, News America Publishing Inc., to Brenda Dean, General Secretary, Sogat '82, ref. WAO/sm, 24 December 1985.

50. 'Statement on Post talks failure', *The Times*, 30 December 1985.

51. Letter from Bill Gillespie, Managing Director, Times Newspapers Ltd, to Bill Miles, General Officer, Sogat '82, 31 December 1985.

52. Barrie Clement, 'NUJ may be open to separate Post deal', *The Times*, 8 January 1986.

53. Letter from Bill Gillespie, Managing Director, Times Newspapers Ltd, to all Sogat Chapels, except Clerical, 9 January 1986.

54. Barrie Clement, 'Sunday Times to docklands', *The Times*, 13 January 1986.

55. *Ibid.*

56. 'Crisis weekend at the Wapping plant', *UK Press Gazette*, 20 January 1986.

57. Patrick Wintour, 'Bouquet of Barbed Wire', *Guardian*, 22 January 1986.

57. Letter from Rupert Murdoch to all News International employees, 22 January 1986.

Index